THE PEACE CORPS IN ACTION

THE
PEACE CORPS
IN ACTION

by Velma Adams

Follett Publishing Company

Chicago, 1964

Library of Congress Catalog Card Number: 64-23606

First Printing

Designed by Gordon Martin

Manufactured in the United States of America

FOLLETT PUBLISHING COMPANY
1000 West Washington Boulevard
Chicago, Illinois 60607

To

John Fitzgerald Kennedy

President of the United States
January 20, 1961–November 22, 1963

ACKNOWLEDGMENTS

I want to thank all Peace Corps Volunteers but especially those who answered my questionnaire, wrote to me, or talked with me while I was overseas, whether or not they are quoted by name; the parents and the friends of Volunteers who gave me insight into the character of the PCVs; and the many members of the Peace Corps staff—the Reps in the field and the desk men in Washington—who answered my questions, discussed the program frankly, furnished photographs, and aided me in innumerable ways.

Specifically, I acknowledge the assistance of: Mrs. Ruth Arthur, my mother, who provided me with a clipping service; Robert Bryan, Public Information, Peace Corps, Washington, who either furnished the information I needed or referred me to the persons who gave it to me; George G. Dawson, Associate Professor of Social Studies Education at New York University and University Administrator in Somalia; Mrs. Bernice Kelly, who often housed and fed me, then stole quietly away to leave me at my typewriter near a window with an ocean view; Miss Irene Kline, for her insistence that I undertake the project and for her inspiration while I carried it out; Mrs. Mary Anne Knynenburg, for her work on the manuscript; John L. Landgraf, Associate Professor of Anthropology at New York University and Peace Corps Representative in Borneo; Kellogg Smith, editor of *PCVolunteer;* Dr. Nicholas C. Leone, former Medical Director, Public Health Service Clinic, New York, now Assistant Medical Director, Public Health Service Hospital,

vii

ACKNOWLEDGEMENTS

Baltimore, Maryland; Miss Louise Parker, with whom I was vacationing when I conceived the idea; Mrs. Joan Rich, for background on Nigeria; Vera Rubin, Director, Research Institute for the Study of Man; John J. Sullivan, Associate Professor of Educational Psychology at New York University; Arnold Leo, associate editor, Follett Publishing Company; Louis Zara, my editor-in-chief, who made it clear that he believed I could do it—and then left me alone to prove it; and all the relatives and friends who encouraged me, respected my need to be alone, yet did not abandon me during this asocial period of my life.

May the finished product justify their faith.

VELMA ADAMS
New York, 1964

I couldn't take the life of a Peace Corps Volunteer. I don't know many people who could. It really takes a special breed— dedicated, zealous, and absolutely independent in spirit. We probably have hundreds of thousands of young men and women who would qualify on these points, but to be a PCV calls for even more, for something of that eagerness to confront and conquer the unknown that characterized the finest explorers and trail blazers.

When the Peace Corps was established, I was personally thrilled. I felt that here was, in many ways, the best idea for brotherhood-in-practice that my generation of Americans had ever been offered. Fortunately for the Corps and for me, my enthusiasm never impelled me to fill out an application. For enthusiasm is not enough, and two years of travel and research, during which time I came to know more than two hundred Volunteers, plus a number of staff members, has not changed my original opinion: it takes a special quality to make a Volunteer.

While this book is based on contributions from many Volunteers and staff members, it is entirely an independent study. It was carried on with the cooperation of but *without* the official sponsorship of the Peace Corps. To gather my material, I went abroad, rode in jeeps, skipped lunches, ate local foods which were strange to me, hiked in the mud and dust, often went longer than I like without bathing or sleeping, and tried, amid unfamiliar customs, to reach across language barriers. And slowly I began to sense something of what happens to individuals in isolation as well as in overcrowding, and experienced, almost with chagrin, the enervation that is induced by life in tropical climates.

Volunteers take the position that no one, unless he has spent two years in the Peace Corps on their particular project, can possibly understand what it is like, and I sympathize with that view. I was never more than a transient visitor, yet I was able to feel the spirit of dedication, the drive to improve ways of life that almost defy change, and to sense the loneliness and the hunger for communication. In brief, I believe that I came to appreciate very quickly what I would have had to endure more rigorously had I stayed on for two years in any given locale. I do not pretend to have lived all their problems, but I looked, and I listened, and I have reported accurately.

My self-imposed assignment became a phenomenal task. When I started there were a few hundred Volunteers in twelve countries; a year later there were nearly five thousand Volunteers in forty-one countries.

My goal has been to report objectively and to interpret, as an outsider, for the Peace Corps; but my feelings were, and still are, with the Volunteers, and not only with them as individuals, but also with their ideals and their goals. It has not been easy to reveal also the discouraging aspects of the Volunteers' work and to offer criticism of the Peace Corps' modes of operation. I have done so in the belief that the reader will recognize, as I did, that despite some failures, the Corps is a valuable tool of our foreign policy—and more: it is an outlet for the noblest feelings of our youth. When young men and women are brought up in the service of a worthy cause, the nation has taken a long step toward training responsible leaders for the future.

CONTENTS

The Peace Corps Is Born

The Congress of the United States declares that it is the policy of the United States and the purpose of [the Peace Corps] Act to promote world peace and friendship through a Peace Corps, which shall make available to interested countries and areas men and women of the United States qualified for service abroad and willing to serve, under conditions of hardship if necessary, to help the peoples of such countries and areas in meeting their needs for trained manpower, and to help promote a better understanding of the American people on the part of the peoples served and a better understanding of other peoples on the part of the American people.

DECLARATION OF PURPOSE
THE PEACE CORPS ACT

I have today signed an Executive Order estab-
lishing a Peace Corps on a temporary basis . . .
under existing authority in the Mutual Security Act.
It will be located in the Department of State.
Its initial expenses will be paid from appropriations
currently available for our foreign aid program.
JOHN F. KENNEDY
March 1, 1961

Since President Kennedy signed this order and, subsequently, on September 22, 1961, the "Peace Corps Act," or Public Law 87–293, I have watched the Peace Corps come to maturity. The Volunteers' initial enthusiasm mounts from the first day of training. It is stimulated by their group activities and by the suspense of facing an unknown future; it reaches a high point upon their arrival in an underdeveloped country. Then the Volunteers become impatient, for they are eager to improve the lives of the inhabitants as quickly as possible, and obstacles they never dreamed of rise in their way. Fundamentally, however, I have come to feel about the Peace Corps Volunteers as they do about themselves: they are a breed apart.

The Volunteers insist that there is no typical PCV (Peace Corps Volunteer). Most Volunteers dislike questionnaires, statistics, and generalizations about themselves. They don't care to be asked why they joined the Peace Corps, maybe because so many of them don't really know why. Yet they all possess some indefinable characteristic—call it dedication, the social service motive, the pioneer spirit, or idealism—which armors them against material discomforts and makes them essentially disinterested in monetary rewards. They apparently welcome the opportunity to face hardships, to grapple with the

forces of nature, to give up temporarily the same high standards of living which they strive to help others reach.

In other words, the ideal Peace Corps Volunteer is not at
all the garden variety of average young American.

The Peace Corps idea was first broached publicly by Senator John F. Kennedy in a presidential campaign speech in
October, 1960, at the University of Michigan. At San Francisco, shortly thereafter, creation of a Peace Corps became
a formal campaign promise. The response from all over the
country was enthusiastic. People were obviously ready for
an international program in which American youth could be
of service to the world. From the beginning, the Peace Corps
was conceived as a means of assisting backward areas by direct
contact with the inhabitants rather than with the officials.
The Volunteers would help these people learn to do things for
themselves. This philosophy, although utilized by Kennedy as
a political weapon, was not in itself new. Since 1809 Christian
missionaries had been leaving the United States to teach and
to work in underdeveloped countries. As early as 1901, a group
of young American volunteers arrived in the Philippines to
teach English. Most of them lived outside the cities. They
taught in small schoolhouses and lived as the native teachers
lived, with no special privileges of any kind.

Through the years, dozens of private organizations had been
active in sending out volunteers to work at such grass-roots
levels. The American Friends Service Committee is renowned
for its contributions to programs of refugee resettlement and
of community development. Probably the closest forerunner
of the Peace Corps is the International Voluntary Services,
formed in 1953 and run by a board of both Catholic and Prot-
estant representatives. Non-religious and non-denominational,
it developed because the International Cooperation Administration, as an agency of the United States government, had to
deal in foreign countries on a governmental level, and many
felt that the *people* of those countries ought to be reached.

IVS began to work mainly in rural areas, concentrating on agricultural projects, animal husbandry, crop and horticultural experimentation, home economics, public health, and house building—projects similar to those espoused by the Peace Corps.

Another private agency, Operation Crossroads, was founded by Dr. James H. Robinson, a Negro minister and director of Morningside Community Center in New York. While on a trip to Africa, Dr. Robinson observed the pitiful conditions that prevailed in primitive African villages. Upon his return to the United States he organized a college program to enable students to spend a summer in Africa at work on specific community projects. In 1958, he and sixty students spent the summer in Africa; by 1963, he had 304 students taking part in twenty-seven projects in nineteen countries.

At the same time that these and other private enterprises were sending volunteers to areas all over the world, interest was growing in the United States for the creation of a government-sponsored youth service. One of the principal advocates was Representative Henry S. Reuss, Democrat from Wisconsin, who felt that many underdeveloped nations needed technical assistance on a level lower than that reached with the existing cadres of technical advisors. In early 1960, Reuss submitted a bill to the House calling for a study of a Point Four Youth Corps. Senator Richard Neuberger of Oregon submitted similar legislation in the Senate. The Mutual Security Act of 1960 made $10,000 available for such a study, and the task was assigned to the University of Colorado Research Foundation, under the direction of Dr. Maurice Albertson.

Reuss's proposal was quickly adopted by the Organization of Young Democratic Clubs and the National Student Association. Both promoted it actively on college campuses around the country.

On June 15, 1960, Senator Hubert Humphrey submitted Bill 3675 which asked for the development of a "genuine people-to-people program in which talented and dedicated young

American men would teach basic agricultural and industrial techniques, literacy, the English language and other school subjects, and sanitation and health procedures in Asia, Africa, and Latin America." In essence, Humphrey's bill, instead of calling for a *study* of a Peace Corps, asked for the Peace Corps itself. Since the Senate was on the verge of adjournment the bill received scant attention. However, in the presidential election campaign that fall, the idea was carried into the political debates.

After the election, mail on the Peace Corps poured into the White House and the offices of the Democratic National Committee. Almost immediately after taking office, President Kennedy asked Dr. Max Millikan, director of the Center of International Studies at Massachusetts Institute of Technology, to submit a report on such an international youth service. The President received Millikan's report in January, 1961, and a preliminary one from the Colorado State University Research Foundation in February. Both studies endorsed an organization which would enable the youth of America to serve abroad. It is interesting that neither study recommended a completely independent government agency, which is how the Corps now operates.

A Gallup poll in January showed that 71 per cent of the American people were in favor of the Corps, with only 18 per cent against it. Now President Kennedy asked his brother-in-law, Sargent Shriver, to investigate the possibilities of organizing a Peace Corps immediately. Shriver's report, on February 28, 1961, covered the previous studies as well as the proposed legislation, and gave the findings of Shriver's own task force. The conclusion offered two choices: either the Peace Corps could begin slowly, with few preparatory steps taken until Congress might appropriate funds to underwrite the whole concept, or the Peace Corps could be created immediately by executive order, with funds from existing Mutual Security appropriations, and several projects could be launched

that summer. Two days later, the President issued his executive order establishing the Peace Corps, and on March 4, he
announced the appointment of R. Sargent Shriver to the post
of director. Though it would not be regarded as a permanent
agency until authorized by Congress at a later time, the Peace
Corps was now a reality.

Everything moved so rapidly that the Corps was at first
in a state of complete disorganization, or rather, un-organiza-
tion. Mail deluged the new headquarters at 806 Connecticut
Avenue, N.W., in Washington. It was heaped onto desks that
had just been brought into the building. The new telephones
rang incessantly. Shriver was in command, but he had no
staff, no operating procedures, no rules or regulations, no
channels for clearing matters, no schools to conduct training,
indeed, no method as yet of recruiting any trainees. And
despite such handicaps Shriver had to prove, to those who
believed as well as to those who did not, that the concept of
the Peace Corps was viable. Since the avowed purpose was
to "help the peoples of interested countries and areas in meeting their needs for skilled manpower," Volunteers would have
to be rushed into the field as soon as possible, as soon as
suitable trainees could be obtained, as soon as they could be
trained. There was no question that there would be a demand
for them.

Sargent Shriver had a reputation for getting things done.
Apparently it was a well-earned reputation, for somehow order
began to appear. Quickly the new director handpicked a number of assistants and delegated specific areas to them: recruiting, public relations, evaluation, programming, etc. He made
all the final decisions himself. Only he could cut through the
complicated red tape in Washington and encourage his people:
"Get it done first, and worry about it later." They could have
confidence that he would support them.

With the help of his aides, he speedily tracked down certain
people whom he judged suitable for particular assignments.

For example, when Borneo asked for more than a hundred PCVs, Shriver realized that he would need a man who could speak Malay and was familiar with the culture of the area. One day, Associate Professor John L. Landgraf, in his office in the anthropology department at New York University, received a phone call from a friend. "John," the other said, "I just want to let you know that you're going to get a call from the Peace Corps. Shriver's trying to fill a job in Borneo, and I mentioned that you'd lived there for a number of years and spoke several dialects."

Fifteen minutes later the call came through from Washington: "How soon can you get down here for an interview?" the voice asked.

On his arrival at PC headquarters, Landgraf was quickly processed all the way up to the Director. He and Shriver had a pleasant chat and agreement was quickly reached that Landgraf would take the job in Borneo. With that settled, Landgraf went to the waiting room to complete the technical details related to his hiring. As he sat there, he heard a secretary gasp at a man who was about to crumple and throw away an envelope. "Don't throw that away," she begged, "I need it for the files. It's the only authorization I have to hire this man." Curious, the professor leaned over and saw that Shriver had written on the envelope: "Get Landgraf. He's terrific." Nine months later, John Landgraf and his wife, already in Borneo, were welcoming the first plane load of PCVs.

There were dozens of similar cases. Shriver and his assistants used no ceremony when they wanted to hire a man who had the qualifications they were seeking. In those early days, before a method of recruitment had been fully instituted, applicants, too, were often notified by Shriver, with astonishing speed, of their acceptance. David King, later a PCV in the Philippines, was teaching in Stuttgart, Germany, under contract to the Army, when a telegram from Shriver instructed him to report for training at Penn State five days later. Marion

Ford, in Paris, Texas, got his telegram of acceptance at six o'clock one morning, "Be at University of Puerto Rico in five days." He typed out a resignation from his job and never had another chance "to draw my breath," until he landed in the Dominican Republic a full-fledged PCV.

As Shriver and his small band of dedicated aides rapidly sought out and hired additional workers, the Peace Corps began to take shape. Today the Corps may be divided into two main categories: administrative staff and field people. (See chart, p. 11.) The administrative staff, located at Washington headquarters, is limited to 275 persons, many of whom were transferred from Civil Service assignments in other government departments to bring the Corps into immediate operation. In addition to Shriver and his assistants, there are recruiters, training supervisors, evaluation officers, and public information people, as well as doctors, psychologists, and clerical helpers. There is also the so-called "back-up service" which handles requests from PCVs in the field and supports them in every way possible, including helping them to get jobs after their tours of duty are over.

The field organization consists of Field Representatives, the Volunteers, and their team leaders. A Field Representative accompanies each group of PCVs and acts as a liaison man between them and the host country. His job is to oversee the group's activities, and to deal with the local government, to watch over the health of Volunteers, and through contact with the nearest American Embassy, to be informed of the diplomatic situation between the host country and the United States. Principally, he is a counselor.

In Togo, all the PCVs were invited to the home of their Representative for Thanksgiving and again at Christmas time, though not all were able to travel there for the holidays. In St. Lucia, PCVs see their Representative and his wife daily, walk in and out of their house and office freely, ride in the

van with them or borrow it, and generally have a close relationship. On the other hand, in some places such as the more
remote regions of Tanganyika and Ghana, PCVs have not
seen their Representative since the time he welcomed them
to the host country. Some Reps sign up for two years, some
for one, though the ranks are occasionally thinned by dropouts. One Rep in West Africa was so revolted at the sight of
women with naked, pendulous breasts, men urinating and
people picking over garbage in the streets, that he came home
after three days.

Each group in the field has its team leader. He is, of course,
one of their own number, but he receives a slightly higher
living allowance and termination payment and is selected by
the Corps presumably because of his superior knowledge of,
or experience with, the kind of project in which the group
is to be involved.

The PCVs are instructed by a doctor, nurse, or other qualified person in first aid and preventive medicine so that they
may be able to cope with minor accidents and illnesses, but
the services of a doctor must be available in case of serious
illness. The doctor, also a Peace Corps employee, in addition
to his responsibilities to the Volunteers, usually works in local
hospitals and medical stations. However, he visits the PCVs
periodically to give physical examinations, immunizations,
and when required, medical care in addition to what may be
locally provided.

At the bottom rung of the field hierarchy is the Peace Corps
Volunteer. He, or she, is assigned for a two-year tour of duty
in a country which has asked for Peace Corps assistance, and
works with the local people on projects that range from teaching to road building. There are many more male Volunteers
than female; indeed, men outnumber the women two to one.
Moreover, the men are a bit younger, the average age for
men is twenty-four, for women twenty-six. The total age range
stretches from eighteen (the Peace Corps minimum) to sev-

PEACE CORPS ORGANIZATION PLAN

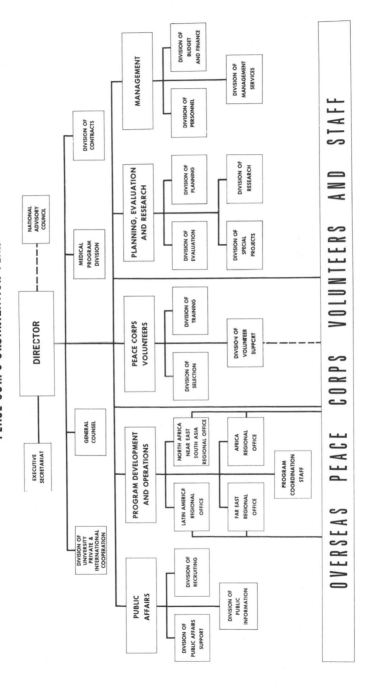

enty-six; the oldest PCV is a seventy-six-year-old engineer who
is working in East Pakistan. One hundred and fifty-four Volunteers are over forty, and there are more grandparents than
teen-agers.

Eight out of nine PCVs are single, but married couples
are accepted if both qualify. In spite of the busy schedules,
there is romance in the Peace Corps. Ninety-eight couples
have married since they joined up, sixty-six while still in the
Corps, thirty-two after they left the Corps. The first Peace
Corps baby was born on May 16, 1962, to a Volunteer-couple
in Nigeria. Since then, twelve more Peace Corps babies have
been born—including a set of twins, to a PCV and his Irish
nurse bride in Tanganyika. Eighteen other couples returned
to the States prior to the wife's delivery date.

Peace Corps Volunteers come from all the fifty states, plus
the District of Columbia, the Commonwealth of Puerto Rico,
and the Virgin Islands. As of April, 1963, California had the
most Volunteers overseas (510), New York State was second
with 358.

The job skills vary from homemaking and surveying to
plumbing and fishing; the majority have teaching skills. As
of June 30, 1963, eighty-one Volunteers and trainees had
their doctoral degrees, and 540 had their master's degrees.
Only 202 had no education beyond high school.

The recruiting program of the Corps is active and in evidence everywhere. Publicity material and application forms
can be obtained from many local libraries and post offices,
from county agricultural agents, from Congressmen, or from
many colleges. Most student centers have Peace Corps information booklets; most university bulletin boards display
Peace Corps posters. Indeed, one can scarcely avoid en-
countering information on the Peace Corps. Shriver's staff
issues reams of press releases, folders, and brochures; national periodicals as well as the press accommodate by publishing one account after another of Peace Corps activities.

Nearly all of the latter are written in a favorable tone.

The information booklets answer about every question a potential Volunteer could ask: who is eligible to apply; what experience or education is necessary; what arrangements are made concerning living allowances, vacation privileges, and medical care. One booklet deals exclusively with older people in the Corps and gives case histories of those who have joined and tells of the special fields where older people can serve best. Since there is no maximum age limit, a number of people in their seventies have been assigned to overseas duty.

On the first page of the application the primary qualifications are stated: one must be a citizen of the United States and eighteen years of age or older. One may be single or married, as long as there are no dependents under eighteen. The application includes thirty multipart questions designed to elicit information on the background and experience of the applicant as well as on the areas in which he may have special interest, skill, and education. At the end of the questionnaire, the applicant is asked to state what he hopes to accomplish by serving in the Peace Corps.

Questionnaires are returned to headquarters in Washington. There they are evaluated by the Divisions of Selection and of Planning and Evaluation. Applicants who have the skills needed for projects which are already in operation or are being planned in the near future are invited to take the Peace Corps Placement Test.

The Placement Test, originally four and a half hours long, was cut to one and a half in 1964. It is divided into two parts, one to gauge the general abilities of the applicant, the other to determine his language aptitude. Because these questions are reused, they are secret; but sample questions are issued so that the applicants may get some idea of what is expected of them. The Corps stresses that the Placement Test is not the sort of examination that can be passed or failed; it is intended solely to help the Corps decide in which countries and in what kind of work a Volunteer might be most effective. However, the score on the language section is closely examined by the selection officers. An applicant with a low score may be assigned to an English-speaking country, where he will not need a second language.

When replacements are needed, when plans for a new project are approved, or when a country requests additional Volunteers, qualified applicants are given strict health examinations at a federal medical facility, if the applicant lives within a hundred miles of one, or by a private physician. The examining physician fills out a form that covers the applicant's complete medical history.

Psychological screening is done by a psychiatrist also engaged by the Peace Corps. A psychologist on the faculty of the college that is responsible for the training, or one who is hired from outside, counsels, tests, and closely scrutinizes each Volunteer during the training period. The psychologist may advise that a Volunteer be dropped, but Washington, at its discretion, may overrule him. The Washington headquarters includes one or more psychologists; during the first two years of the Corps, a University of Michigan psychologist—Lowell Kelly—was chief of the Division of Selection.

Volunteers must have excellent physical health and be emotionally mature if they are to contend with the hardships they may encounter while living in underdeveloped countries.

When the applicant has completed these examinations satisfactorily, he moves into the training program for his group. He is informed at that time of the country where he will serve and the job he is to perform. However, the Corps notifies each applicant that the training period is considered an extended comprehensive test of the candidate's suitability for service. The training is both rugged and rapid, and some trainees cannot keep up the pace.

Volunteers recruited for any given project are trained

together, but no two groups follow exactly the same schedule. The programs depend upon the facilities and the faculty available at the training institution and on the type of assignment and work to be carried out in the field. However, all groups are trained according to a three-phase pattern: the basic training, which is eight to ten weeks long and is taken in the United States; the field training, usually given at the Peace Corps Field Training Center in Puerto Rico; and finally, the overseas training.

Phase I includes grueling work sessions that average about ten hours a day, for six days a week—double the load carried by regular college students. The courses are held at a university selected for its eminence in a particular field, i.e., engineering at Texas Western for Volunteer surveyors and geologists destined for Tanganyika; education courses at Columbia Teachers College for Volunteers who will teach in Nigerian secondary schools. The training programs may differ considerably, but certain basic courses are given to all Volunteers. "The trainee must understand the project, its place in the total development picture of the host country, and his place within it," says the Peace Corps manual. "He should understand the relationships between the Peace Corps and the host country, the arrangements that have been made for the actual operation of the project in the field and specific information about precisely what he will be doing. He should understand how the project emerged and where it is intended to lead."

Toward this end, Phase I includes studies of the language and the background of the host country, of American politics and history, of world affairs, and of the technical knowledge and skills required overseas. In addition, there is health and medical training (first aid plus rudimentary treatment for various unfamiliar ailments), physical training and recreation, and general orientation to acquaint the Volunteers with the organization of the Corps, the administrative procedures, and the role of the Volunteer overseas.

After completing Phase I, the Volunteers are usually sent to Puerto Rico for field training at either Camp Radley or Camp Crozier. (These camps were named after PCV Lawrence Radley and PCV David Crozier, both twenty-two, who were killed in a plane accident in Colombia on April 22, 1962.) Most trainees are sent to Puerto Rico, although field training has been conducted in other places. The principal objective of Phase II is to make sure that the trainee can perform effectively under totally different cultural conditions and in situations of unusual stress. Therefore, emphasis is placed not only on physical conditioning, but on fortifying the trainee's confidence in himself. The course seeks to develop those qualities that will give the Volunteer the know-how to adjust to a more difficult way of life and the perseverance to stay with his job in spite of the numerous frustrations.

Trainees are sent out on expeditions, sometimes alone, sometimes in a small group, into the wooded mountains around the camps to spend the night, or several nights, shifting for themselves. Time is spent on map and compass exercises, on advanced first aid, on all kinds of water activities such as lifesaving and artificial respiration, and on rock rescue techniques. Under the heading of community development, everyone gets a glimpse of what it will be like to go into a strange town, survey its needs, and enlist the help of townspeople in a community project. There are also continuing language study and lectures. This demanding program gives the supervisors an opportunity to observe the physical and psychological capacities of the trainee and his ability to work with others.

In the final week of Phase II, a resumé is prepared on each candidate. It includes information gleaned from the questionnaire in the original application, from the Placement Test, from letters of reference, from medical records, from a thorough investigation by the Civil Service Commission, and from ratings by the supervisors of the training program. Then a selection board, consisting of representatives from the Peace

Corps, from the training institution, and from the embassy of the host nation, meets to examine the complete record of each trainee and to recommend those candidates who should be assigned to specific projects.

Those selected are sent to the host country for Phase III of their training. This period can take from two weeks to three months; the average is about a month. Phase III is conducted by the host government, and its content, format, and the personnel involved are chosen by that government in consultation with Corps officials. Generally, this final phase includes an orientation to the host country together with introductions to the people with whom the Volunteers will work. There is often additional training in language and in the special skills required for the various projects.

The PCVs—now full-fledged Volunteers—disperse to their final destination, the place of assignment. Usually they serve in teams, but there are instances where a Volunteer has lived and worked entirely alone.

Once in the field, the PCVs are under the supervision of the local government, with the Field Representative acting as intermediary. PCVs have no diplomatic immunity and no other special privileges; they receive the same treatment in the host country as would any other foreign visitor, and they must conduct themselves accordingly.

During their two-year service in the Corps, they are not allowed to return to the United States on leave. However, they do accumulate leave at the rate of two and a half calendar days for each month of satisfactory service. On the approval of the Field Rep, they may use this time to travel, for which purpose they receive a special allowance of five dollars per day while they are on vacation.

Otherwise, the PCVs—although they are given allowances for food, clothing, housing, and incidental expenses—receive no pay while abroad. These allowances average about two dollars a day or sixty dollars a month, but may be higher,

depending upon the conditions in the particular country and
the needs of the PCVs.

A sampling of the allowances in American dollars that were
granted in May, 1963, will indicate how the allowances vary
from country to country:

Nigeria—reduced from $163 to $149 a month; Tanganyika
—from $182 to $160; Bolivia—from $150 to $125; Colombia—
$150 to $119.

India and West Pakistan allowances had to be raised;
India from $63 to $70, in Pakistan from $75 to $81.

In two Venezuelan cities—Caracas and Maracaibo—the
PCVs are allowed $189, but those in the rural areas of Vene-
zuela are allowed only $167. In the Philippines, some get as
little as $53 a month. In Nepal, where living quarters are
free, the monthly allowance is $46; contrast that with Niger,
which has the highest allowance rate: $220. From Jamaica,
one PCV wrote: "Our daily allowance at Chestervale Youth
Camp is a little over two dollars a day plus an additional
twenty dollars a month for food (which we sure use!). Our
allowances are different from those of the Volunteers in town
since they need more money for transportation to and from
work, rent, etc."

Since the allowances are usually paid in local currency and
according to local pay scale the PCVs are on an equal footing
with the local people in relation to budgeting, shopping, and
daily living.

In addition, PCVs are credited with seventy-five dollars a
month, deposited for their return, to help tide them over while
they resettle in the States and look for new jobs. Team leaders
are paid a hundred dollars a month in addition to their
monthly allowance. The Field Rep is salaried. His family
may accompany him at government expense, and although
there has been some criticism of this, it is actually no different
from the payments for moving the families of armed forces
personnel and diplomats. PCVs may allot any portion of their

monthly seventy-five-dollar termination payments to support of a parent, to pay insurance premiums, to help pay for the education of a member of his family, or to meet other commitments. PCVs are also allowed to receive from local people gifts of books, materials, and money given for use in the local projects.

Compensation to the PCVs and the Reps is only a small part of the expense of the Peace Corps program. The cost of training, equipping, and setting a Volunteer down in the field is estimated at about $10,000 per recruit per year. Shriver asked the Eighty-seventh Congress for an appropriation of $63,750,-000, but was granted only $59,000,000. The Peace Corps therefore had to decrease the number of Volunteers for which it had planned—from 10,000 to 9,000. (In 1963, applications flowed in at the rate of 3,000 per month, up from the 2,000 a month in 1962.)

According to PC headquarters, only one out of ten applicants reaches the field, and among these there are probably some who are not as well qualified as they should be. In early 1962, 698 Volunteers were serving abroad in twelve host countries: Chile, Colombia, Ghana, India, Malaya, Nigeria, Pakistan, Philippines, Sierra Leone, St. Lucia, Tanganyika, and Thailand.

Since then the number of Volunteers has increased seven times; the number of host countries four times. As of April, 1963, about 4,000 PCVs were serving overseas. In addition, 877 Americans were in training prior to being sent out to their assignments in seventeen countries.

By June 30, 1963, 4,379 PCVs were at work in forty-five countries, and 2,000 trainees were enrolled in PC programs at various colleges and universities.

Among these trainees was the tenth group to be scheduled for Peru (referred to as Peru 10); Philippines 9 was in training, as were Colombia 8 and Pakistan 7; and a sixth contingent was being trained for each of three other countries—Nigeria, Thailand, and the Dominican Republic.

PCVs are sent only to countries whose governments ask for Volunteers. Such suggestions or requests may come in through the American Embassy or the local Agency for International Development (AID) mission, through private agencies or universities, through personal contacts with Peace Corps officials who may be visiting an area, or directly from the country. In deciding which applications to accept, the type of project is considered. According to the Peace Corps' definition: "To be eligible for Peace Corps participation, a project must make a contribution to the economic, social, cultural or political development of the host country . . . It must require primarily 'workers' or 'doers' with skills not sufficiently available in the host country, as distinct from advisors or consultants."

"The Peace Corps emphasizes projects which have an impact upon development of the host country or upon an activity being undertaken to foster that development," Shriver told Congress in his presentation on December 31, 1961. "It also favors projects which involve maximum contact between Volunteers and the people and the society of the country served. Where possible, the host country nationals [acting as counterparts to the Volunteers] participate in the work, for every project looks toward their taking over eventually the jobs of Peace Corps Volunteers."

Once a country has put in its request, the Peace Corps consults the American Embassy and the AID Mission to assure coordination, and to ascertain whether or not this particular project will duplicate or counteract other American work in the host country. An exchange of diplomatic notes follows between the American Embassy and the foreign ministry of the host country before an agreement is drawn.

An agreement was made with Ghana—the first country to receive PCVs—in an official document signed at Accra on July 19, 1961. On September 12, Tom Livingston, the first

OVERSEAS VOLUNTEERS BY CATEGORY OF PROJECTS
AND GEOGRAPHIC AREAS

CATEGORY OF PROJECTS	AFRICA	FAR EAST	LATIN AMERICA	NEAR EAST & SOUTH ASIA	TOTAL
Agricultural Extension	28	—	239	64	331
Community Action:					
Rural	74	108	572	103	857
Urban	—	—	265	—	265
Education:					
Elementary	76	399	9	—	484
Secondary	980	190	104	133	1,407
University	4	106	66	98	274
Adult	8	—	—	—	8
Vocational	16	46	48	7	117
Physical	33	32	27	9	101
Health	80	95	154	32	361
Multi-Purpose	—	—	—	64	64
Public Works	94	—	—	16	110
TOTALS	1,393	976	1,484	526	4,379

From the *PC Volunteer*. A quarterly statistical summary, compiled by
the Division of Volunteer Support, June 30, 1963.

Volunteer to start work, began to teach in a secondary school
in Ghana. (The Tanganyika group started training first, but
the Ghana group beat them to the field.) Ghana paid the
entire living allowance of each Volunteer, the same amount it
pays its own teachers. This type of contribution is encouraged
since it makes the host country an active participant in the
project. Other countries have contributed training programs,
transportation, housing, medical and hospital services, or
whatever else they are able to offer.

Some countries have relatively simple needs, others very
complex requirements. (See table above.) Borneo, for example,
asked for special, highly individual skills, which it was impossible to fill completely from the ranks of the PCVs. Among

the specialists needed were: an agricultural economist to set up a system of reporting agricultural statistics; a hydrologist to measure the rise and fall of rivers; a supply officer for a malaria control team; an entomologist. To meet the 102 skills enumerated, Field Rep John Landgraf arrived in Borneo with ninety-six PCVs commanding skills that might cover any imaginable task.

Frequently, the Corps cannot meet the numbers requested with PCVs who have the special qualifications desired; in such cases a smaller number is sent. When both Brazil and Togo asked for fishermen, neither request could be filled. Eventually, an American recruited his own team of fishermen to go to Togo.

The projects can actually be handled in several different ways. The Peace Corps seeks to reinforce existing programs of voluntary organizations and therefore provides Volunteers for work through contracts for Peace Corps type programs carried out by private agencies; through contracts with colleges, universities, or other educational institutions; through the programs of other government agencies; through United Nations programs and those of other international agencies; and through directly administered Peace Corps programs with host countries.

This framework, established by the original planners, proved amazingly successful. It surprised even Sargent Shriver, who is reported to have said in the early days, "We don't even know if we'll be in business two years from now." But the Peace Corps is still here, apparently, to stay.

PART I

The Early Volunteers

1

I could live comme les Africains *for a few days . . . with no real ill effects; but two years? We were all wondering how the Peace Corps was going to make out. One could exist, but there was a risk that the enthusiasm, which got us to Africa in the first place, might gradually drain away. And what use would we be then? Our pioneering youth is too valuable to be unnecessarily de-energized. The world needs the creativity which comes from well-being.*

RUTH T. PLIMPTON
from *Operation Crossroads Africa*

Lomé's airport is too small to accommodate large trans-Atlantic jets, so PCV Mike Ruggiero, a fishery expert, arrived for his preview of Togo by way of Liberia, Senegal, and Ghana. From the Accra airport he made the last stretch of the trip to Lomé in a rented car.

To his eyes, accustomed to the miles of irregular, ever varying New England coastline, tiny Togo—smallest independent country in Africa—looked like "nothing." A four-hundred-mile strip of brownish-green land, sandwiched between Ghana and Dahomey, the coastline is only forty-one miles long, but with no harbor and not a single docking facility. Foamy surf pounds against sugar-white beach which is dappled with dug-out canoes and grass fishing shacks. Togo is an Ewe word for "behind the sea."

How did forty-one-year-old Michael Ruggiero from Peabody, Massachusetts, suddenly find himself five thousand miles away on the coast of Africa? His story is unique in many of its details, yet representative of the amazing transplantations that the Peace Corps effects with its volunteer personnel.

When the Peace Corps was first organized in 1961—and most people believed that the ranks of the Corps would be filled with adventuresome college students only—Mike, a Civil Service career man with seventeen years of professional experience, sent in an application, "just for kicks," as he put it. Then he waited eagerly for a reply. Several weeks went by, but no word came from Washington. Almost daily the newspapers carried stories about men and women who had been accepted and were being sent off for Peace Corps training—and still no word. Six months after he had sent in his application, Mike decided to take action. He telephoned the Washington headquarters of the Peace Corps and asked, in effect, "What happened?"

"You're the only fisherman who has volunteered," someone in the Division of Selection told him. "We can't send you out alone."

"Then how about letting me recruit my own team?" Mike retorted, without realizing what he was letting himself in for. "There are dozens of men here in New England and in all the coastal towns who've fished either on trawlers or draggers or on their own small boats. I'm sure there are men who'd like to share in the work of helping others."

The voice at headquarters sounded enthusiastic, and Mike, after some additional reflection, liked his idea enough to go forward with it. He began to ask around among his fisherman friends. There was definitely interest. Then it was not long before United States Senator Benjamin A. Smith 2nd of Massachusetts heard about his project and offered to back it.

"I discovered that things *can* happen fast in the Corps," Mike described the incident later. "Shriver gave his approval right away, and even President Kennedy heard about my plan. Then Richard Bowman, special assistant in the Corps' Division of Agriculture, came up to work out the details."

Mike's chief at the United States Bureau of Commercial Fisheries in Gloucester, Massachusetts, naturally did not share the general enthusiasm. In fact, he tried to neutralize Mike's interest in the whole venture by offering a promotion and a raise. "That was understandable," Mike told me. "There are only twenty-seven of us in the whole country with my particular specialty. Mostly the fisheries have to use biologists to do their exploratory fishing."

By April 15, 1962, Mike on his own time was working unofficially to recruit the other men he would need to make up his team. The New York *Times* of that date published his picture together with his request that fishermen write to him about volunteering for service in the Corps "to help hungry people learn to take more food out of the sea for themselves." The applications were to be sent to Mike at his address in Peabody.

"What a telephone and transportation bill I ran up that month," Mike said; since he was still unofficial his costs were his own to bear. "I was on the phone to Washington or talking to applicants and meeting with them all the time."

In talking to the men, he explained his purpose was two-fold: To get a wide spread of fishing skills and to select a group of men who could work together compatibly.

"I didn't have to worry as much as most recruiters do about how Volunteers would stand up under isolation," Mike explained. "Fishermen are a breed apart. And morale isn't a big problem. They're used to being alone, yet if they have to, they can also live in cramped quarters. They just like to catch fish."

Within six weeks, Mike Ruggiero and Richard Bowman had screened all the applicants and carefully selected eight.

In the meantime, the government of Togo, as if it had been waiting for Mike Ruggiero to volunteer, filed a request with the Peace Corps for men who could teach modern fishing techniques. Headquarters decided that Mike and his eight fishermen would be assigned to Togo. First, however, they would have to complete the normal Peace Corps training program at Howard University in Washington, D.C.

Before Mike left for Howard, he spent a Saturday afternoon telling me about his fishing experiences, about the Peace Corps, and, also, about his love for music. The handsome six-footer with slightly graying curly hair talked eagerly; he looked forward to the opportunity to teach the Togolese how to obtain more from the sea.

He was amused by a packet he had just received from Peace Corps headquarters. The Corps, suggesting the kind of clothing and equipment he should bring along, also recommended various reading materials that might help him prepare himself for his assignment. On the list of fishing instruction booklets was one booklet that Mike himself had written! Five others had been written by the man with whom he had been working at the bureau in Gloucester. Just before leaving his job, Mike had finished a paper on lines and had started another on New England trawls. As he showed me various of his writings, he talked animatedly about the gear he had described from every kind of fishery in the world, the experimental cruises on which he had gone, how he had developed a plastic (polypropylene) twine which is easier to tow and which makes it possible to catch more fish. He was proud of his work, yet his pride was tempered by a certain modesty, for Mike still did not realize that there was no one on the staff of the Peace Corps, or on the faculty of Howard, who could teach him and his fellow Volunteers anything about fishing that they did not already know.

Several of the Volunteer fishermen had been Mike Ruggiero's friends or acquaintances for years. They admitted that they had joined the Peace Corps primarily because of Mike's enthusiasm and leadership, only secondarily because of the goals of the Corps itself.

One potentially valuable member of the group would probably never have been accepted had Mike not sponsored him. Mike declared in pleading for him, "Even if he is practically illiterate, he's one of the best fishermen I know."

Headquarters took him on Mike's recommendation, and the man reported at Howard University with the others late in June, 1962. That was approximately one year after Mike had first mailed in his application. The accelerated program of college courses was tough—technical studies, area studies, world affairs, and French conversation (while there are forty-four local dialects spoken in Togo, the primary language is French.)

"He understood everything that went on," Mike said about his friend, "and he remembered more than most of us. I suspect that he pretends to be less literate than he really is. Of course, his biggest problem was making the psychological adjustment to life on a college campus. But guess where he really showed us up? In conversational French. He beat us all and it wasn't because we weren't trying," he grinned. "We had a doll of a Wellesley girl named Martha Noel for a teacher, so there was no lack of motivation for any of us."

Mike knew everyone on his team. He and each of the other eight men—they ranged in age from nineteen to fifty-seven—was already an expert in some type of salt- or fresh-water fishing—seining, gill netting, trawling, clam digging, lobstering, oyster culture, etc. They all knew how to build boats, to mend nets, to develop gear to fit the needs of the locale, and to process fish. But no one, including the instructors at Howard University, knew what fishing conditions to expect in Togo—the depth of the water, the kinds of pots, the size of the nets that would be needed; not even the kind of fishing methods that were being used now. Togo has no fishing regulations, so these factors alone could determine the type of gear to be taken along and the different techniques that could be used.

The Peace Corps had decided that as soon as Mike had completed the program at Howard he should spend two weeks in Togo. While he was evaluating the fishing conditions there, his fellow fishermen could begin the second stage of their training at the Peace Corps camp in Puerto Rico. Suddenly, this plan, too, was changed, and even before the program at Howard had ended, Mike was told to get ready for immediate departure to Togo. He packed his bag and went to claim the money he would need for the trip. But someone in the accounting office remembered that Volunteers are not full-fledged government employees until they have completed the training program, have passed a security check, and have embarked for the host country. Therefore, the government could not pay Mike's transportation; no travel funds had been allocated for trainees.

"I don't know from whose pocket my trip came, but somebody dug up the money," Mike explained later. "All I know is that I went with expenses paid."

Mike took to Togo from his first day, registering all the sights and sounds with which he and his men would be living for the next two years.

As is traditional in West Africa, the women own all the vehicles of transportation—old trucks, buses, and lorries known as "mammy wagons." Usually overloaded with people, goats, pigs, chickens and with all sorts of goods on the roof, the vehicles are never so crowded that room can't be made for "just one more" rider. Not even a full load slows them down as they jounce along, throwing up clouds of dust on the dirt roads.

In Lomé, capital city of about 78,000—swollen now by several thousand exiles from Ghana, mostly political refugees who fled without their wives and families and are now unemployed—the women also operate the markets. The stench in the fish market is unbelievable even to a fisherman. For here the fish are not cleaned; they are just dried in the sun with the heads left on, and the smell, as Mike put it, is "never to be forgotten." Some fish is salted or smoked, but most of the catch is ground up, head and all, for food. Of course, there are flies over everything.

The Togo government had made its request of the Peace Corps hoping that the team of Volunteers might help in developing a full-fledged fishing industry. Such an industry would be an economic boon to a country whose economy is based on coffee and cocoa production. Even more important, a fishing industry would improve the health of the populace by supplementing the meager native diet with an abundance of inexpensive fresh fish.

For two weeks, while his "boys" were still in their classes in Washington, Mike traveled Togo's dusty roads, from south to north and north to south. He observed the local fishermen as they used their trial-and-error techniques and inadequate gear to fish the lakes, the rivers, and the ocean.

"We can probably increase the catch two or three times," Mike concluded quickly.

He talked with the men who were building an irrigation dam at Lake Togo (Le Lac) about introducing food fish into the lake. He also visited a reservoir where he was immediately convinced the Peace Corps should start fish culture. Out on the lake, men were fishing with barricade-like weirs and doing cast netting. "Great spot for oyster culture," Mike, who enjoys diving and is a qualified Navy underwater swimmer, pointed out. "I lived with oysters for months when I was a Navy diver on Long Island, experimenting with oyster beds. I used to check them every day."

When Mike finally boarded a plane to take him back to the States and to take over the vocational training sessions at Howard, his report to the other fishermen was brief but graphic: "The food is lousy, mostly starch and no protein. There's no water fit to drink without boiling, filtering, and putting in pills that make it almost unpalatable. There are bugs and disease and an uneasy political situation. Actually, I'm scared—but we're going anyway."

Under his direction, the men converted the lawns of Howard University into practice fields for net casting, and used nets that Mike had brought back with him from Togo. "We might as well get the habit of doing everything with people watching us," he told his teammates. "I think visual education will work best, especially with the children. We'll make nets, we'll repair equipment, or we'll build boats, and we'll let the Togolese watch us. Some of them may get interested in learning."

Mike had already seen enough to convince himself that it would not be hard to get people in Togo to gather around for a look at anything new. "During one of my stops an announcement was made that a film would be shown by a United Nations representative. Five or six hundred Togolese showed up. They'll come to see us, too."

Deciding what items—personal and professional—to take along for a two-year stay in an underdeveloped country with a tropical climate is not easy. Each fisherman had been allotted a thousand dollars for equipment, and a number of American companies had donated out-of-date gear to make up a sizeable cache. Having concluded that the native dugouts used by the local fishermen were less efficient than Gloucester dories, Mike also decided to take along two dories.

"The dories need less lumber and they're cheaper," Mike explained. "Those dugouts of theirs are made out of the trunks of huge trees and involve a lot of time and waste."

In addition to the fishing gear and personal items, the Volunteers packed quantities of assorted vegetable seeds. Regardless of their specialties, most Volunteers in underdeveloped countries sooner or later take up gardening, for the produce is usually needed to relieve the monotony of the local diet. Sometimes the vegetables are also important for trading purposes.

From his firsthand observations, Mike told his teammates about some of the local customs: "The babies on their mothers' backs are cute. But never pat one of the children with your left hand or put your left hand out toward any person. Togolese believe the left hand is bad, dirty, and you mustn't touch anyone with it. As far as food goes, the first rule is never throw anything away. When you're eating a sandwich, the children will all gather round, just waiting for you to give them the bits that are left over. Every crumb is precious."

Finished with the classes at Howard, Mike went on his week of home leave; all Volunteers get home leave before they report for their second stage of training in Puerto Rico. His enthusiasm ran higher than ever.

"The Peace Corps is so fouled up," he said, in a sort of reversed compliment, "and, at the same time, it's so great."

He scoffed at the suggestion that the training of Volunteers improved as the Peace Corps gained experience: "Are you kidding? It's terrible. They're all mixed up. But Howard's the greatest. Is it ever tough! They did everything for us; it must have cost a fortune—all those lectures, trips and everything. The Peace Corps is a lousy outfit, but I love it."

Of the nine fishermen who arrived in Washington late in June, there was one dropout—a nineteen-year-old who turned around and went home almost as soon as he got to Washington. His was completely a personal reaction: he knew at once that he would be too lonely without his family and his girl friend. Mike concurred; that one would probably be of no help in Togo. A replacement, Jackie Theriot from Louisiana—described by Mike as "a great boy who already speaks French"—was recruited to fill the vacancy, and as planned, nine members shipped out for Togo four months later. All were proud that they had made it "through Puerto Rico."

"It was a great conditioning course—mountain climbing, swimming, camping," Mike said of the second-stage training in Puerto Rico. "The best part for us was La Parquera where we spent a full week observing local fishing methods, scuba diving, and living on a little island owned by the University of Puerto Rico."

Early in November, 1962, I received the first of several letters Mike would write me from Togo. As the return address stated, Mike was now a full-fledged member of the *Corps de la Paix*.

"We arrived in Lomé at 6:45 A.M., October 23, and were met by the Field Representative who is responsible for Volunteers in Togo. It was damp, but the sun was just coming up. We're putting up at a local hotel until our home and equipment are ready. For now, we're eating all French food, but this will be too expensive for the long run. Each day we make field trips to local fishing villages, just to get the lay of the land. Eventually, after our gear arrives, two of the men—Vito Blonda, who's a granddad, and Keith Keller, who had his nineteenth birthday during training—will be in Togoville on Le Lac; two others—Bill Outten and Jackie Theriot—will work near Dapango in the north, and five of us (Pat White, Frank Ciaramitaro, George Toneatti, Merton Plume and I) will be at Anécho.

"We've met local officials, and best of all, the U.N. adviser to the Togolese government, whom I told you about, gave a party for us, so we met all the local fishing chiefs and tribal chiefs from the villages. We've received a very cordial welcome and got a big play in the local paper, both in French and in Ewe.

"So far, we've done no fishing, but four of the boys went out in dugouts—two to a dugout—for red snapper. They were allowed to paddle but not to fish. They left at 6:00 A.M. and returned at 5:00 P.M., claiming that the local fishermen are highly skilled seamen and their dugouts very efficient and seaworthy. These boats, without any navigational aids, go over twenty miles to sea and return safely. They're guided only by the wind and the sea, which are always in one direction.

"Few young people are learning to be fishermen, but we hope to change this. My men love the local sights, especially the women carrying everything on their heads and the babies

on their backs. "We all feel great about the project."
Mike's entrance into the Peace Corps had not followed the
usual pattern: no other trainee had been permitted to assist in
recruiting or been sent to preview the host country; few got
so much publicity. And since the Corps has not adopted
either practice for general use, Mike's early experience as a
PCV remains unique.

Nevertheless, his comments reveal some of the attitudes that
are characteristic of Volunteers during the training period.
Trainees are extremely enthusiastic; the Peace Corps seems
to offer them unlimited opportunities to use their initiative in
serving a real need. At the same time, they tend to belittle
the competence of both the administrators and the training
staff of the Peace Corps. This generally critical attitude
toward official disorganization may inspire some Volunteers
to take matters into their own hands in the host country, but
Peace Corps officials say they welcome that. As one trainee
candidly said to me, "As long as we're griping about headquarters and insisting that our group is the greatest in the
Corps, there's nothing to worry about."

Trainees, most of whom have not seen their host country
beforehand, are often quite uneasy as the day for their departure nears. This is understandable, for they are to leave for a
strange new country, one in which they are expected to perform valuable services, perhaps a country where left hands
are "bad," where proper etiquette requires that food be eaten
with the fingers, where there may be political unrest.

Soon after meeting Mike Ruggiero, I joined a Peace Corps
group that was training with the faculty of New York University in New York City. The forty-five members of this group
were destined for Somalia.

The Somali Republic, formed in 1960 when British Somaliland and Italian Somaliland united to become independent,
is an East African country about the size of Texas. Bounded

on the north by the Gulf of Aden and on the east by the Indian Ocean, its borders also touch Kenya (to the south) and Ethiopia, where disputes over possession of a few miles of arid desert continue to rage. In the south, where the economy is supported chiefly by the banana crop, Italian influence is still strong.

I first met the Somalia group on May 5, 1962, a Saturday afternoon, on the New York University campus. The group was being trained for teaching in the intermediate and secondary schools of Somalia. Most of the Volunteers would teach English, and others science, mathematics, education, commercial subjects, and industrial arts. In preparation, the trainees were obliged to take seventy hours of Somali, which is a spoken but not a written language. During the practice sessions each student, wearing headphones, sat in a separate booth and listened to tape recordings of words and sentences spoken by a native Somali, which they, in turn, had to repeat back to the teaching machine. The instructor checked each student's progress by plugging into the different booths.

It seems to me now that my reactions after my first visit with the Somalia trainees, indicate that I lacked insight into the potential of the Volunteers. I was soon to learn that the qualities we associate with success in business situations, for example, are not those that necessarily make for successful Volunteers. My first impressions underestimated what two months of rigorous training can do to develop confidence, muscle, and tolerance for the discomforts and frustrations to come in the field. Fortunately, those at the top level in the Peace Corps and in the universities which contracted to train Volunteers had a clearer vision of what intensive training could accomplish.

The first afternoon class was in World Affairs. The room was nearly full. I slipped into the nearest vacant chair and took a look around.

Fat, skinny, light, dark, white, colored, quiet, noisy, one

beard, several pipe smokers, one cigar, several cigarettes (despite a "No Smoking in this room" sign up front)—probably much like any classroom of college students, except for a wider age range. I knew that three young married couples were in the group. What impressed me most was everyone's friendliness. There seemed to be no constraint, even though they had met each other only recently and they showed no fatigue from a schedule that provided them with activity from eight in the morning to ten every night. Later, they introduced themselves. They were as curious about me as I was about them. They wanted to know what did I do? Whom did I write for? What did I think of the Peace Corps?

The young instructor said little; he was pleasant, even jocular as he listened. He asked the PCVs for ten oral reports on books about various countries in Africa. The trainees quickly accepted assignments to give seven-minute reports at the next several meetings of the class. One eager recruit offered to do two reports, but the instructor said no, one to a customer.

Six Volunteers gave their reports during the afternoon. I recall that the report by William "Bill" Levine, a University of Pittsburgh graduate, was outstanding for content, general knowledge of the subject and ease of presentation. Speaking without notes and illustrating his subject with charts and drawings that he made on the blackboard, Bill talked for more than the allotted seven minutes. But the instructor did not interrupt him. One girl read her entire report, while seated, glancing up only now and then at her audience. Again, no comment from the instructor. A boy made several grammatical errors as he spoke. Still no comment or correction from either the instructor or the trainees, although I was sure the latter would have questioned and criticized had they been given the opportunity. Lack of time apparently made class discussion impractical.

After the World Affairs class, we all walked over to the

gym for physical education. In this setting, the Volunteers—
especially the girls—appeared self-conscious. They were less
at ease with each other and with themselves than they had
been in the classroom. Perhaps they were not used to mixed
sports.

The obvious lack of physical fitness in several PCVs concerned me. Although I was aware that they had not been
selected for athletic prowess but for other skills, the sight of
spindly legs, weak, flabby bodies, a paunchy gray-haired man
(he wasn't bad at basketball), an over-forty woman with a
limp from a recently broken ankle, all made me wonder if the
recruiting system had really selected a group of men and
women who could be molded within two months into hardy,
healthy, well-adjusted, and self-confident persons capable of
surviving under hardship conditions.

Near the close of the session the coach, a rugged, deep-
voiced man, with whistle in hand, came over to me.

"What do you think?"

"Oh, average," I replied noncommittally.

"Too average, that's what worries me," he muttered. "I'm
disappointed. Most of 'em I don't want representing me."

"Don't you get to grade them?"

"No. The Peace Corps doesn't even ask me to take attendance. That's why I object to the program. I made them sign
up in the beginning and I make them work. I won't just let
them sit around."

I was disturbed. Are we all expecting too much, I asked
myself. These people are bright, outgoing, friendly, easy to
get acquainted with, eager to talk, and yet my first impression
was that some of them were less than "all 'round." Then I
recalled that we were not, after all, training a team for an
Olympics competition. Volunteers are selected primarily to
export the ideals of American democracy, and not for the
purpose of proving to the world that all Americans are perfect
physical specimens. There is no point in creating an image

of Americans that is false; we would never be able to live up to it. I remembered now with a smile that a PCV had once said to me, "The Peace Corps is right—we should send out idealism wrapped in realistic packages."

As the study sessions at NYU drew to a close, I questioned several trainees about the value of the Peace Corps training program: Did they feel it prepared them for their assignments? They weren't sure, and they wouldn't be until they had had a chance to put their training into practice. What the trainees did convey to me was a feeling of huge optimism. As Bill Levine later told an audience of relatives and friends in NYU's auditorium: "When we arrived we wondered if we could possibly teach. We were told, 'I know it—you can all teach.' And we found that we can. We've had an opportunity to teach in the local New York City schools, and we're confident now—at the end of our training period here at NYU— that we can do what Somalia wants."

Enthusiasm among the Volunteers mounted as they left for the week's home leave prior to their departure for Somalia. Instead of the usual training in Puerto Rico, these Volunteers had been scheduled to receive their second-stage training in Somalia.

The next we hear of the group is on July 14, at 5:30 in the morning. Bill Levine wrote:

"We were over Egypt. Looking out, I could see nothing but sand and bare mountains. Many thoughts ran through my head, the most prominent one being whether we had made the right choice in coming.

"Around 8:15 A.M. we crossed into Somalia. The scenery was better and we may have even convinced ourselves that there was more green than there really was. The touchdown at Mogadiscio was especially exciting. Everybody was keyed up; terrible jokes got rave reactions. Some were silent, others were sneezing or scratching, but most of this disappeared as soon as the plane rolled to a halt. Baggage was handled well and the only confused ones seemed to be the Volunteers themselves."

Boris Sojka, who kept a diary for himself and his wife, Carole, recorded the experience as follows:

"*Forty-five Minutes from Mogadiscio in the air.* Brown and barren country. Flew over Hargeisa. Could not believe it that small and desolate. Lot of scrub bushes. Reminds me of the Mojave Desert from the air.

"*Reactions:* I generally feel good. Terrific anxiety in the group. Some kept drinking the liquor served almost all the time across. Rest requested bar be closed for the good of the group. Yesterday before Bierut, many had butterfly stomachs. Tons of Alka-Seltzer consumed. We all see how rough it will be. The reality of it has been hitting for the past twenty-four hours. Now that we see Somalia, the reality hits even more. God, what a desolate country. We all seem better than yesterday though. Four continents in thirty hours, rather shocking. Clouds completely covering the land. Volunteers reading or light talking. No talk about our landing or what we'll do there."

Bill Levine's wife, Maryl, also described the flight, going on, however, to depict the group's arrival at Mogadiscio, its first destination in Somalia:

"As we flew over the Somali Republic, I felt that the land was extremely barren and there were few signs of human civilization. Even the cities noted on maps seemed very tiny; if we didn't look quickly from the plane, they were out of sight! As we moved further south, the land appeared greener and more fertile, and when we saw Mogadiscio, I was very surprised at its size—larger than I expected.

"It was a beautiful sight—the city glistened and sparkled because many of the roofs are metallic and the sun was bright and strong. We approached from the Indian Ocean, which was a lovely bluish color with occasional white speckles and streaks. The city was white, clean and fresh. At the airport, we were met by our Peace Corps Representative, a few Somali officials, a newspaper reporter and photographer, some Americans and some Somalis. We stared, and they stared.

"The next forty-five minutes were spent getting instructions, filling out forms, unloading the plane, and checking our baggage. The Somalis were well-organized and things moved swiftly and well. From the airport, we were to take 'buses' to our hotel. These 'buses' turned out to be two lorries (truck-like things). As I stood there in my new white drip-dry dress and looked at those high, muddy lorries, I thought that this was a big joke, and then, of course, I remembered that I was in *Africa* and it was easy to climb aboard and forget the white dress.

"When we arrived at the hotel, I was surprised to see how lovely and modern it was. It was certainly a comfortable way to begin life in a new country, and besides, it was the only place in the city that could accommodate forty-five people.

"From the time that we left the plane until we came back to our room tonight, the Somali people have been wonderful hosts to us. They are patient, warm, eager to help us, and have really made our first day in their country an unforgettable one.

"The city is busy but not fast. Here in Mogadiscio, we are quite a spectacle because we greet the people in their own language and attempt to carry on simple conversations with them. This is unusual for most Western people to do, and the local people are surprised and very pleased.

"The main streets of the city are lovely and modern, but it only takes a few minutes to walk to the areas where most of the Somali people live. They are pitifully poor and the main parts of Mogadiscio are not very representative of the country and its citizens."

After two days in Mogadiscio, the forty-five Volunteers were moved to Sheikh where they were given a formal reception. PCV John Bayer had memorized a speech in Somali:

"Good Evening. How do you do? We are Americans and
Peace Corps teachers. We will be teaching English, carpentry,
mathematics, and science. We want to learn Somali. We will
be here two years and we want to be your friends. Thank you
very much."

As he had climbed upon a bench to deliver his salutation,
a hush had fallen on the audience. It was the first time a
foreign visitor had addressed them in their native tongue. As
the speaker began they listened eagerly. Then words seemed
to fail the newcomer and he paused. The pause became a
great gap of silence. Suddenly the audience broke into laughter and hand clapping. "Thank you!" said John. Relieved at
the friendly tone of the applause, he sat down. The Somalis
loved it.

Their first days in Somalia were exciting. They found
Mogadiscio and Sheikh charming, the Indian Ocean magnifi-
cent, the people friendly; but the Volunteers were in Somalia
to render service, not to sightsee. For two weeks, in Sheikh,
they received their second-stage training; then, much to their
relief, they were given their individual assignments.

Boris Sojka recorded the event—and its frustrating after-
math:

"*Sheikh*. Group finally got their assignments and are split-
ting up.

"These were the days we have been looking forward to for
four months, yet it was very sad. We formed a very strong
bond—we lived together, had fun together, fought together.
We were all working for the day we'd split up and go to our
assignments, and now many have left. Only the southern
group is left. When the loaded lorries left, most of the girls
cried a little. We have a really great group, now we won't see
some of them for at least a year.

"*Mogadiscio five weeks later*. We're still in Mogadiscio,
doing nothing. We have to wait for the houses to be ready,
our goods to come back from the north, our refrigerators, and

our furniture. We haven't been doing much of anything. Swimming, going to the (Italian) movies and reading. We're very happy that we're in the south and not up north. It's all very green down here and we do love the ocean.

"Carole and I will be in Merca—a really beautiful old town— by ourselves. The reaction [with the people] has been worsening ever so slightly. The Somalis—that is, the people in the street—want to know when we will get to work. How can we explain all the red tape? Our morale is low from stagnation. We've all lost the drive. A general day for us goes like this: Sleep late, have light breakfast, go to the beach, have lunch, read and nap in our room, have supper, go to movies, talk for a while, read and sleep. We want to do something, but there's nothing to do."

An enthusiastic Volunteer is easily frustrated—he expects, or has been led to expect, so much of himself; and the people in his host country also expect a great deal of him simply because he is an American. Even a small delay is frustrating, but finally the Volunteer is transported to his place of assignment to begin his actual service in the Peace Corps. Three teachers in the Somalia group—Dave Dalcanton, Greg Smith, and John Bayer—were sent to one of the most remote schools in the country, the Dayahe Intermediate School about fifteen miles from Erigavo, the nearest town. John described the journey:

"Erigavo, up north in the country's highest mountains, is about three hundred miles along what the Somalis call a road, but what we might call tire tracks, ruts, and holes.

"Actually the bumps weren't too bad; it was the dust that really got to us after a while. We left in the morning and it took us a little over nine hours to get from Mogadiscio to Erigavo. We were supposed to go by Land Rover, but we had so much baggage that we couldn't fit it in, so we had to go on a lorry. With the three of us PCVs we thought we would take turns sitting with the driver while somebody sat on the top.

"As it turned out, there were ten of us—the driver, three of us, a family of five including two women, two little babies, and a clerk that worked in Erigavo, and another fellow. So we gave the women and babies the front seat and climbed up on the top, with our mattresses, trunks, and everything else. The family, I think, had all the possessions they owned with them, so it was really a packed truck and an unusual, funny-looking group.

"When we started there were three white people and seven dark ones; when we arrived, there were ten dark people, we were all so covered with dust. It was an experience I will never forget, but we hope that, when we go back to Hargeisa, the ride will be a little smoother."

After weeks of delay, Boris and Carole Sojka finally went to their assignment in Merca.

From there Boris wrote:

"We finally arrived, and we think we're the luckiest of the whole group. We have a beautiful house near the ocean in a grove of trees, with a view of the city and ocean. Merca is really beautiful, a far cry from our original ideas of life in the Peace Corps.

"People in Merca are the friendliest we've met in Somalia. There's a new school. Carole will teach the kids English during the day and has a class of girls at night. I have three adult English classes from 4:30 P.M. to 7:00 P.M. six days a week. I have all the officials, police, *municipia*, some Egyptian teachers, and the town doctor. Everybody, including the Italians, wants to learn English. Many people speak it, more than in the north, we've found, and they all want to learn more. The school has turned away more than two hundred people already.

"We're the only Americans in town and we're riding on a terrific feeling of pro-America. There were six families here with the International Cooperation Administration, and they were all liked. Everyone knows us and tries to help us. We

were taken on one of the banana ships for lunch by the harbourmaster, one of my students. This was the most wonderful
time we've had in Somalia so far.

"Our biggest problem is the lack of books. Went to the
U.S. Information Agency to beg, borrow, or steal all I could
get. Got some but not enough.

"We've got a monkey already and I've passed along the
word that we want all the animals we can get.

"Next week we're having the harbourmaster for dinner,
along with the Inspector of Labor and an official of the banana
industry. They've all heard great things about the U.S. and
want to go there. For food, they're most intrigued by sandwiches, so instead of the sumptuous dinners that we've enjoyed as guests, we'll have to serve sandwiches, hamburgers
and french-fried potatoes."

Thus life begins for a Peace Corps Volunteer, whether in
Togo, Somalia, or elsewhere. At this stage, his hopes are still
high, his vitality is undiminished. His enthusiasm still has to
face the challenge of hard, cold reality. Just how much can
he accomplish? What are the odds against him? This conflict
between hope and actuality, between desire and possibility, is
the story of the Peace Corps in action.

2

In some small village they [the Volunteers]
will lay the seed which will bring a rich harvest
for us all in later days.

JOHN F. KENNEDY
June 24, 1963
Bonn, Germany

To enable the Volunteers to plant that seed, Sargent Shriver organized a reasonably efficient staff which, in a remarkably short time, trained and sent into the field an impressive number of Volunteers. All, like those who trained for Togo and Somalia, were highly enthusiastic. The underdeveloped lands appeared to offer them unlimited opportunities for their work.

Each Volunteer, following Shriver's example, threw himself energetically into the task of creating order out of chaos. Thus begins every Volunteer's two years of service in the Corps. My first contact with Volunteers in action in this early stage was in the Dominican Republic.

On September 25, 1962, the Field Representative for the Dominican Republic—Andres "Andy" Hernandez—and I set out by jeep stationwagon from Santo Domingo. Along the roads, especially on the outskirts of settlements, men, women, and children were carrying jars or canteens of water, or were queued up, standing barefooted in the mud, waiting to fill a container from the trickle of water at a single faucet or pump. A few were leading burros that had two or four saddlebags slung across their backs. In the fertile Cibao valley lands we drove past hundreds of families who were planting rice on plots that had once been the property of the Trujillo family but which now belonged to the local people working the soil.

A year had passed since Dictator Trujillo had been assassinated, and pending the democratic elections scheduled for December, a seven-man provisional government was running the country.

At noon we arrived at an old farmhouse about five miles north of Santiago. Here a number of local merchants and businessmen hoped to establish the first agricultural college in the Republic. Six Volunteers—Edward Brand, Donald Close, Jose Garcia de Rosa, Jerry Dupuy, Bernard Isaacson, and Marion "Tex" Ford—out of the group of twenty-one that had arrived only two months earlier, had been assigned to this project. Tex Ford had emerged as the natural, though unofficial, leader.

As Andy and I drove up, several of the Volunteers were working in the garden, hoeing, planting, and weeding. Inside the farmhouse, the cook, a local woman, was instructing her two children, who were helping put the finishing touches to a rather lavish meal, one that had probably been prepared in expectation of guests.

As we hiked out to join the PCVs they greeted us warmly. They immediately began to talk about their plans, their problems, and the materials they needed. I am sure that they knew that Andy had brought their mail, but no one inquired although he did not distribute it until after we were seated at the table and Tex had asked the blessing.

Each PCV had a letter from *Time* magazine announcing the end of a complimentary three-month subscription. None of the free copies had arrived, but the letter—which afforded one PCV his only bit of news from the homeland—went on to urge each man to continue his subscription at a special rate.

As Tex, the lanky twenty-six-year-old from Paris, Texas, read aloud from one of his letters, I thought that Representative Hernandez had described him well as "a six-foot-sixer" in cowboy hat and chinos who had set out to make friends in the tense city of Santiago and had quickly become a hero to

Dominicans young and old. "He's dynamic enough to be a
deputy representative. He learned his Spanish in the Peace
Corps. He probably needs a little more experience, but I'd be
willing to have him for an assistant right now," Andy had
told me.

Tex had graduated from East Texas State in 1955 with a
B.S. degree in vocational agriculture. Around Santiago, where
"Yankee go home!" was the only English expression many of
the people knew, Tex appealed to everyone with his frank
smile, his easy conversation, and his obvious honesty. His
cowboy hat and the movies he had begun to show for fiesta
every Wednesday night seemed to speak for the *Cuerpo de
Paz*. He described one of his first shows: "This was the first
time most of these people had ever seen a movie. They
laughed, yelled, screamed, got up and pointed and tried to get
into the act. When a Greek bishop with a beard came on the
screen, they really cracked up."

Tex liked a good time—"You should have seen me dancing
the *merengue* with a five-foot tall Dominican girl"—but his
dream was to play an active part in establishing and running
the Dominican Republic's first agricultural college. Indeed,
Tex had talked of little else ever since he had heard that
Asociación para el Desarrollo, Inc., of Santiago, under the
leadership of businessman Luis B. Crouch, was eager to establish a technical school for boys. I was impressed that there
was a tenacity and a thoroughness in his thinking that is not
characteristic of all PCVs. "I just wish I could be on the first
faculty," he said wistfully. "I'd like nothing better."

He took me on a walking tour of the campus-to-be. We
climbed a steep hill across the road from the house, and I
tried to see the grounds through his eyes, for the site was still
no more than an open field. Tex pointed to the splendid
panorama of the Yaqui Valley and of the city of Santiago in
the distance—then he became absorbed in the weedy field in
which we stood. Not a spadeful of dirt had been turned, not

a building had been staked out, yet he assured me confidently that the school would open on schedule in less than a year with seventy-five boys enrolled.

"The businessmen themselves already have given $30,000 to help get started," he said. "They're not often so generous and community-minded in Latin America, even in a relatively rich country like the Dominican Republic [which, despite its sugar, bauxite, and bananas and other fruit, still depends heavily on the United States for financial aid]. These men take the time to meet on the planning board, and they've succeeded in interesting technicians at Texas A & M in advising on curriculum and in helping to staff the school in the early days. The Agency for International Development has pledged $500,000 for the buildings, the Ford Foundation is interested, and now the Peace Corps has come along to talk it up and to help out where we can. The *Asociación* has even adopted some of our suggestions.

"There's no problem about generating interest. Word has gotten around, and the local people are already proud of their agricultural school before it's even built. Everyone in Santiago has been out here at least once to see what we're doing. We have visitors all the time. Even the youths are interested and they'll be more so when construction actually begins. There's going to be a lot of competition for admission.

"The school buildings will be up here on the hill, overlooking the Yaqui Valley. In three or four years [he seemed to have forgotten that he had volunteered for two years only] we'll have two hundred acres under cultivation and a dairy big enough to be self-sustaining. That's one point on which I was able to influence the *Asociación*."

"In what way?" I asked.

"We'll have a model dairy, a really modern one with a milking machine. They hadn't thought of making this a show place, but there's no electric milker anywhere in the country, and the bacteria count in the milk is very high. So I con-

vinced the planning board of *Asociación* that the school
should serve as the example for the whole country."

There had been little publicity, but Dominican youths had
evinced so much interest that Tex felt there would be tough
competition for admission when the selection committee
finally got to work. Seventy-five boys would be accepted each
year for a three-year course, to form a student body of 225.
The students would attend classes in livestock, poultry, general
farming, or truck gardening for only part of the day—and
would work for the rest of the time in the tree nurseries, on
the experimental plots or truck farm, or caring for the animals. Tuition would be free, but the school would try to be
self-sustaining. As Tex described it all, it was clear that he
could think "big" about the future while contenting himself
with the small tasks that had to be done day by day.

"We'll clean out the area," Tex continued, gesturing from
where the dormitory and the classrooms would rise, "and put
in a garden up front. We'll put in a good road where the
present turnoff comes in. There'll be a farm manager, a foreman, and a mechanic to run the machine shop, and probably
fifteen to twenty people in the administrative and teaching
staffs. They'll be mostly Dominicans and Puerto Ricans, and
some Americans, at least at first.

"One way in which the Peace Corps has contributed by
being here: Texas A & M can rotate their staff more frequently,
sending more personnel for shorter periods of time, because
we'll be here to keep the school going. There's talk now of
sending instructors for only a month at a time. This will give
the students more contacts than they'd have otherwise.

"The big problem for us, once the *Asociación* agreed to let
us come out to the farm and get started was to decide exactly
what and how much we were going to attempt to do. Since
the planning board hadn't been formed, the *Asociación*
couldn't buy equipment to start any large projects, so we had
to be content to do what we could with what we had."

While waiting for the work to begin on the agricultural school, the PCVs had completed many small projects. The farmhouse in which they were living had been painted a neat white with green shutters, repairs had been made on the thatch-roofed barn, a fence had been built, irrigation ditches had been dug, and pineapples, poinsettias, and a few coffee trees had been planted. PCV Don Close, an agronomist, was experimenting with lemons, cashews, oranges, and mahogany. The Volunteers were giving away tomato plants which they had cultivated from fifty dollars worth of seed that had been donated by businessmen in Santiago. Tex later wrote to me that they had given away most of the plants, although many who were interested had no soil in which to plant them. "We told them we'd give them all the plants they wanted. With a little supervision from us, about twenty families have tomatoes growing. The season has been very favorable."

I asked Tex why he wanted so much to see the agricultural school succeed. In reply he told me of his own early life. His parents had owned a small truck farm twenty miles northeast of Paris, Texas. Here, Tex, his two brothers—"if you think I'm tall, you should see them"—and his three sisters had been raised.

"My twin sister and I are the youngest. It was very difficult for my father—a tenant farmer on rented land—to keep us all in school. At times, it looked as though we might not make it, but we always did. There was always someone around to give a helping hand.

"I went through the tenth grade in one- or two-room country schools. I finished the last two years at Paris High School. I had to walk two miles to catch the bus to ride twenty miles to school. I graduated at sixteen years of age and entered Paris Junior College. During the summers, I raised cucumbers and tomatoes on rented land. During the school term, I worked on the college dairy farm.

"After two years at P.J.C., I transferred to East Texas

State College, where I continued my studies in vocational agriculture. For six years after graduation, before joining the Peace Corps, I worked for the North Texas Milk Market Administration as a milk tester, auditor, and milk plant investigator.

"Except for my oldest brother, who lives in Kansas City, the rest of the family have stayed in Texas. They've been very helpful in sending down baseball equipment for some little league teams we've organized. Now I'm hoping my Dad can send us an auger bit, so we can test to see how deep we have to go for water and what kind we'll hit."

Perhaps the summer of 1962 was a fortunate time for the Peace Corps to have arrived in the Dominican Republic. The seven-man provisional government was eager to show accomplishments: it needed evidence of progress, and it needed ideas. Although about 70 per cent of the Dominicans worked in agriculture, there was no extension service to teach and supervise agricultural and homemaking projects in rural areas, and the Peace Corps was prepared to help until the government could organize its own service. While the Santiago businessmen had often talked about doing something for the community—such as building an agricultural college—no one had ever proposed a feasible plan.

This sort of vacuum called forth the ingenuity and skill of the Volunteers in many ways. They were fortunate in having Andres Hernandez for their Representative. Bilingual from childhood, familiar with the local culture, and experienced in agrarian programs from his years of work in Guatemala, Andy was a pragmatic individual. In the first weeks Andy consulted with the government officials when he could reach them. When he could not reach them he simply approved small programs himself and deployed Volunteers into areas where he felt they could serve best. Later, when the opportunity came, he casually mentioned these programs to the officials. In most instances they gave him their approval to continue the work.

"Mostly we're doing what the people want," Andy said. "When there's nothing at all being done, it's not hard to find something to do."

The provisional government had assured the Peace Corps that the local extension service would be ready in January, 1963, and that the seventeen Dominicans who had been hand-picked by Representative Hernandez would be hired to work alongside the PCVs and to take over when the PCVs left. These people—referred to as "counterparts"—had trained with the Volunteers in Puerto Rico, but much to the disappointment of the PCVs none had been hired by the government as agreed. However, one man, Luis Grullion, became so enthusiastic about the agricultural school that he wanted to work with the Corps while still waiting to be hired by his own government. The Santiago businessmen arranged to pay him a stipend and he joined the PCVs at the farm.

Not all the undertakings in those first weeks were as exciting as the project for the agricultural college. But each PCV had been making a place for himself as Tex had done in Santiago. The concrete gains were modest, but the effect was noticeable.

"It's incredible," commented the American ambassador's wife, "what they've accomplished in a few weeks. Since the Peace Corps arrived, there's a different atmosphere. The spirit of anti-Yankeeism is gone; already the people see Americans differently."

I could testify to this. When Andy or the Volunteers drove by, even the little children recognized the Peace Corps jeeps and called out "Peac-a Cor-a, Peac-a Cor-a."

Such acceptance was welcomed, of course, by the PCVs. However, not one felt that the reason for his presence had been justified simply because a favorable image of America had been created. At the end of their second month in the country, this was a gratifying beginning. Inspired by visions of more solid achievements to come, they were willing to start with small-scale projects—many woefully unsophisticated by American standards, but which in such an underdeveloped land could help to bridge the difference between a poor diet at high cost and a good diet at low cost, between sheer idleness and productive work.

I was in the office in Santo Domingo when two PCVs—Charles Debose from Louisiana and John Geisweidt from Texas—came in to ask permission from Representative Hernandez to spend fourteen dollars for a hundred runty chicks. "They're not first-rate chicks, but they're cheap, and it'll help us get going," they said.

Andy explained that the two Volunteers were asking for the money to start a local operation of what later was to be called Plan Avicola. If all went well, this plan—which had been initiated by PCVs with the aid of a hundred-dollar loan from a local businessman—might eventually be instituted over the entire country.

Charles Debose gave me the details: "A group of boys raises 100 chicks, sells them or the eggs, puts the money back in to buy 200 chicks, and so on, until each boy can take 50 for himself. We show them how to build feeders and watering troughs, elevated to avoid disease, and teach them how to raise healthy fowls. The plan is carried out with members of local 4-H clubs. John and I are hoping to work with the 4-H boys in the Pedernales district."

"The goal of Plan Avicola," Andy said, "is to distribute 100,000 chicks during the first year of operation. The profit on chicken raising in the Dominican Republic is about 100 per cent. Eggs cost ten cents each. We think we can cut the price as low as four cents."

He looked at John and Charles. "O.K.," he said, "fill out a voucher for the fourteen dollars."

Later that day, I met with the two Volunteers. Charles Debose had joined the Corps three weeks before he would have graduated from law school; John Geisweidt had joined when he still had a year and a half of studies to complete at Texas A & M. Upon arriving here, they discovered that the provisional government had no assignment for them. They were disappointed until they found an official in the Department of Agriculture who was willing to introduce them to the people in Pedernales.

"There are about three thousand people in Pedernales," John said, "and it takes only two hours for word to get around about what we're doing. If we're going to show a movie, we just start the word around in the morning and everyone shows up in the evening. They love movies and funny books, but they get all their wrong ideas about the U.S. out of the cheap movies we send abroad. Dominicans are very interested in money. They ask us: 'How much money do people make in the U.S.?' 'How much does a chicken cost?' 'Why did you volunteer to work for nothing when you could work in the U.S. and make money?' But we think we really got a good thing started in Pedernales with the chicken raising."

"Our toughest problem," Charles said, "is that the people think all Americans are rich and that we can make everything right. We can't, of course, especially without supplies and equipment, and this creates a bad situation. We need a well pump, animals, chickens, seeds right now. It's planting time; later, there'll be too little rain and then it'll freeze. We've started a baseball league, but we need gloves and bats. The Peace Corps should have equipment at local headquarters so we can just come in and requisition it."

Representative Hernandez explained the procurement problem to me. "We need money. All we can provide is the enthusiasm, the leadership, and the labor. We have to go to other agencies or private sources for every item we need."

John and Charles, naturally, cared most about the work they had mapped out for themselves. I found this true of Volunteers everywhere. Where or how they got the tools to do

their work was of little importance. They asked for help
unashamedly. Sometimes they got a "yes," other times they
were turned down flatly, but they kept right on pursuing their
plans and pleading for support.

On the outskirts of Santiago, another pair of PCVs, Wesley
Stewart and Jon Fosdick, started a Baby Ruth League. They
had seventeen baseball uniforms and some equipment sent in
by friends in Toledo, Ohio. Then Wes and Jon decided that
Santiago ought to have an outdoor basketball court. They
borrowed a mechanical shovel from U.S. Steel, got a man to
operate it on a Sunday, solicited the assistance of twenty local
trucks, collected as many workers as they could who owned
shovels, picks, or wheelbarrows, and made the basketball
court. "Even the little naked kids tried to help us," Wes said.

I questioned Jon why all the activities seemed to be planned
for boys and youths. "Dominican girls don't do much outside
the home," he shrugged, accepting local custom as a fact of
life. He explained that the sports programs were designed to
reduce the hoodlumism that was common among the unemployed young men. "A gang of hoodlums said they were going
to burn the clubhouse in town that belongs to a group of Santiago boys. So we invited the gang out to the farm for an
outing, talked with them, took them swimming, showed them
movies. Now they want to build their own clubhouse in Santiago. They've forgotten all about the burning. Now another
group is threatening to burn the clubhouse, so I guess it's time
we invited them out to the farm. But you can feel the attitude
changing: now we're *Americanos* instead of *Yanquis*."

No discussion with PCVs in the Dominican Republic continues long without talk of the acute water shortage, and what
they may be able to do to relieve it.

At a meeting of the Volunteers, Tex Ford told about the
auger bit he hoped to obtain from his father. With it, Volunteers could determine how deep they must dig and what kind

of water they would get in a given location.

"This is the sort of practical problem technically trained Americans should be able to solve in any underdeveloped country," Andy Hernandez maintained.

Shortly after returning to the States, I read the following statement in the New York *Times* of October 30, 1962, under the headline "Ford Foundation Gives 13 Million"—"Two grants, totaling $218,500, have been made to the Association for Development in the Dominican Republic to support the development of a vocational agricultural school and demonstration farm in the Cibao district."

So the Fords—Tex and the Foundation—had joined forces, and Tex would get his college.

However, for the various participating agencies to join forces to implement the plans for the school more time was needed. In November, Tex Ford wrote to me that in the meanwhile he was working with other PCVs—many of them newcomers—throughout the Republic:

"I've been spending quite a bit of time in the other provinces and in the capital, assisting some of the boys with 4-H Clubs and helping to expand Plan Avicola. Involved is AID, Heifer Project, Business Council for International Understanding, Dominican Department of Agriculture, and the Peace Corps.

"Some chickens are bought, some incubated here, some sent by Heifer Project. They're kept in Santo Domingo and in Santiago, until they're distributed to the people. Volunteers in the field select the families and instruct them in the building of low-cost bamboo chicken houses. Already more than 100 families have 50 chickens each, and we're just getting started. Later some families will expand to 100 and 150 chicks, some for eating and some for egg production.

"Also, I'd like to mention the Rabbit Project which started when I went to Puerto Rico on vacation. I bought ten does and two bucks, all registered New Zealand Whites. The people at the Pan Am desk in San Juan went into utter confusion, but I arrived in Santo Domingo with the rabbits.

"We' ve constructed hutches out at the home of Wes Stewart and Jon Fosdick near Santiago. The interest is tremendous. Sometimes as many as 150 people come out in a day to look at the rabbits. They've been amazed to find out how good rabbit meat is and how quickly and easily it can be produced. Things have been a little slow around the farm, but they're about to start with a bang. The technicians from Texas A & M are arriving November 15 and actual construction and development will start soon."

Regardless of what role they play in the actual operation of the agricultural school, Peace Corps Volunteers believe that they have already made a significant contribution if only by arousing local interest. "It's the talk of the town in Santiago and the Cibao," Tex said. "We proved that such a college was wanted and needed, and no doubt this helped to influence the Ford Foundation to make the grant."

3

Dem wish de 'Merican nice things,
An gi him pridefully
A Jamaica pair a shoes
Fe keep we in him memory.

Ah hope dat him wi memba us
Widout sorrow or pain,
Dat him wi have a good time an
Come look fe we again.

Song by LOUISE BENNETT COVERLY
Jamaican poet
from *"Distinguish 'Merican"*

To visit the Peace Corps in Jamaica immediately after leaving the Dominican Republic was a startling experience.

The first Volunteers I met in Jamaica were working at the Institute of Jamaica in Kingston. The Institute, which is like a small-scale Smithsonian Institution, has three departments of public information: a general lending library, a science library, and the West India Reference Library. It was to the last of these that Marvin Smith, Janet Earnshaw, and Barbara Nolting had been assigned four months before I arrived.

Marvin Smith lived in a flat in a pleasant residential area about four miles from the downtown district of Kingston. If Marvin was not up by 7 A.M., the arrival of the milk man would awaken him. Once aroused, Marvin would make his breakfast of fruit and coffee, and dress, putting on a clean white shirt. Within a half-hour he would board a bus that was already crowded with commuters like himself. When he got off, usually about 8 A.M., he would walk the two blocks to the Institute of Jamaica on East Street.

If the local laborers were not on strike, Marvin might look

to see how the construction was proceeding on the new wing
of the building. Inside, he would greet several members of the
library staff—Jamaican, English, and two American non-
Volunteers—on his way to the rear of the building where he,
Janet, and Barbara had their desks.

During the morning and again in the afternoon, the three
might take a short break for tea or coffee and buns in the
cafeteria; at lunch, they would probably eat there, too, rather
than go out into the hot sun. At about 4 P.M., they would
board the bus with other commuters for the trip home.

Sounds just like a job in the States, doesn't it? It is, out-
wardly at least, and that's what disturbs the Jamaica Volunteers
and makes them ask, as Marvin did: "What am I doing living
and working with middle-class people who are not unlike those
at home?"

Jamaica is a former British colony which consists of about
four thousand square miles of mountainous tropical land,
lying in the Caribbean south of Cuba. The PCVs had arrived
in time to participate in the island's first Independence Day
celebration on August 6, 1962. The customs, manners, and
dress, and even the language, were, of course, not alien to
them, except perhaps for some baffling expressions of British
origin. And while few could grasp everything that was said
in the Jamaican creole, the PCVs were familiar with the lilting,
colorful dialect in the poems of Louise Bennett Coverly, and
during training in New York they had also heard her humorous and sympathetic renditions of creole folk songs. They
were prepared to feel warmly toward the people.

The three Volunteers assigned to the Institute had studied
library science at the graduate level. They worked without
Jamaican counterparts. Marvin Smith's job was to classify and
catalogue several thousand valuable maps and an unknown
number of unusual early prints. The collection—of English,
Spanish, French, and Dutch origin and going back to the
sixteenth century—had been accumulating in drawers for sixty

years. Whatever degree of order might have existed was upset during the 1907 earthquake.

"I'm adapting the State Department method," Marvin explained, "and writing myself a procedure manual, so I'll remember what I'm to do. First, I try to locate the map in a bibliography. Many come out of atlases, so finding the page may be a clue. The older maps have no co-ordinates, no degrees north-south, no date or name of the cartographer, and the place names are in archaic spelling, so it's a little like a treasure hunt. I have to be careful that some don't crumble and fall apart. They need restoring by a specialist. Also, there must be fifteen to twenty thousand estate maps. They're important to Jamaican history, but it'll take someone with surveying experience to identify them."

Janet Earnshaw, who joined the Peace Corps just two months before she was due to complete her studies for an M.A. in library science at the University of California, was trying similarly to classify old manuscripts and letters.

"We're trying to make the collections usable," Marvin said. "Once I've identified a map and made a record for the card file, I put the map in a folder in a drawer cabinet. The outcome may be a published bibliography. I've written to the Library of Congress, which has expressed interest in some of the maps, many of which are rare and include the southeastern United States.

"Columbus was among the first to discover this area and to take the news to Europe about these rich virgin territories. His report, along with those of other explorers, brought the French, Spanish, English, and Dutch to the Caribbean and, at the same time, to North America. No other area of the New World was as thoroughly mapped as the Caribbean, because it was militarily and economically important to the great world powers of the time. It was rich in slaves, sugar, and rum and was close to the trade routes to South America. Today, the Caribbean is of great military importance to the United

States, and the position of Jamaica is strategic because it guards the Windward Passage and lies directly in the path of the Panama Canal."

To indicate the potential of the Institute—and to show me the backlog of work—Marvin took me on a guided tour. In several rooms in the basement, not catalogued, labeled, restored, or ready for display was a collection of dusty relics to make any museum director ecstatic. I saw prints of three ships, for which Annapolis is rumored to have offered $30,000; dampness had caused foxing on the paper, so they needed reconditioning. There was a metal mantrap, with a tight spring and jaws powerful enough to cut off the foot of a runaway slave. There was an iron cage, with stationary handcuffs, in which to suspend a disobedient slave in a tree— a slave who had dared to assault a white man, for example— to become a feast for the native vultures.

A Roman altar piece, found in Kingston Harbor and identified by the British Museum as dating from the first century A.D., might have been brought over as ship ballast. There were seventeenth-century tortoise-shell combs with elaborate carving of a kind that had not been done since the 1692 earthquake.

The collections of maps, prints, books, and relics—when catalogued and displayed—will certainly be remarkable. Barbara Nolting—who is from Chattanooga, Tennessee—told me that the books she was cataloguing probably comprised the most complete collection of West Indian literature in the world. "At present, when a reader wants material on a particular subject in the library, he must hunt for it. The catalogue will save him a great deal of time. Also, the proposed new copyright law, if it passes, will name the Institute as depository for the West Indies, and a copy of everything published in the entire West Indies will come here to Kingston."

When I expressed admiration for what the Volunteers were doing, they demurred.

"We're not being creative. We can't start anything, no

matter what the Jamaicans may tell you about wanting us to
show more initiative. Besides, shouldn't we be helping the
lower classes?"

Of the Volunteers working outside the city, the largest
teams—nine and seven members, respectively—had been assigned to two youth camps, Cobbla and Chestervale, in the
Blue Mountains north of Kingston.

Chestervale Youth Camp is built on ninety acres of mountain land, three thousand feet above sea level. It looks much
like any summer camp in the United States. In autumn, 1962,
345 teen-age boys (fifteen years and older) were there, the
largest enrollment in the six years the camp had been in
operation. On the morning after my arrival, the campers awoke
at their usual hour, 6 A.M. They chattered and sang in Jamaican creole, and their voices cut through the uneasy silence that
often hangs over these mountains and valleys.

I had arrived at Chestervale about 11 P.M. the night before.
After a brief conversation with the PCVs, it became obvious
that not all the hardship assignments are in remote areas where
there are language barriers.

Each of the seven volunteers at Chestervale had lost weight.
One who had lost nearly thirty pounds joked about the
clothes he had brought. The PCVs told of one Sunday night
supper: a small serving of soggy bread-pudding and some
cooked cereal. The camp, they believed, was saving money
on food in order to contruct more buildings. I suspect that
the camp budget, despite the increased enrollment, had not
been increased. At any rate, the PCVs were forced to buy food
from their meager allowances of two dollars a day plus their
additional twenty dollars a month. They occasionally prepared
their own meals, which they ate away from the camp dining
room, although they knew that this might be construed as
standoffishness.

Their questions told a great deal. They wanted to know did

other projects have similar problems? Didn't I think they would be doing better in a hardship post far away from the States? Would they be making out better if they had not bypassed the Puerto Rico training camp? Did I believe that the Peace Corps really ought to be in Jamaica at all?

I found the food at Chestervale during my stay adequate: the bread and rolls—made by boys in a kitchen which would never pass a health and sanitation inspection—were palatable. Basil Ferguson, Chestervale camp director since February, 1962, described with considerable pride the menu they had served on the day President Johnson—then vice-president— came to visit. Due to weather conditions, Johnson had left before the lunch hour. "He missed a great meal," said Ferguson. "The Peace Corps Volunteers can't say they didn't have enough to eat *that* day."

Campers do not get the same food as the thirteen-member staff and the Volunteers. The chief dishes are rice, beans, porridges and cereals, plus carrots and other vegetables which the boys cultivate on the twenty acres of hillside they have terraced under the supervision of Assistant Director Bennett. Jamaican authorities complain, according to Director Ferguson, because production is too low to make the camp completely self-supporting. Each boy—or his sponsor—pays only a hundred dollars a year, so that some government support is necessary. "The authorities fail to take into account that we got 170 new boys in September," said Ferguson. "The seniors, who've been at Chestervale for six to nine months, will just be becoming productive when they leave."

The thirty-eight pounds of meat allotted to make a meal for 345 boys seemed to me to be an amazingly small ration. How, I wondered, can growing boys be expected to have enough energy to learn and to work on so meager a diet? Then I talked with an Englishman, formerly a photographer for *Life* and *National Geographic*, who owns two coconut farms near Ocho Rios, employs about a hundred Jamaicans, and who now has three boys, sons of his farm workers, at Chestervale.

"How many meals a day do they get?" he asked.

"Three, of course."

"That's probably one or two more than most of them ever had at home," he said. "Furthermore, you can't get some of them to eat meat or fresh vegetables. They won't touch lettuce. They like fish, rice, and beans because that's what they've been brought up on. I've tried with the families at my place. I've begged the boys to eat some meat or chicken first, and then they can have all the rice and beans they want, but it's no good. They like bulky foods."

After breakfast on my first day, Ferguson called an assembly of campers and staff. It was held outside, and we all stood for an hour in the sun while he delivered a speech: "We're going back to the old menu and the quantity the government authorized. I've heard complaints about the kind of porridge and that you weren't getting enough food. I've changed from rice porridge to oat porridge to wheat porridge, and you're still griping. I've increased the amount of food and you still say it's not enough. Now I'm sick of these complaints, and I'm going back to the original amounts. If anyone wants to go to the powers-that-be and tell them he's not getting enough food he can do so."

During the rest of that long meeting, the director discussed a variety of misdemeanors. Campers were instructed to lace their boots, to stop looking sloppy, to wear clean clothing (they do their own laundry). Light bulbs, they were informed, had been covered with screening so that they could not be stolen. The tailor shop was declared off limits, although PCV Elsie Tanaka locked up the supplies anyway and every night took home her thread and steam iron for safekeeping. No one, it was emphasized, was to go near the toolshop except to attend a class—some of the boys had taken the plywood that Volunteer Dick Grobe intended for ping-pong tables and had sawed it into paddles.

After the meeting, Director Ferguson offered to explain to me the camp's system of self-government.

"There's more free discipline at Chestervale than anywhere else in Jamaica," he said proudly. "The boys do everything for themselves. They're free to select the classes they want to attend, and they discipline themselves. The postal service is heavy and the letters are not censored. We're not concerned about what they write home. They can say whatever they want."

The system is textbook perfect. Campers are divided into ten-man leads, each with an elected leader and subleader. Twelve leads—or three dorms—make a round of 120 boys. In the dorms, each senior man occupies an upper bunk, and has a "dog"—a junior boy in the lower bunk—for whom he is responsible. The "dogs" get to do most of the work.

At a round meeting, members elect a prefect who has "authority" over that round. Above the three prefects is a senior prefect and deputy, elected by secret ballot. His job, entailing considerable responsibility, is to act as liaison between the boys and the staff, to conduct visitors around the camp, and to take campers into Kingston on holidays. On Thursday nights, the boys hold a group meeting. No staffer may attend unless he is invited.

"The minutes, however, come to me," said Ferguson. "Nevertheless, the boys speak very frankly, have some hot discussions."

Considering that the system of "self-government" seemed to mean that the boys may say (but aside from choosing their own classes, not do) what they want, I surmised that the campers used their group meetings to let off steam. Perhaps they even enjoyed provoking Director Ferguson by complaining endlessly about the food even though they did not dislike the diet at the camp.

If the authoritarian atmosphere brought complaints from the campers, it caused frustration among the PCVs. There seemed to be no time in the daily schedule for new projects.

As soon as the Volunteers planned a new program, the director found that the program was impossible within the framework of the camp. For example, at the beginning of their stay in Chestervale, the Volunteers initiated a literacy class which was attended by a hundred boys. This class was cancelled by Ferguson, at the insistence of Assistant Director Bennett, on the grounds that the boys were needed to work on the farm.

The PCVs were encouraged to operate within existing camp programs. "I'd like to see the PCVs getting groups together to take them swimming or on hikes," the director said to me. "They don't have to wait to be assigned; they can do it spontaneously. All they have to do is ask me for the truck." So far no one had. It would be unfair, however, to conclude that Director Ferguson was entirely to blame for dissatisfaction of the Volunteers. There was apparently a misunderstanding of the role the PCVs were expected to play. As Ferguson said to me: "The Volunteers thought they came here just to teach; I understood they came to do whatever was needed." But the Volunteers, all of whom were teachers, had hoped to start new teaching projects, of which the literacy class was but one example. Instead, they were expected to teach in the programs that already existed, and not only to teach, but also to work with the campers to produce buildings, uniforms, and food. For instance, if PCV William Robertson is to instruct twelve grubbies (new boys) in plumbing so that the boys can install pipes in a new camp building, Bill will find himself doing most of the work. While lying on his back tightening pipe joints, he tries to explain the technique of joining to one group of boys, but at the same time, he must keep an eye on a second group that is at work on another phase of the job.

Whatever may be the cause of the lack of rapport between PCVs and the camp staff, the effects were evident. When I was there, only one Volunteer had developed what might be called a friendly relationship with the director and the regular staff.

"He'll do anything you ask him," Ferguson said. "If we ask him to do something with us and he says he can't, we know he's busy and really has some other plans. We accept this and we ask him again. We wouldn't feel he refused because he didn't want to come along."

As for the campers, they seemed to respect the PCVs, but they showed little warmth or comradeship. Perhaps the red sign with the white lettering, which the campers nailed to a tree beside the path connecting the two houses of the PCVs, gave the story. The sign read: "Peace Corps Avenue." In any frustrating situation, when it is difficult to make friends, the temptation is great to spend one's free time with persons one knows and understands. That is what the Volunteers were doing.

However, despite the uneasy situation at the camp, I was impressed by what the Volunteers had achieved.

One of the busiest PCVs was petite Elsie Tanaka. Formerly an instructor for Singer Sewing Machine Company in Hawaii, she was now in charge of the camp's tailor shop which was open all day six days a week. The shop consisted of a porch—which contained three treadle sewing machines and a pile of the coconut fur or kayak which the boys make into mattresses—and a dark, windowless room which Elsie and the boys had painted white to lighten it because the electricity is off most of the day. I walked in as the class was gathering at 8:30 A.M. Seventeen boys showed up—all calling "Sir" at Miss Tanaka. There is no creole word for woman teacher. Tailoring would eventually be a vocation for some of these boys, and a few had already started to earn money by their skill. One student was doing well by altering the dungarees which his fellow campers got from the camp store.

Richard Grobe, who had worked at home construction and cabinet-making in Boulder, Colorado, was supervising the laying out of a building which was to be used as a shop. Supervising is hardly the correct word for what he was actually doing. When I saw him, he was down in a muddy ditch, lining out the building foundation and, simultaneously, directing about a dozen boys in the manipulating of plumb lines to get the walls straight and the corners true.

"Just put it in your book," said Director Ferguson, "that the camp director and Grobe quarrel at least once a day. Isn't that right, Mr. Grobe?"

"Sometimes more," said Dick, grinning.

"Yet we always clear it up and are friends again," Ferguson added.

Two Volunteers—Dick Grobe's wife, Ruby, who was a nurse, and Rita Villicana, an art teacher—didn't have enough to do. There was never much sickness among the campers; besides the camp already had one nurse. Ruby, therefore, drove down the mountain to help in a local clinic. As for the art classes, they were small and Rita had to fill in her free time in any way she could—a difficult problem considering the rigid schedule at the camp.

Probably the most popular course was Joe Murphy's class in mechanics and welding. On Fridays, the newer boys, who had not yet decided what trade to specialize in, could visit any class they wished. On that day, Joe's supply of tools was totally inadequate.

"They love to get their hands greasy and mess around with equipment," explained Director Ferguson. "I know the PCVs think I'm backward because I don't encourage the boys to select these trades to specialize in. But lack of money is the problem. It's no use to expect mechanization in Jamaica yet. Even if these boys learned to use tools expertly, it wouldn't be practical. They may never see or get to work with similar equipment after they leave camp."

In addition to showing boys how to use a blowtorch, Joe Murphy had started a camp library. Books were kept in the tailor shop, but as soon as the campers, under the tutelage of Volunteers Dick Grobe and Bill Robertson, had finished the new building for PCVs, the present PCV quarters would become a student union and library.

Yet the fact remains that the PCVs in Jamaica—whether at a camp or in a city—were dissatisfied because their assignments were too much like regular jobs in the States. Many told me that they had been regretting it ever since they had learned that they had been assigned to a country better known for tourism than for underdevelopment.

However, the Volunteers in Jamaica were one of the first groups to be sent to a relatively prosperous, sophisticated society, and several of the original forty-one—like Marvin Smith, who had a master's degree in library science—were assigned to professional jobs in a period when the public image of the Peace Corps seemed to portray it as favoring physical hardship and primitive living.

Later on, doctors, nurses, lawyers, and college professors accepted assignments in city hospitals and colleges, but in the summer of 1962 the Jamaica Volunteers were sensitive that others in the Corps considered that they had drawn a "soft" assignment, and were self-conscious about it. While preparing, under the direction of the Institute for the Study of Man in New York, to spend two years with our newly independent, English-speaking neighbors, they had frankly envied those Corpsmen who were studying little-known languages* and were to embark for remote settlements or "bush" country.

"But we can't go home and face people now after they've given us a send-off," one girl told me. "We'd be quitting before we ever got started."

This lack of belief in their own mission was a handicap. They had been told by their instructors that they had a tough

---

*Dr. Edwin R. Henry, Director of Selection, later told me that these applicants were offered an assignment in an English-speaking country partly because they had shown no marked aptitude for languages on the language aptitude test which the Corps considered to be very reliable. I do not know if the Volunteers were aware of this.

job before them, but they had not realized that it was also to be a subtle challenge in public relations.

Besides the lack of enthusiasm—maybe because of it—the Jamaica group had been short on self-confidence, even after two months of training.

No wonder that I found morale among these Volunteers in the field unusually low for any PC group at so early a stage in their adjustment. Several had already returned to the United States and a husband-and-wife team—"so nice that they could get along with anyone"—flew home the day I arrived.

The problem in Jamaica, it seemed to me, had many causes. First, jobs were rigidly defined within the existing framework. To independent young Americans, the job supervision appeared to be authoritarian, or at best, an inconsistent mixture of an authoritarian and a democratic approach. They found it hard to please their local bosses and counterparts, even though their work—in museums, libraries, youth camps, and schools—was as skilled as any being done by Volunteers in other countries. Administrators who issued mandates and then maintained that, nevertheless, they wanted everyone to make suggestions baffled the Volunteers. They felt damned if they did come forth with new ideas, and damned if they did not.

And the opportunities to start anything new were rare. Volunteers could join groups already organized—the local drama group, an extension class in art—but the need to initiate extracurricular activities, to organize ball teams, or to stimulate other types of recreation did not exist.

One of the most difficult obstacles was that the Volunteers were expected to teach and to produce goods at the same time. At youth camps like Chestervale and Cobbla, they were expected to complete buildings by certain dates, although the boys in the plumbing class might all be grubs. PCVs were responsible both for finishing projects on schedule and for instructing the boys in the very skills they needed to do the work. While trying to teach the people in Jamaica how to help themselves, the Volunteers were doing the work for them.

Close people-to-people relationships—that intangible which is at the heart of the Corps' impact in most countries—were uncommon in Jamaica. Most of the contacts were with the emerging middle class, whose feelings of nationalism and pride in class were intense. The Jamaicans themselves wished they were a hundred years further along in their development. The presence of skilled, young Americans—so like themselves, yet so different—who had come to *help* them, only emphasized painfully the tremendous amount of progress Jamaica still had to make.

The PCVs, on the other hand, felt they were neither needed nor wanted. "The Jamaican government never had any idea why they wanted us," I was told. "They took us because we're free and they wanted to get into the act. But it's pretty difficult for us to bring anything worthwhile to a sophisticated society."

Cathy Cobb, who worked as a student on the Crossroads Africa project in Nigeria during the summer of 1961, experienced similar difficulties. With real insight she described it in a letter quoted by Ruth T. Plimpton in *Operation Crossroads Africa:*

It's with the educated groups . . . that national pride interferes. We're part of a country whose strength and whose culture are established and accepted, but these [Nigerian] students have a double dose of national pride because their country is so new, and they have to believe in its potential . . . very strongly. Thus, they were not as anxious as we to act as peers. . . . Gaining some kind of rapport with the university students, was not at all easy, but if we had never come in contact with this segment of the Ivory Coast population we would have avoided some of the most important, influential parts of the country's future.

The challenge is great in trying to help relatively sophisticated societies advance even further into the twentieth century, but during the first two years of its existence, the Peace Corps received most of its requests from relatively unsophisticated countries where the need for teachers, academic or vocational, was greatest. In the coming years, the Peace Corps will undoubtedly be asked to supply an increasing number of non-teaching professionals: doctors, nurses, lawyers, city planners, engineers, etc. As this trend accelerates, both the Volunteers and the public will be forced to broaden their image of Peace Corps service to include any task which an emerging country needs and wants, and which Americans can do.

PART II

Volunteers in Transition

*I heard nothing but praise for the
Peace Corps in my country.*
A HIGH MILITARY OFFICER
Somalia

There was a rumor that a hippopotamus had been ravaging the crops in a Somali village not far from Mogadiscio, where PCV Jack Magri was teaching. The hippo was a menace, and the terrified inhabitants wanted the beast killed. Jack was eager to try hunting in the bush—although he was not an experienced hunter—so he left his wife, Diane—also a PC teacher—at home and started out with their houseboy as his guide. In Mogadiscio they took a bus as far as it would go.

"Now we have a thirty-minute walk," the houseboy said.

"The Somalis are great walkers but a little vague about time," Jack related later. "After two hours of walking we came to the village. I was exhausted, but news that I was coming to kill the hippo had somehow preceded us, so the villagers had prepared a big welcome.

"I had to eat a progressive dinner—the same meal seven different times in seven different homes. It was something called *sure* (pronounced 'tsurah') which can best be described in American terms as hominy grits and rancid melted butter, and it's eaten with the fingers.

"I finally got to bed. Frankly, I didn't believe there was any hippopotamus, but I left word to call me when the scavenger showed up. Early in the morning, while it was still dark, I was awakened. 'The hippo is eating the vegetables,' I was told. 'Time to get up and shoot him.'

"I got up, put on my cartridge belt and gun, and went out, never expecting to see anything. I figured if the hippo had really come, he would be gone by the time I got out there.

"Well, I met him face to face, two eyes in the dark. I didn't even know where to aim, and what was worse, I was standing between him and the river.

"I shot twice and waited to be charged by the hippo as he went to the river. I thought I was as good as dead. Then something zoomed by me but missed. Blood spurted all over the place, and bloody tracks led to the river."

Jack assumed that he had merely wounded the beast, sufficiently, he hoped, to keep him out of the villagers' gardens. But two days later, the news came from a town farther down the river: A dead hippo had been found.

This popular story was related to me by several Volunteers in locations outside Somalia before Jack himself filled in the details. The Somalis, too, loved the story, for it was a demonstration of the friendly relations that existed between them and the Volunteers. I could not help but think that the PCVs in Jamaica, who were longing for adventure, would have been very happy suddenly to find a hippopotamus or two wandering around on the outskirts of Kingston.

I had met the Somalia PCVs earlier, when they were going through basic training. They had spent their early months in the host country much as had the Volunteers in the Dominican Republic. Since all were teachers, they got acquainted with their students, established pleasant relations with the local people, and began to consider what additional projects they might initiate.

The routine at most of the Somali schools—where the PCVs were expected to teach the established courses such as English and mathematics—was neither so strict nor so strenuous as to hamper Volunteers from carrying on activities outside the regular classes. Thus they did not experience the kind of frustration that had plagued the group in Jamaica. Of course, there were some difficulties in the early months: assignments were delayed, thus leaving many with too much time on their hands; some PCVs had an uneasy relationship with their Representative; and the poor liaison between the Corps office in Mogadiscio and the administrators on the project often led to confusion. Because of these situations, plus various individual problems in personal adjustment, nearly 25 per cent of the original group went back home early.

Those who remained, however, still had much of the confidence they had displayed during their training. They went on with the same enthusiasm that had spurred them to launch their projects, and they continued to believe in the worthiness of what they were doing. As they finished their sixth month of service, they were intent on completing as many of their plans as soon as possible, but they were beginning to realize the depth and extent of the obstacles they would have to overcome.

Geographically and culturally, Somalia breaks into two regions. Before it achieved its independence in 1960, the southern portion of present-day Somalia was the Italian Somaliland. Consequently, those PCVs who were familiar with the Italian language were assigned to the towns around Mogadiscio, where, except for the vegetation along the rivers, the land is barren. Bananas, the main crop, grown on the fertile banks of the Scebeli River, are sent chiefly to Italy. The only other exports are skins and hides, which are sent to Arabia and the Middle East. However, the export revenue scarcely covers the cost of the goods which Somalia must import.

Northern Somalia—mountainous country not unlike New Mexico—was formerly British Somaliland. And so English is spoken here. The nomadic people in the area seldom come down from the hills where they live. Their diet consists mainly of meat and milk, which they obtain from their camels or goats, and their only occupation is tending this livestock.

In this region—around Hargeisa close to the Ethiopian

border—John Bayer, David Dalcanton, and Greg Smith spent their first months in Somalia teaching English, chemistry, and mathematics at the Dayahe Intermediate School, which is about fifteen miles from Erigavo.

The school is located in excellent oasis-like surroundings. Even during the dry season, when drinking water is rationed in the towns of Northern Somalia and the only water for washing is brackish, Dayahe always has enough water for showers and for the PCVs to water their garden of beans, squash, melons, tomatoes, and lettuce every night.

As Volunteer Bayer described it: "We have a fine stream here, with an endless supply of water, which even gives us a natural swimming pool only about a mile from the school. This is unusual because there is almost no swimming in Northern Somalia unless you're lucky enough to be on the Gulf of Aden or the Indian Ocean. We once followed our stream down into its gorge. In many places it was so deep and the walls of the gorge so straight, that we were forced to swim. Farther up the gorge there were two other swimming holes, both with small waterfalls down one side. I should mention that during the winter rainy season, there is too much water— more than our garden can absorb. So our meals consist of meat, potatoes, and onions for weeks on end.

"Not too far from Dayahe is a cedar forest. One day we went for a walk there. The cedar trees smelled wonderful. Suddenly we came to a cliff, probably three thousand feet high and equaling the Grand Canyon in grandeur. It was amazing.

"We could see all the way to the Gulf of Aden, which is about forty miles away. It took a stone about twenty seconds to go all the way down. What a tremendous place!"

For the three Volunteers, the highlight of the first term at Dayahe was a visit by the President of Somalia, Aden Abdulla Osman.

"It was truly a festive occasion," said John Bayer. "There was no school for three days before his arrival. The buildings here were whitewashed; we put up posters on the trees and hung big banners over the road. Even the road, which was unbelievably bumpy, was smoothed with a bulldozer—we don't know where they got it—and every rock along the road was straightened and whitewashed.

"At nine o'clock, the students, dressed in their white shirts and brown shorts, lined up on both sides of the road, about twenty feet apart, with flags and palm branches. After forty-five minutes, the President finally came. Everybody cheered and waved, and as soon as he went by, all the kids ran over to the school where they were to put on a program. The President observed some classes (they were planned, of course), inspected the dormitories, and watched the students put on a tumbling act and several plays. The plays were quite funny, and I think the President and his ministers were genuinely amused. He was supposed to stay an hour, but he stayed two and a half hours because, according to the Minister of the Interior, he was enjoying himself so much. In the end, the school gave him a little plaque. It was probably the biggest event that's ever happened at Dayahe."

After the program at the school had ended, the PCVs received a special invitation to a dinner that evening in the President's honor.

"The dinner was a real opportunity!" related Greg Smith. "I was only one seat away from the President. I only wish that I'd had more knowledge than I do. We started talking about the climate and his trips, but then we discussed the status of the Somali Republic, including the Kenya border problem. I brought it up—probably I shouldn't have—but he took it well. He was very, very pleased when I asked about his family. He said he had six sons and two daughters, and that two sons are in Italy, and that one of the daughters had just been married. It was amazing how the family talk livened up the conversation.

"We got onto the subject of monogamy and polygamy, and

the President explained in his rather halting English that we, since we're unmarried, couldn't go out and look for *another* woman, but that he was thinking of taking a second wife.

"Then he told a parable concerning the true religion. Many men, he said, were once put in a dark room and told that a gold chain was suspended from the ceiling and that whoever found the chain would have the true religion. Actually, there were a great number of iron chains suspended from the ceiling, so everyone thought he had the true religion."

Most days for Dave, Greg and John, however, were not as exciting; their problems were those of Peace Corps teachers everywhere: not enough books and supplies; students so used to rote learning that they cannot or dare not think and reason; and delays and frustrations in whatever they attempted to do.

"The teaching here hasn't been too hard," said John. "We've fallen right into the schedule without too much trouble. In fact, we haven't had many of the culture shocks that we were warned about."

"I was a little shocked to see everyone in one of the tea-houses eating with his fingers," put in Dave, "but that's minor. The food had an odd smell, too, a charcoal smell typical of Somalia."

"I guess the biggest shock is the way the teachers use force to discipline the children," John went on. "They don't hold back at all. One teacher at Dayahe seems to love hitting the students, yet the boys don't hate him for it; they seem to respect him. But sometimes it's amazing how he hauls off and hits them."

One day about ten students were caught smoking. A couple were eventually expelled, but all were immediately subjected to a paddling before the student body. "With big boards," John described the scene, "just like a fraternity. The students who were watching got a big kick out of it. They realized the boys had been caught and had to be punished."

On the other hand, students in Somalia can be shockingly

undisciplined. In a pupil strike at one school, students threatened to lynch the headmaster. Another group went to Mogadiscio to complain to the Minister of Education.

Volunteer Ruth Evans, who weighs about a hundred pounds, was one of the first women teachers ever to face a class of Somali boys. Her class once became so unruly that she had to walk out. Before long one of the boys came to her with this note:

DEAR MADAM:
As we are the class, we make a great noise which was not good for us, but now we are going to apoligise our bad behavier (especially I Ahmed Jama Abdi) and Basha Mohamed Adan.
YOUR PUPILS
(in class)
(We beg your pardon, Evans.)

Despite their attitude on behavioral problems, the Somali people are happy, witty, humorous, and gay. "It's almost impossible not to have a close affinity for them, especially the students," said John. "When we go into the classroom, they stand up, this is their tradition or custom, like calling us Mr. John, Mr. Greg, and Mr. David. We've tried to keep a teacher-student relationship and not get too friendly with them. Life in Somalia can take a lot of patience. The Somalis are new in administration and management, and I'm sure they'll improve. But in many ways, they are as inefficient as can be. They're never on time. They usually do things wrong the first time and have to do them over. They're always late, and it wasn't easy for us to get used to this. I suppose we were this way when we were a young country."

This habit of procrastinating affected everything the PCVs tried to do until it became impossible to tell who or what in the host country, or in the Peace Corps' own administration, was to blame for the delays. Even after several months in the field, the books the PCVs had packed while they were still in training at NYU had not arrived. Their refrigerators—promised—had not come.

"John's right about the Somalis," said Dave. "Every time they try doing something, or we try doing something, and it doesn't come out right, they say, 'Oh, that's good enough.' And really it isn't good enough, and this is aggravating, trying to instill in them the idea that they should and can do better.

"But they're very friendly and it's easy to make them laugh. They all have big smiles and their teeth shine through. Students like to be kidded in class. I'm having trouble with my class, though. They aren't studying and they can't reason or make connections very easily.

"For instance, one day I brought a cube to class—a box—to show how many sides a cube has. I showed them the sides of the box and tried to get them to deduce the formula for finding the total surface area of the cube by taking the area of one side of the cube and multiplying it by six, the number of sides a cube has. But they just couldn't do it. I went over it and over it, but they couldn't get the connection. I had them come up individually and count the sides of the cube. This is typical— this inability to reason.

"As one of the Somali teachers said, the students want to be spoon-fed. The three of us have refused to do this—spoonfeed them—because they should learn to think, to make connections for themselves.

"Also, they just refuse to study. I've given several tests in mathematics and they refuse to prepare. I can tell them the diameter is twice the radius, and tell them and tell them and have them come to the board and do the problem and give them nightwork, but they'll miss it on the test again and again. I can't figure out how else we can do this, except to keep telling and telling them.

"Some of the students, though, are very bright and have a lot of initiative. There are a few math books around and some students have spent money to buy one for themselves, and to take the time to work out the problems."

"There are many good students," John put in, "but it's too bad that so few of them will ever get a chance for higher education in England or the United States."

It was frustrating for the PCVs to see this waste of good minds in an underdeveloped country that needed all the brain power it could muster. I read an essay which a boy student at another school, not Dayahe, had written in a class taught by a PCV. The text speaks for itself:

I am here to get from darkness of ignorance into the light instead of being in country looking after the camels and sheep and thus missing all civilization light. I am not learning English to get a better job, but I only wish to speak it. I want to live a good life as all Somali people do. I don't like to live under nations. Living a bad life is better to be dead, so I think bad life is like death.

Dave told me about the difficulties he had encountered in his science classes.

"There just aren't any science supplies. My Standard Seven class is very far behind, and I'm going to have to go over with them what I've been teaching my Standard Five.

"I tried teaching chemistry and of course there are no chemicals. We have a little sulphuric acid, but it's so contaminated that it can't be used. There are a few beakers, most of them broken.

"So what do you do? Just keep trying. Put your head down and charge ahead, and hope for the best."

Since the school had no textbooks, Dave and Greg Smith had to teach certain subjects from memory. In his classes, John Bayer wrote everything on the board so that the students might copy it into their notebooks. Each student was allotted a sixteen-page book for each course, but often the supply ran out.

"This lack of materials—paper, pencils, texts—is probably our biggest complaint," said John. "You can't give students homework or anything to copy down. The schools just don't receive enough money from the government to carry on."

There were 250 boys at the Dayahe Intermediate School, although the actual capacity was only 200. During the first two months of the term, forty students slept on blankets and coats piled up on the floor or on top of bed springs until the headmaster could make arrangements for extra mattresses. The boys were thin, but this was understandable if the diet they got at school was any indication of what they had been fed all their lives. At Dayahe they had jawardi bread for breakfast; rice, meat, and, occasionally, a vegetable for lunch; tea and bread for supper.

Most of the boys wore the white shirts and khaki shorts which were furnished by the school. About half the students appeared without shoes, and most went without socks. (Sargent Shriver, during his tour of Africa in 1962, surprised the Somalis by not wearing any socks. "They really expected President Kennedy's brother-in-law to be more aloof," reported a PCV in Southern Somalia.)

However, the Somali youngsters, despite their delicate appearance, are very athletic. "The students play soccer," Dave Dalcanton told me, "better with their bare feet than we can with shoes. In fact, it hurts our feet, but there's no end to the way they run and kick. They just go and go and go. We get tired playing with them after the first ten minutes. So far Greg has managed to score two goals and John and I are still scoreless. But we're improving and this is really the only athletic diversion at the school.

"We've introduced softball and the boys like it, but nobody catches the ball. They're very enthusiastic about competition; show them some activity in which they can excel over somebody else and they're all for it.

"They congregate in front of our house and do exercises, and we show them tricks, which they like to do. There's a rock called the 'lifting rock,' but Greg is the only one who can lift it. None of the Somalis can get it up in the air. They're thin and they don't have very well-developed torso muscles. But they try and try, grunt and groan, and laugh and kid each other when they can't lift it, and they enjoy this. Perhaps the way to get them to learn is to make it competitive and funny. This is the way I'm trying to approach them. When I give the tests at the end of the year, we'll find out if it worked."

And so life went for the Volunteers. Each day the frustrations and difficulties of teaching at Dayahe were felt more keenly. The PCVs began to be aware of a fatigue that might eventually overwhelm them.

"I can see," said Dave Dalcanton, "that things are going to start wearing thin. The experiences won't be new and everything will be drudgery. The routine will be the same day after day, the food will taste the same, look the same, and even smell the same. This will be a test of *us* more than anything else. We'll have to search within ourselves to find new resources, new diversions, new methods of entertaining ourselves so that we won't 'crack up.' "

"We'll probably teach in Dayahe a year," added John Bayer, "and then, unless we really want to stay, I suppose everyone will be transferred around. PCVs in the south will get a chance in the north and vice versa."

About two months later I received the following letter from Greg Smith: "The harvest season is over and the rainy season has just begun. The vegetable gardens are barren, and existence is more difficult. There's no variety in our meals. Last night John remarked that the only thing that could happen now to make things worse would be for the electricity to go off.

"About one minute later, the lights went off. Both generator engines had broken down. The nearest mechanic is in Burao, 230 miles away, and the road is impassable during the rainy season, so it will probably take two or three weeks to get the mechanic up here to repair the electricity supply. Well, this is life in the Peace Corps."

The headline in the *Somali News* of December 7, 1962, read, "English teaching programme at Intermediate School, Merca." The story went on to describe the work of a husband-and-wife team who, after several months of bored waiting, had finally begun their assignment in Southern Somalia.

This year two American Peace Corps teachers, Mr. and Mrs. Boris Sojka, have joined the staff of the Intermediate School and have launched an extensive programme of English language teaching both for the students of the school and for adult classes in the evening. In all about two hundred people in Merca are now attending the classes. Mr. and Mrs. Sojka are also conducting classes in singing and dancing for interested students. . . . The director of the Inter-mediate School and the two American teachers are currently exploring the possibility of setting up a programme to teach basic reading and writing to students who are unable to attend school on a full-time basis.

"Don't be too impressed by the article," warned Boris. "It's not all that good, but Merca is happy with Carole and me, and we're happy with Merca.

"I'm very pleased with the results of my classes. I can really tell the difference from when I started. I'm rather poor in English myself, so I'm learning a lot while I teach. I try to keep out my accent and pronunciation, but I find myself saying *yeah, wader, brudder,* and so on. When Jack and Diane Magri were last here, Hamka, the harbormaster, told them, 'Mr. Boris is changing the English language for us.'

"The police need English for promotions, officials need it for better positions, shopkeepers need it for better business, some students need it in order to get scholarships to the United States."

"It's a difficult setup," said Carole, "with kids learning three languages plus their own and trying to think in a language not their own. But I've observed that my kids know as much English in a year as I knew Spanish, and that's the only criterion I can judge by."

Like the three Volunteers at Dayahe, Carole and Boris were completing their sixth month in the field. They could be proud of the good relationships they had established with the inhabitants. Their house—which at one point was embellished with a private "zoo"—was a popular place.

"Not everybody can mix with the Somalis," Carole said. "If we weren't teaching, where would we begin to make contacts? It's through people like the headmaster that we even met any Somalis. And the adult classes we teach at night give us just so many more contacts. Our Italian neighbor, who teaches in an Italian school, has no social contact with Somalis, except perhaps to say *Buona sera* to them on the street. We're probably the only Americans who ever lived in this town, the only ones the Somalis in Merca will ever meet. The best thing we're doing here is being ourselves."

"When I walk down the street," said Boris, "the kids call me 'beard,' in Italian instead of Somali. The Somalis rather like my beard. All the sheiks have them and dye them orange with camel urine."

"And you have people who adopt you." Carole went on. "Boris has had several. One boy adopted him, used to come to our house all the time. When he got busy, he stopped coming. Another used to come and stay, and he'd go away and come back again. And Mohamoud used to come and sit. He hasn't been here for a while, but he'll be back. They don't care if I'm writing letters or cleaning or what—they just sit. If I talk, I get monosyllabic answers. I'm probably the first white woman who talks that most Somali men have ever met.

"People are in again, gone again. Police transfer constantly; teachers are transferred; people go to Mogadiscio, come back, go and get a job, lose the job, come to class, stay away from class. Your sphere of influence is always changing."

"We've shown films from the United States Information Agency," Boris said, "and we get great turnouts. For awhile we had a 'zoo' at our house: a monkey, two dogs, a hedgehog, and two Guinea vultures.

"We let the birds go, the hedgehog escaped, and one of the dogs was run over. Our monkey, Daniel, disliked Somalis. He bit a few people, including our houseboy, who teased him, so we decided to let him go. An Italian friend took him to his banana plantation and set him free.

"We had a baby ostrich for a day, but the owner wanted him back. Now we have a baboon named Gina. She's afraid of me—we think it's the beard. And we have a new baby monkey with big eyes, named Nutmeg, and the remaining dog, Punch. He's going to the States with us when we finish here. I'm still trying to get a cheetah and a desert fox."

Carole referred to their pets to illustrate her revised thinking about Americans abroad. "True, our monkeys eat a lot more than the Somali settlers' kids, but if we didn't feed our monkeys, those kids still wouldn't have more to eat. People criticize Americans for having big cars when people are starving, but if I bought a Ford instead of an Imperial, it's not true that fewer people would starve.

"There are people in the Embassy—really great people—who're making big salaries and driving big cars. This is their prerogative. This is an American, this is the way Americans act who have a good position. Why shouldn't they do this? I don't think everybody overseas, just because they work for the embassy or USIA is ugly at all. I think there are Americans here who are good at what they're doing and ones who are not, and this is true in the Peace Corps. But I don't agree with the Rep who thinks an American should be someone without this, without that, without the other thing. I've come to feel that everybody should reflect his own culture overseas —come with the trappings you have."

"Back in the States we talked about the right of all countries to their freedom," said Boris. "Naturally, we still feel this way, but we know now that not all the Europeans here are a bunch of dirty colonialists. I have much more respect than I did for the Italians. They are just as right or just as wrong as we were in our expansion to the west.

"They made arable this semidesert. Before them, there was only the pastoral nomad. Whether it's right or wrong to change the country is another matter, but they developed the economy for what it is: Somalis realize this and let the Italians stay peacefully. Many decent white men consider Africa to be their home."

The Sojkas had obviously undergone a change in their thinking. However, this was inevitable. After all, Boris and Carole had arrived with a set of assumptions which had been formed on the basis of secondhand information. The reality of life in Somalia was bound to alter those assumptions, for each new day brought unexpected problems. It might be the kind of minor problem described by PCV George Bond, a friend of the Sojkas who was teaching at *Collegio Professionale Agrario* in Genale, Southern Somalia: "At least one important thing is *non c'e* (Italian for 'there isn't any') each day. Monday it may be water, Tuesday electricity, Wednesday meat, and so on. For these occasions we have no solution but to scour the community for a substitute commodity, and that takes precious time from our work schedules."

There might also be the kind of serious problem that had plagued the three Volunteers at Dayahe Intermediate School: the shortage of teaching supplies. The Sojkas, in fact, had only two textbooks and therefore had to write the lesson for each day on the blackboard. This was especially frustrating because a set of books which had arrived for Boris had been sold by the school librarian before Boris could advise her that he had ordered them.

Perhaps the most serious frustration was the realization that progress would be slow in Somalia.

"I'm afraid the future of Somalia is rather nil," said Boris. "In the south, there's a one-crop economy—bananas. The fruit is smaller than the American kind and bruises very easily. Italy pays twice the world-market price for it, as we used to do with Cuban sugar.

"Away from the river, there is need for lots and lots of water. All this will cost a great deal of money, which Somalia does not have. Salt water purification costs are prohibitive. The farmers could raise cash crops, but most plantations are Italian owned and there aren't enough agricultural experts. So right now and for a long time to come, Somalia will have a one-crop economy. Oil in profitable amounts still has not been found.

"When we came to Somalia, we felt that we were unique, that we could do things for Africa. The people in AID and USIA were just not doing things right. Well, it's not so. Some of them really work, and Merca is pro-American largely because of the good work of AID.

"But there's something missing, something we just can't pin-point. Maybe it's a lack of sophistication in the system, maybe too many people are trying to get their fingers into the pie. But we find ourselves in the same position as AID— we're putting out but the Somalis are not helping themselves.

"For example, part of Merca—including us—is out of water. The wells have filled in with sand. Everyone knew it was happening but nothing was done to prevent it, and so far nothing is being done to remedy the situation, even though there is drilling equipment in Mogadiscio. And there's nothing quite as bad as a bathroom equipped for running water but not having it.

"Or, take another example. If our houseboy would save his earnings from us for two years, he'd have about fifteen hundred shillings. He could then buy a donkey or a piece of land and go into business for himself. Instead, he spends all his money on clothes, movies, and girls. So he'll have nothing.

But he's not looking to tomorrow. That's part of his religious background. Tomorrow he may be dead, but if he's not dead, then Allah will take care of him.

"I have this empty gnawing feeling about us and the Peace Corps; its press is so much better than the actuality. The actual concrete help that we are giving is miniscule. The biggest thing, and maybe the best, is acting as public relations men, showing what Americans are like. This I think is a complete success."

Despite every obstacle, the PCVs in Somalia could point to a rather impressive list of accomplishments, including the building of basketball and volley ball courts, and other athletic fields; the organizing of clubs in cooking, sewing, model airplanes, and photography; the starting of school newspapers; the preparation of texts for English classes; the teaching of English with Italian texts which had to be translated each night for use in class the next day; service as scout masters; the building of a science laboratory; an oratorical contest in which girls participated for the first time in Somalia; teaching accelerated classes for girls; building a library; wiring schools for electricity; conducting adult education classes; reorganizing the library of a government department; assisting the U.N. in housing surveys; measuring and screening the windows of a hospital in Hargeisa; instructing workers in a hospital in chemistry during vacation from regular Peace Corps activity; conducting an evening school in Hargeisa to prepare students for college entrance examination (subjects taught were algebra, science, history, geography, English, psychology, current events, and pedagogy); obtaining one of several windmills, furnished by AID but left rusting in Mogadiscio, and setting it up in Northern Somalia where water was needed desperately; working in a mental hospital in Berbera during vacation and organizing a local women's club to raise money for clothes for the mental patients, who had no clothing and no bedding and were kept in cement cells (the women's club made twenty-eight dresses in a month, visited patients, and overcame their fear of the institution).

The female Volunteers in particular had made a mark on one aspect of Somali life. After attending a wedding in Burao, PCV Janet Shomaker received the following letter:

My wife and I are sincerely thanking you very much for your very kind and respectable attendance to our wedding celebration both in the first and last day of it. Indeed you have given a remarkable feature to our tea party which was the first of its kind in the history of Burao inhabitants. In the past it was very rare for Somali ladies and gentlemen to sit together in the same party and in this case you have also constituted a great encouragement to the Somali community in the field of social activity.

Considering the difficulties of working in an underdeveloped country, the accomplishments seem more than satisfactory— and indeed, most of the Volunteers were content with their individual projects. It was rewarding for the PCVs to see the gradual improvement in the use of English, to realize that the Somalis had come to have a better impression of America, to guide gifted students along the right path, to help in the preparations for a local festivity, or simply to make friends with the neighbors. However, the Volunteers no longer viewed the future with unabated optimism, for the achievements that had been made in Somalia were the result of six months of arduous labor. It had been necessary to overcome an endless number of obstacles to get even a small project into motion.

This was indeed a dangerous time for the Volunteers: as I noted before, 25 per cent of those in Somalia had returned home after a few months of service. Although it was easy to be discouraged, those who stayed on struggled to ignore their dismay and to do their best under the prevailing conditions.

5

When we came they laughed at us.
But I think what impressed them
most was that we worked right along
with them. We joined in every mean,
dirty job that had to be done.
PCV MICHAEL RUGGIERO
Togo

By the time I landed in Togo, Mike Ruggiero's original team
of nine fishermen had dwindled to five—two at Dapango in the
north and three at Anécho on the coast adjacent to Dahomey.
They were now serving their eighth month in the field. The
other fishermen had returned to the States, and it had therefore not been possible to assign any Volunteers to Lake Togo
as planned.

Mike had lost thirty pounds and his curly hair was really
gray now. The Gloucester dory and about half the equipment
he had been promised—and around which he had built the fishing program—had never appeared. His later request for a
thirty-eight-foot Navy boat, to be used for training purposes,
had also been ignored; he did not know why. As late as March,
1963, five months after they had arrived, the Volunteers still
believed the Navy boat would arrive. Mike had written to me:
"What our counterparts want most is to see our small dragger
arrive. You see, these fishermen are fully aware that better
techniques are used throughout the world. They have never
been introduced here because of the surf which runs the full
length of Togo. No one could operate a vessel here without
docking facilities. We plan to moor our boat outside the surf."
But the Navy craft never came.

So instead of training local fishermen on a modern boat,
the PCVs had spent their time mastering the Togolese dugout-

95

canoe methods. And the daily catch had not been increased appreciably.

The much-publicized fishermen, their numbers depleted, were no longer receiving extensive press coverage, for in the meantime, the Peace Corps' first medical team had begun work. It had been stationed in central Togo and was doing an impressive job, as were some of the newly arrived teachers. Many of these other Volunteers felt that "the fishermen had always received too much publicity." It is unfortunately true that Peace Corps projects which originally seem highly promising do not always turn out as anticipated. Similarly, PCVs who seemed to be outstanding while in training, and make the best copy for publicity writers and photographers, are sometimes unable to carry through, and cause their Reps many a sleepless night.

The morale of the fishermen was, if not low, certainly not high. They had been reassessing their goals, evaluating their own accomplishments and—regretfully—shelving some of their plans. But they continued within the limitations.

There had been administrative problems, too. The PC Rep who had come over with the first group had been recalled after three months in the field. He was not a good administrator, and his wife, according to PCVs, had tried to run the group by "playing favorites." C. Payne Lucas, who had worked both at headquarters and in the field, inherited the responsibility. "Luke," was being assisted temporarily by Sandy McCaw. Sandy had been diverted to Togo as she was returning to the States from the PC public works project in Gabon.

In spite of the numerous disappointments, team leader Mike Ruggiero could look positively at his work in Togo. "Jackie Theriot and Keith Keller are doing a great job with fish pond farming up in Dapango," he enthused. "You should see all the ponds they've cleared and stocked. Here at Anécho, the first full season of fishing is just beginning for us. We're still negotiating a deal with the Dahomey fishermen whereby our

boys [the native fishermen] can go out on the Dahomey dragger and get used to a big boat and different gear. I think we'll
complete the arrangements soon."

Sharing his hopes were Bill Outten and Vito Blonda. Bill—
who sported a heavy reddish-brown beard he had not worn in
training days—and Vito had quarters with Mike in a two-story
house in Anécho. Like Mike, they felt that they were not ac-
complishing enough. If the cutbacks had affected Mike's self-
confidence, they had not affected his standing with the local
people. With them, the big fisherman was still first-rate.

"Mike's biggest contribution is in public relations," said Acting Representative Lucas. "In relating to people, he's the best
in Togo, maybe in the whole Corps. In Anécho, where he lives
and works, everybody knows him. He calls most of them by
name, talks with them in French, wanders in and out of their
compounds exchanging small talk and joking as easily as
though he were one of them."

I accompanied Mike for several days, in the market place,
at the beach among the fishermen, in the natives' compounds,
and in his own quarters where people strolled in and out
freely, asking questions, selling eggs, collecting money for
past services, delivering messages, and when I was there with
my Polaroid, getting their pictures taken.

To me, Mike appeared happier and more at ease with the
Togolese than with his fellow Voluntcers. When he smiled or
kidded, even when he argued and disagreed with them, the
strain of the eight months of frustrations seemed to vanish.
Tété, the fishing chief at Anécho, and Tété's big family, were
his friends. So was Jenny, the slender young Togolese woman
who with her husband and children and perhaps fifty other
persons lived in the walled compound next to the Volunteers'
house. The women in the market place were his friends and so
were dozens of the children. "It's easy for the children to love
us," Mike explained, "because we don't deal with them like
the teachers do. We work with the men."

I observed Mike's work with the local fishermen when an unexpected drama unfolded on the beach. The cast of characters included:

Têté, Mike's local boss and a rich man, who, the PCVs said, could go to France whenever he chose. Têté had a house. He also had several wives and a large number of children, including a son whom he hoped woulc' become a chief fisherman. Têté spoke good English and French, plus four of the forty-four Togolese dialects. He was a judge in the tribal court at Anécho, where a verdict of guilty usually carried a fine of enough whiskey for everyone present at the trial. Grey-haired and intelligent, Têté had learned fishing from his father, and he was proud of his heritage—especially of the records which showed that each of his parents had lived to be over a hundred years old.

Têté's boys, the local fishermen with whom Têté had an economic relationship. They used his equipment and shared the day's catch with him.

A *U.N.-FAO adviser* to the Togolese government, a so-called fisheries expert. Intensely disliked by Têté, this man was responsible for training the apprentice fishermen who were employed by the *Service de Pêches,* a branch of the Togolese Department of Agriculture.

Assorted boys who were working for the *Service de Pêches,* but who were receiving their practical training from Têté and the PCVs because their supervisor, the FAO adviser, never ventured out on a fishing boat himself, presumably because of the danger.

The coastal fishing village of Anécho has a population of 10,430. Aside from the market place, the center of activity in Anécho is the beach, where the local fishermen make their headquarters.

Mike and I arrived at the beach by jeep at about 7:30 one morning. Têté and some of his men were already at work. They were burning the outside of two new dugout canoes they had brought back from Ghana. Afterwards, they would install seats in them. PCV Bill Outten was there, too. It was a gray day and the surf was high, too high to go out, according to Têté. Besides, the mackerel were not running, although the season would begin any day.

Bill explained to me what was going on. "They fire the boats to drive out the little animals so the wood won't rot. Each canoe is carved out of a whole tree. Notice how high they are in both the stern and the bow. They're strictly utilitarian; no fine craftsmanship here. It takes about two months for the canoe makers to go into the Ghana woods and truck the trees out to the coast. They cost about $175 each, and Têté had to pay some of that in advance."

We started the day by taking a few pictures, a mistake at almost any hour in Africa but certainly an error so early in the morning. Têté had been photographed before, but had never seen a finished picture of himself. Mike told Têté we would give him a picture to keep. The chief posed readily. Then we took shots of Têté and several fishermen against a background of a huge seine net that was piled on the sand. Bill and Vito had worked for hours making the net—it was as large as a football field—but it still needed leads and rings before it could be used.

I passed out the first pictures. People crowded around us; they all wanted to be snapped by my fetish-camera. Women swarmed out of the grass-roofed mud huts, carrying their babies. Men and boys, who previously had been wearing nondescript shorts, reappeared now in colorful *pagnes*. Naked and half-naked children crowded around. As I was trying to figure out how to rid myself of this sudden popularity, a jeep drove up with the FAO adviser and several apprentice fishermen from the *Service de Pêches*. They proceeded to unload a blue nylon net which they had repaired. Têté said something under his breath, but I had no time for questions since the U.N. fisheries expert soon began a long lecture in French. He wanted the men to go out immediately, and to go out every day, regardless of the threatening weather and high surf. He told them that they should mechanize the canoes by building platforms on which outboard motors could be attached. He especially wanted the men to try out a lightweight Japanese net which he had brought along.

Têté's men and the PCVs had already examined the Japanese net. They had decided that it needed heavier leads to carry it down underneath a school of fish; the net was tied and hung so that all the weight of the catch would pull on the lighter line with the heavier line serving no purpose. Têté would have none of it, and stubbornly refused to send his men out. He said that the surf was not right and that the boats would tip over and the gear be lost. "I've fished these waters for fifty years," he told me in English, "and my father before me. I worked with him back in 1914. That man knows nothing about this. There's no use going out today. Better to work on the dugouts."

There was disagreement, too, about the use of motors—"a real Guinea rig," Bill Outten whispered to me. The opinion of both the PCVs and Têté was that the canoes, if thrown even slightly off balance, would capsize in the surf, and the motors would be buried in the sand and lost forever.

"I'll take that chance," yelled the FAO man. "Just get out there as I told you and let's see what you can do."

But he did not wait to see what they could do; he left to go on an errand in the village. The PCVs and the local fishermen discussed the problem. Têté was furious. While Mike agreed with most of his contentions, he tried to calm Têté down.

"This is tough fishing," Bill said to me. "You can't use the same methods here you would elsewhere. We learned that the hard way after we first got here. Most of us had worked on trawlers or draggers—big motor-driven boats—but we'd never paddled through surf like this."

"The *Service de Pêches* fellows get a good salary," said

Mike, "so they have to go out if their boss says to go out. But they don't have a good captain, so they can't go out without one of Têté's men as captain, and his men can't be pushed. A good captain, like Têté's No. 1 nephew—Amegbo, who's fifty years old—makes all the difference in the world. Timing is terrifically important. The captain has to call for the men to paddle or to jump overboard at the right time. Why, one of those guys the fisheries man wants us to send out can't even swim.

"You don't necessarily have to be a strong swimmer, but you've got to be a cool one to bring in the paddles and all the gear. You have to jump clear of the boat so that it doesn't turn over on top of you or hit you in the head. But it's too dangerous out there today. Somebody might get the net wrapped around his neck in that surf."

Before Mike and Têté could agree on their course of action, the FAO man was back, shouting his instructions once more. He and Têté got into a noisy argument. Mike tried to placate them. "Since it's so late today, why don't we plan to go out early tomorrow?" he suggested.

His idea was finally adopted; but before the adviser departed, leaving his apprentice fishermen behind, he shouted a few orders to Mike. "Don't argue with 'em, just tell 'em to go! And work 'em hard as hell."

Têté's anger was undisguised. Mike and Bill looked tired— or was it disgusted?—and somewhat embarrassed. One reason, I discovered later, was that the adviser was often mistaken for an American.

"Just another bad image the Peace Corps is supposed to compensate for," Bill said, as we walked back to the jeep.

Têté was still repeating, "I was born with this. I know about it. I fished with my father back in 1914."

The house where the Volunteers lived was large and airy. The second-floor balcony was an excellent point from which to project movies on the whitewashed wall across the way.

Lunch was waiting for us. Vito Blonda had prepared curried chicken, rice, and a crisp green salad. Best of all, there were tall bottles of cold water. Drinking water had to be boiled, filtered, and refrigerated. It was partly because of the water that Vito had fired the cook about three weeks earlier.

"He used to get up very early," Vito told me, "and spend an hour boiling the eggs until they were like rocks; but we could never train him to boil the drinking water twenty minutes before filtering, and this has to be done three times a day. He'd cook lunch early, get it all ready about 11 A.M., and put it steaming hot in the refrigerator. All the ice cubes would melt, and the lunch would be ruined. I couldn't teach him anything, so I decided to do the cooking myself."

I asked about the marketing, since I had noticed people going back and forth continually from their compounds to the market place, where small lots of sticks, coconuts, matches, fruit, and so forth, were spread out on the ground. "Oh, everyone makes a separate trip for each item that's needed. They'd never think of picking up two or three things at once," Vito explained.

At lunch, Mike and Bill reviewed the scene at the beach for Vito. The three men rehashed the problems that had bedeviled them since they had arrived in Togo.

"Sure, I could *order* Têté," Mike said, "but I could do it only once. He'd do what I said, but it would ruin our relationship. We have to work with the local people, not tell them what to do. That's why Têté hates the FAO adviser, and these people don't hate easily. But I'd rather have them like us. Our creed is to work with them, not to give them some gear and say 'Go use it.' "

"Têté fishes for five families and the five all help make the nets," Bill added for my benefit. "He's the acknowledged chief of the fishermen in our area, and one of the most respected elders—probably the best educated. It's kind of an incongruous society at this stage—part capitalistic, part socialistic. The men work for money, but they can't keep their earnings because they can't refuse to help their relatives."

"Besides Têté," Mike went on, "we have to work with the *Service de Pêches,* too. We have an obligation because of the equipment they give us. They send boys in training from fishing stations all over the country to learn from the Peace Corps —three months with the *Service,* seven weeks with the local fishermen and the Volunteers."

"They get a good salary," said Vito. "8900 francs [$36] or more a month."

"Vito, you should see the Japanese net they're going to try out tomorrow. It's lightweight nylon, one-inch gauge, all hung wrong, and the weights will never carry it. It'll just float on top of the water. Not only that, but they didn't wash it after they got it wet once, so rats ate it and now it's all mended. Took them hours to fix it."

"O.K., so let's do what the FAO man wants. Let's go out tomorrow and try it out."

"We could have had a nice self-contained fishing unit for $10,000," Mike said to me. "We haven't increased the catch a bit yet, and we still don't know if motorization will work, but we have gained the people's confidence. They're peaceful and shy, and I believe they're friends of the U.S. now.

"During the first three months about all we did was uncrate and send out household articles, fix screens, and get acquainted. We had to start sending Peace Corps fishermen on trips to see other projects, sort of as consolation prizes."

Mike had made a trip to Ghana and had taken Têté with him. "He was thrilled to see large fishing vessels for the first time. But what really got him was the fact that they were run by his own people—Africans—yet he knew nothing about those boats and considered himself a big fisherman. Now he wants a large boat, so we made our point."

"Well, *we've* learned a lot," Bill sighed. "We discovered that the Togolese know the different types of knots American fishermen use, but they have good reasons for doing things differently. Ability to get in and out of the surf is the important factor, something none of us had any experience with previously. And long lines are no good in these waters, because of the danger of getting tangled up in hooks when the boat turns over. But these men are aware that more productive techniques are used throughout the world; they've just never been introduced to them."

"Well, we'll try again," Mike said, "Our first full fishing season—June through January—is just beginning. We ought to bring in herring, tuna, jacks and mackerel. If the cooperative deal with the Dahomey boat comes through, some of our Togolese men can go aboard. Of course, if we get the boat, there'll be the problem of who's going to run it. And if we land large quantities of fish on the beach, this is going to bring up more problems. Now the fishermen use some of the fresh fish for eating and selling in the market. The rest of the fish they dry and smoke by burning coconut husks in those ovens along the beach that look like beehives. An increase in the catch will throw this balance off.

"We'll have to work with the *Service,* but we'll stay away from AID as much as possible. It's better public relations. Reps don't judge PCVs by what they do, anyhow, but by the noise they make. The quieter the better. They prefer Volunteers who don't make any ripples and they definitely don't want anyone making waves."

"We agreed to go out tomorrow at 6 A.M.," Bill put in. "That means if conditions are right, if weather is good, if people show up, and if everything works out. But how can we make people back home understand this? These people aren't lazy, but they don't really want to change, and we can't go any faster and get cooperation from them."

"I can show you fishermen in Maine the same way," said Mike. "We once tried introducing long-handled clam rakes. Got a good mess of quahogs, but the natives never used rakes again. Went right back to the old back-breaking way of clamming."

With their program so severely hampered, the PC fishermen might have resigned and gone home, or they might have asked for a transfer to another location. But Mike and those who stayed were not willing to give up. "I still like it," Mike insisted. "There may be a big gap between the idea and the carrying out, but I think the Peace Corps will succeed in spite of itself."

Up at isolated Dapango, in the northwest corner of Togo, nineteen-year-old Keith Keller and twenty-two-year-old Jackie Theriot were rehabilitating a fresh water fish hatchery. They had few opportunities to fraternize with anyone but their Togolese counterparts on the job. However, work on the fish hatchery had progressed more rapidly than had been expected.

The living quarters of the two PCVs was situated about three hundred feet above the mountainside village of Dapango. Their house had two bedrooms, two baths, a combination living-dining room, as well as a kitchen, a storage room, a big veranda overlooking the village, and a garage, used as a workshop, where Jackie had started to build a boat. The huge grounds surrounding the house included a chicken yard, two vegetable gardens, several flower beds, rock fences, and a great variety of trees.

"We have everything from sisal for rope-making to orchids for parties and cactus for prodding animals," said Jackie.

"And we have Coo-coo (that's Moba for 'cook')," added Keith, "He's really not bad except that he starts cleaning about 5 A.M. He's crazy for leaving the guts in chicken when he cooks them, and he manages to get insects in everything he cooks. Aside from that he's O.K."

For diversion, Keith and Jackie turn to sports—football, tennis, basketball, volley ball, ping-pong. They swim in the lake except in the rainy season. When they want a harder ex-

ercise—I wouldn't think this would be often—they sometimes
pace themselves on the road.

"There are fewer recreational outlets here than anywhere
else in the country," said Keith. "I've read over fifty books
since I arrived, including a good deal of the *World Almanac*."
Keith, who hopes to go to Massachusetts School of Art when
he leaves the Peace Corps, also paints during his spare time.
"Up until the last month I wasn't at all satisfied with the art
work I was doing," he told me.

The fish hatchery had been initiated in 1955 by SEMNORD,
a French organization. Before abandoning it five years later,
SEMNORD had built twenty-five barrages for the purpose of
storing water for the dry season. The small reservoirs of water
were obviously suited to fish pond farming, but the French
experts did not have enough time or money to pursue that
possibility. Under the Togolese Water and Forest Department, maintenance on the water sheds was neglected. Levees
broke, spillways washed away, and ponds dried up or silted in.
Some fish breeding had been attempted; but a few months
before the PCVs arrived, a section of the breeding station had
choked with weeds.

"The Water and Forest Department wouldn't release the
ponds to us," Jackie recalled. "The government just didn't
understand what the Peace Corps was trying to do. Our Rep
and the newly formed Fisheries Service had to help us per-
suade the officials.

"I told the director of the department that members of our
organization didn't shout commands, but that we had come to
work. He's convinced now."

First, the PCVs cleared the weeds from the levees around
the fish stations. There were ten breeding ponds, but only
seven were even in partial operation. The other three had
dried out; bamboo grew in the empty basins, and dead stalks
matted the ground. After several weeks of clearing, Jackie
and Keith—eager to get some results—decided to stop cleaning

and to stock the three ponds with various species of *Tilapia* which could be obtained from other Togolese water sheds.

Then they went back to clear more of the station. They had been asked not to disturb any of the seven operative ponds where the government was running tests, but they did get permission to feed and care for the fish in them until the experiment was over. One pond was stocked with *Heterotis,* an indigenous river fish which had not bred in seven years.

"After our partial clearing of the pond, the addition of water and two months of supplementary feeding, we noticed a very exciting development," Jackie wrote to Acting Representative Lucas in Lomé. "The parent fish were building nests. There were four nests close to the bank—round, about eighteen inches in diameter, with elevated ridges of debris cleared from the center. About two weeks later, we spotted a black ball in the water—1,500 to 2,000 small *Heterotis* frys swimming on the surface. After two days they disappeared into the dirty, unsettled water, presumably to swim closer to the bottom."

Thus the small effort proved a point: A little care and feeding in a fish pond could provide Togo with a much-needed increase in its supply of fresh fish. In any case, the PCVs tended these fish as if they were pets.

By the time the *Heterotis* hatched, the tilapias in the three ponds stocked by the PCVs were raising small fry. *"Tilapia macrochir* seems to be the most prolific, but *Tilapia zilli* is by far the fastest growing," reported the two fishermen. "Their ability to eat algae, plankton, phytoplankton, zooplankton, as well as higher plants and partially decomposed manure makes them most suitable for artificial lakes. At present we're feeding crushed cotton seed sent to us by the Togolese Fisheries Service. This seems to attract tilapias more than the cassava and banana leaves we pick from the local trees.

"Another fortunate characteristic—their breeding habits are such that they will not overpopulate the lakes, preventing rapid and larger growth. This might be a problem where fishing is a new idea and people are hesitant to leave their farms to learn a new trade."

A newly hatched tilapia, the fishermen told me, will attain a size of eight to ten inches and be edible usually within eight months under natural conditions, or five to six months under fertilization and artificial feeding.

"This is the size we Americans think of eating, and we try to teach people here to accept this size," said Jackie. "But the Togolese eat all the fish they catch, regardless of size. It's just like the farmer who grows a crop year round on the same plot of land until it's depleted of nutrients."

There were fifty-four lakes from Lama-Kara to Dapango, a distance of about a hundred miles, but few had been stocked. Only three lakes in the Dapango area had fish of edible size. A number of government employees were helping to stock more ponds, and during school vacations, many students were learning how to throw and mend cast nets.

"We're trying to get the young people interested, because they are more apt to forget their fathers' trade and learn one of their own," said Jackie.

"But one problem in the north of Togo is the number of people unable to speak French. Probably 90 per cent of the Hausa, Moba, and Gurma tribes talk only the local languages. This is really frustrating as we can never get a straight answer from the rural people."

The Volunteers had two Togolese fishermen from the coast working with them, supposedly learning techniques which they could demonstrate to their own people. But—

"This is one of the more disappointing things," said Keith, "the African's seeming disinterest in other Africans. For example, these two Togolese were taken from two small fishing villages in the south and trained by *Service de Pêches* in the use of advanced fishing equipment and in the basic techniques of fish farming. A plan was worked out for them to come up here and live in the village, which is just like their own. They were to train the local people and to work with us in fish culture.

"However, they wouldn't live with the northerners whom they considered beneath them. They have shown no patience in their work with the villagers and they work grudgingly. When we're working with fish culture, Jack and I wear blue jeans; they come to work in new shirts and white bermudas. If the African won't help the African, what are we doing here?"

"Sometimes, though," Jackie put in, "they just don't know what to do. My first day here I saw ten sacks of ammonium sulphate which were half rotted. I asked the director of Water and Forest if he had used any fertilizer in the ponds. He said it was for use on trees, not in the water. I tried to explain that the water is also deficient in sulphates and could use nitrogen from the ammonium. He was astonished and wouldn't believe it. A French technician had given him the fertilizer, which is somewhat rare and expensive in Togo, but he'd never used it. I have since used some along with phosphate to induce plankton blooms in the breeding ponds."

Jackie and Keith wondered who, if anyone, would continue their work after they returned to the States. They estimated that a staff of six would be needed, but they doubted that more than one or two would be hired. Assuming that most of the lakes in the north would have edible fish, the work could be carried on by: two teacher-demonstrators who would teach the making, casting, and mending of nets; a guardian for the station; a warden for the lakes; and two workers at the breeding station.

"Perhaps we can keep up our counterparts' motivation through correspondence," Jackie said. "If we can encourage them to use the knowledge they've gained, there should be no recurrence of the deterioration that happened from 1955 to 1962, and Togo's inland fisheries industry should have a good start."

Then he added, "We can only hope for the best." Keith agreed.

At one spot on the road which runs parallel to the sea, from Lomé to Anécho, the sand trucks of a local concrete maker back up to load. Women and children, with pans of sand on their heads, march endlessly up to the trucks and back to the sand pit. They earn 125 francs a day, or about fifty cents.

African men rarely do this sort of labor. But not far from the sand depot, the males were openly smuggling bootleg liquor and cigarettes. The big red and yellow plastic bags that bobbed up and down in the water like lobster buoys were easily identified. All day the men ran their motor boats back and forth between Togo and Ghana, since the land border between the two countries was closed. The smugglers were paying twenty-two cents a pack for cigarettes in Togo and selling them for fifty-five cents in Ghana; gin or Scotch at 750 francs ($3) in Togo might bring as much as seven dollars in Ghana.

There is always activity along the coastal road between Lomé and Anécho. When the fetish season is on, as it was when I was in Africa, the people in the settlements along the road may be seen in their ritual costumes, dancing to the beat of drums to influence the gods. At any time of year, the road is crowded with women carrying goods on their heads and children on their backs. The pedestrian traffic moves very slowly, but news travels fast.

The distance from Lomé to Anécho is about forty miles. At 7 A.M. one morning, Mike Ruggiero and I left Lomé in the baby-blue Peace Corps jeep. We arrived in Anécho at about 8 A.M. As we drove up to his beach headquarters, more than fifty people were standing around on the sand; many were dressed in bright colored *pagnes*.

"Who are all these guys?" Mike asked. "Some of them I've never seen before and others not for months."

Then he glanced at my Polaroid. "It's your camera again."

They had heard that Mike was coming and had guessed or got the word that I was coming with him. The word-of-mouth communications throughout the country seemed to be amazingly effective; the PCVs confirmed that.

The day was sunny. The Volunteers and Têté consulted. Because of bad weather, the Japanese nylon net had not yet been tried. But the sea was fairly calm now. Several of Têté's men prepared to launch a dugout. Five men from the *Service de Pêchés* and three from Têté's group would go out.

About thirty persons surrounded the canoe as if to push it down the beach and into the water. But instead of pushing, most of them looked over their shoulders at me.

"If you don't put away that camera we'll never get this thing launched," Mike hollered.

The launching was perfect, and under the direction of a capable captain, the canoe cut through the surf without mishap. Têté and some of his boys went back to work on his two new boats. Everyone was still concerned about the Japanese net: how unevenly it was hung, how wrong the stress would be, how the net was too light to sink beneath the fish.

The team came back early in the afternoon. We were on the beach to watch them land. So were their families, friends, and the other fishermen, all curious about the size of the catch and eager to see if the captain could bring the canoe through the surf without capsizing.

The catch was small. The Japanese net had floated too close to the surface to pick up many fish. However, the men had seen whole schools of mackerel and had watched other fishermen take in a big catch. The season had started.

Têté's surly mood did not improve at the news. He was angry now that he had not sent out more of his men with gear that would be effective. He and Mike immediately planned to begin fishing again on a daily basis. To get a better share of the catch, they would get up at 4 A.M. and go out at about

5 A.M. each morning—which makes it easy to understand why Mike wrote to me later:

"I must be going to bed now. It's 7:30 P.M., long past my bedtime. We may not be producing much—there's so little we can do about that—but we are getting the Togolese to know and like Americans."

Friends today, enemies tomorrow.
From a song at a Togo
graduation.

To drive the thirty miles from Lomé to Tsévié took over an
hour in the PC jeep station-wagon. Sandy McCaw, assistant
to Acting Rep Lucas, and I sat in the back seat, talking while
the red dust settled on our arms, faces, and clothes.

It was graduation day at the government school where PCV
Gerald Paré was teaching. There was also a graduation ceremony at the local Catholic school, and the people in Tsévié
were unusually animated. However, since time means little in
Togo, the two graduations had been scheduled for the same
hour, and many people were expected to appear at both
ceremonies.

We heard cannons fired. A prominent man had died in
Tsévié, and a two-gun salute was being fired every hour until
after the burial. The status of the deceased determined the
number of shots; shortly after Gerry Paré had arrived in
Tsévié, there had been a seven-gun death.

At the government school, Gerry Paré was about to take off
on his motor bike to fetch from home several books which
were needed for prizes at the graduation exercise. One hundred and fourteen prizes were to be given, but the school had
only ninety-five items to hand out.

"Did you bring any books with you?" he asked immediately.

We had none. Gerry was under the impression that the
Peace Corps had been retaining books which should have been
forwarded to him.

"I went through my own library this A.M., but guess I'll
have to go through it again," he said. So we all went back to

113

his house. He found eighteen that were suitable for prizes.

"These really aren't right," he grumbled. "We should give little books in easy English to all those who came out first in English. But I just don't have them. These will have to do."

He excused himself, ran from the house, jumped on his bike, and rode off with the books. He returned quickly and asked us to stay for lunch.

"You'll have to excuse the looks of my house," he apologized. "We had a little party here last night. In fact, since I'm leaving for the summer, I've had two weeks of celebrating, with all the local traditions."

As he cleared the glasses and ashtrays, Gerry explained that before the drinking of beverages, local custom requires that some be poured from the bottle into the first glass, then from the first glass into the second, from the second into the third, and so on around to prove that no one is being poisoned. Then a few drops are spilled on the floor or ground to appease the spirits.

"Before this round of parties began," he continued, "I was visiting and eating with local people on both sides of town in order to patch up a feud. A Navy helicopter had landed in a big field on one side of town. That set up an immediate feud since the other side of town felt slighted, so the only thing for me to do was to make peace by visiting on both sides of town. Several times a week I would eat a meal of slightly cooked chicken (it's split open and you eat it with your fingers) and *fou-fou* (manioc which you dip in tomato sauce)."

For lunch, we shared the last of Gerry's supplies—beans, spaghetti, bread, and soft drinks. As we sat down to the meal, word came that the ceremony at Gerry's school would be postponed an hour to permit the Minister of Education and the other officials to attend both of the exercises scheduled for the day.

We settled back, and Gerry told of his life in Tsévié. He lived alone, without even a house boy for company.

1. *(l. to r.)* PCVs John Shearer of Santa Rosa, California, Carole Sojka of San Francisco, Diane Magri of East Norwalk, Connecticut, and Somali friends are given a "joy ride" in a banana bucket at the port of Merca.

2

2. PCV Marion "Tex" Ford takes a breather with a Dominican farmer, who has just opened some fresh coconuts with his machete.

3. PCV Bennie J. Barela of Las Cruces, New Mexico, playing with a group of children in Boni, Dominican Republic, where he does community development work.

4. PCV Wes Stewart of Toledo, Ohio, teaching English to his class of adults in Santiago, Dominican Republic.

3

4

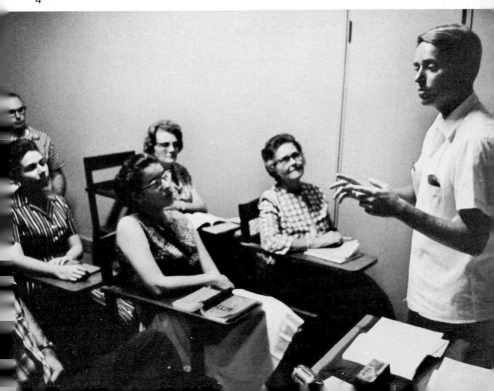

5

5. Andres "Andy" Hernandez, Field Representative for the Dominican Republic.

6. PCVs John Greenough, Vernon Guilliams, and Hill Phillips *(first three from left),* watch Dominican boys try baseball, which PCVs introduced by giving the boys a ball and encouraging them to make bats and gloves.

6

7

7. PCV Joe Murphy of Buffalo, New York, teaches Jamaican students at Chestervale Youth Camp how to read. He also conducts classes in metal and iron working.

8. PCV Marvin Smith, cataloguing maps at the Institute of Jamaica.

8

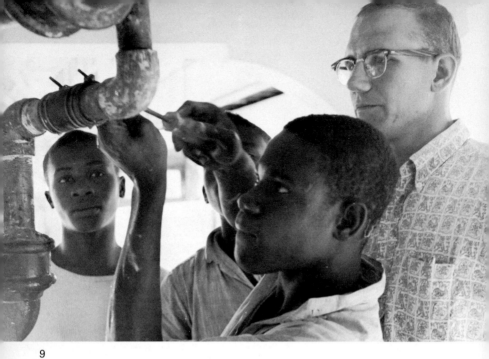

9

9. PCV William Robertson of Malvern, Ohio, with apprentice plumbers at Chestervale camp, Jamaica.

10. PCV Elsie Tanaka of Papaaloa, Hawaii, teaches sewing to Jamaican youths who may become tailors.

10

11. PCV Mike Ruggiero, in Togo, casts off set lines which will angle for fish while the fishermen work nets.

12. PCVs Ruggiero and Vito Blonda *(third and fourth from left)* were part of the team of fishermen sent to Togo to help increase the fish catch.

12

13

13. C. Payne Lucas, Acting Field Representative for Togo, in his office in Lomé.

14. PCV Jon "Mike" Hofgren of Syosset, New York, a mechanic, is connected with the medical team at Sokodé in Togo. Here he restores power line that had been knocked over by a truck.

14

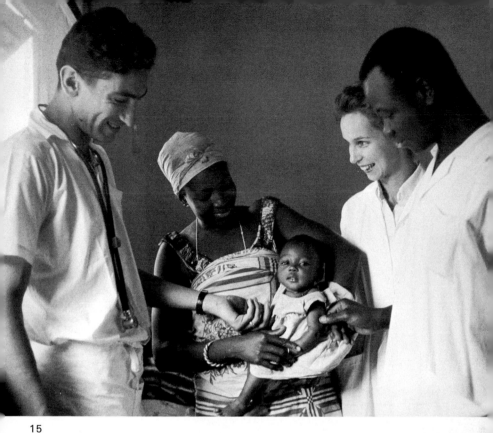

15

15. Dr. Merton Koenigsberger
and his wife, Dorcas, part of
the seventeen-man medical
team in Sokodé, admire a
healthy infant.

16. Dr. Nicholas Cunning-
ham, leader of the medical
team, hopes the municipal
hospital in Sokodé will be
developed into a model medical complex.

16

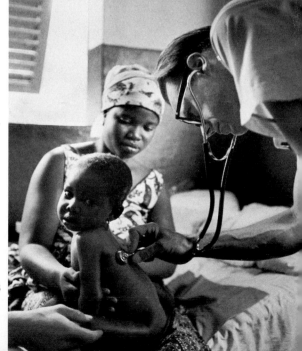

17

17. Mrs. Ann Moore, a PC nurse, at baby weighing station which is part of the Sokodé infant-care center she helped set up.

18. PC Nurse Jean Hewitt of Cambertsville, New Jersey, assisting a Togolese doctor give free check ups.

18

19

19. Fred Brancel, Field Representative for St. Lucia, and his family.

20. PCV George Askew *(right)* with his St. Lucian counterpart outside the house which they share.

20

21. PCV Bill Hundley and St. Lucian farmers, making a pen ready for Heifer pigs.

22. PCV Gene Hunter explains his experimental vegetable garden to a St. Lucian agricultural officer.

23. PCV Merlin Skretvedt of Gary, Minnesota, and St. Lucian farmer check some of the Heifer geese brought to the island to help diversify the mainly fish diet.

22

23

24. PCV Carol Watkins, in her classroom in St. Lucia.

25. PC Nurse Karelyn Hodges, of Lansing, Michigan, gives public health instruction to young St. Lucians. She also helps local nurses prepare prenatal instructions for expectant mothers.

24

25

26

27

26. PCV Arthur David Thaeler, of Kearney, New Jersey, works with the agricultural extension service in St. Lucia.

27. PCV Roberta Napier Thaeler, a teacher-trainer, married Dave during their PC tour of duty.

28. PCV Gloria Houston trains St. Lucian youngsters in home economics.

28

29. PCV David King, a teacher of English and literature in the Philippines, enjoys the company of a local belle during farewell festivities in his honor.

29

Photograph 13 by Velma Adams. All others by the Peace Corps: 1 Boris Sojka; 2, 3, 6, 21 Paul Conklin; 7, 9, 10, 27 Phil Hardberger; 11, 12, 14, 15, 16, 17, 18, 22 Rowland Scherman; 19 David Sandell.

"This image building we're doing is phony," he said. "We don't live this way at home. For example, I had my suit pressed for today, but the ceiling leaked. My suit was rained on and mussed up. I needed to press it again to wear to graduation, but I don't even have an iron. So I went over to another teacher's house to borrow one. 'What kind of a life is this you live without even a house boy?' the teacher asked me. I feel we just aren't behaving in ways natural to us. We're very self-conscious about the image we're building but it isn't a true one.

"Actually, I prefer living alone. I like my work, though for the first three months, I wanted to leave. I wasn't exactly a favorite of the Rep's wife, but after they left, things got easier, and I'll stick it out another year if nothing else goes wrong. I've built my own little kingdom but I'm still close enough to Lomé so that I get to see other PCVs sometimes. And the teachers I work with are well educated. I'm the only white person on the staff, and I conduct the entire English program at the school.

"There won't be as big a challenge for me here next year, but I'll be a different teacher. I'll go slower and give more pattern drills—'I am a boy,' 'I am a girl,' 'I am a student,' and so forth.

"My neighbors have been wonderful to me, but I never made the mistake of opening up my house to everyone, as some Volunteers did, so I never had to ask people later on to stay out, thus causing friction. People respect my rule that no one can use my library between 6:30 and 7:30 P.M. when I'm having supper. And when a drunk came around selling pencils, my neighbors came over and sent him away. Sometimes they chase away children when they fall asleep on my porch. I feel that if anyone started anything, the whole town would protect me."

Gerry had also limited his participation in the town's activities. When the local chief—who has so many wives that he

must ask his neighbors to assist in getting them all pregnant—
sent out a call for help, Gerry did not volunteer. Nor did he
take up the practice of some local teachers who, to get the
exclusive attention of a girl student, may expel the girl's boy
friend.

"I frequently get asked why I don't have a woman," Gerry
said. " 'Are you unpowerful?' the people ask me. But if I
had one, or if the townspeople thought I did, they'd be the
first to criticize and gossip."

At 2:30 P.M. we started for Gerry's school. We drove past
a variety of walls, most of them topped with broken glass or
spikes. Each plot in Tsévié has a wall built around it in traditional fort style—even if the owner does not have a house on
his land. If the wall is not complete, Gerry told us, it is only
because the man died or lacked money, or because the summer came and the builder ceased to work. The houses in this
part of the country are square, whereas in the north of Togo
the houses are round.

In the street, the students were lining up to march to the
school. The boys wore white duck pants and white shirts; the
girls (all except one) were dressed in yellow. The boys out-
numbered the girls by about ten to one.

The school auditorium was dark and hot. In the front of
the hall, nearest the stage, were an unusual variety of chairs,
including many that were overstuffed or cushioned; these had
been borrowed from nearby homes. At the rear, set stiffly in
rows, were the straight wooden chairs for the students.

As members of the audience wandered in and took seats,
it became obvious that more chairs would be needed. Then
we saw the chairs from Gerry's house being carried in through
a side door. On the stage, at a table piled high with books,
sat the five local teachers. Gerry took a place beside them.

Finally, singing in harmony as they marched down the road
and into the school to their appointed chairs, the students
arrived. They went through a repertoire of five or six songs—

one in English, the rest in French—several times while we
waited for the authorities to appear from the graduation at
the Catholic school. The English song amused me and I wondered how it happened to be chosen. It ended with the phrase,
"Friends today, enemies tomorrow."

We waited a while longer. The police left the auditorium,
apparently to round up the officials.

The cannons honoring the dead man were still being fired.
They reminded us more of the passage of time than of the
passing of man. Eventually, the program started—though the
Minister of Education and the principal speaker had not yet
arrived.

The headmaster for the school read in French a serious
talk about civilization, and the awarding of the prizes began.
Almost every student received one or more books, although
Gerry had told us that some had passed in only one subject,
and that others had failed in everything and were being
expelled from school. Faces peered in through every open
window and door. When the noise became too distracting, a
teacher arose and temporarily closed a window, thus shutting
out part of the little light and air there had been in the
auditorium.

Several members of the audience—including two Israeli
supervisors from a local farm, a German doctor, Sandy Mc-
Caw, and I—were asked without warning to hand out one or
more of the prizes. The name of a winning student was read,
and as he or she came forward, a teacher went down into the
audience and handed the prize to the chosen guest. That
person stepped forward, handed the book to the student, shook
his hand, and congratulated him.

The ceremony must have been three-fourths completed when
there was a stir at the rear of the hall. The Minister of Education and the commencement speaker had arrived and were
being escorted to the big chairs up front. Now the whole
program had to be repeated. The students sang their reper-

toire of songs, the remaining prizes were awarded, and the speaker was introduced. He graciously asked the headmaster to repeat his speech. The headmaster did, reading it again in French.

The chief speaker gave a witty address in French. He responded so aptly to the headmaster's talk that I judged he had needed the other's speech as a hook upon which to hang his own. Then the Minister of Education was introduced. He talked somewhat briefly and extemporaneously. One felt that he was a pleasant person who enjoyed working with young people.

The program was completed for the second time at 6 P.M.

"It was wonderful to look out and see you in the audience," Gerry said later, and I was glad that we had sat through it. Invitations, I knew, had been sent to all the embassies. The day before, the American Charge d'Affaires had mentioned the school graduations to me, but he had said he was too busy to attend. Apparently, he had not considered it important to send anyone in his place. PCVs are expected to be "loners," but there are many situations, like this graduation, when their aloneness or "minority of one" status is brought home to them rather painfully.

As we drove back to Lomé the sun was setting. The sky had become rosy red. It had taken a whole day to drive thirty miles to see Gerry, to have lunch, and to attend what had been scheduled as a two-hour graduation. We were two hours late for an open house at the home of Acting Representative Lucas, but this concerned no one. In Africa, people are more often late than on time.

After graduation, the schools in Togo were scheduled to close for three months. Since PCVs get only thirty days annual leave, the Volunteers at these schools would spend two months on summer projects which they had devised themselves, with the approval of Acting Rep Lucas.

Gerry Paré was planning to cooperate with AID in a program designed to teach workmen such useful English phrases as "This is a hammer," "This is a shovel." Jean Mammon had agreed to tutor five mechanics and seven university students who were to go to the States in August. The most ambitious project, perhaps, was that which Carol Cox and Margaret Anderson had planned. They were going to research and to write a textbook for teaching English in French. They intended to travel around the country to study vocabulary needs and the popular usages. By determining the frame of reference in which English is spoken in Togo, Carol and Margaret could make their courses in the second year more useful to their students. They hoped to leave behind them a specialized textbook—at least in mimeographed form—for the teaching of English to the French-speaking Togolese people.

Adult language classes—often sponsored by AID, USIA, or other agencies, with PCVs assisting—are very popular because Togo is located geographically between two English-speaking giants—Ghana and Nigeria—and English is needed to communicate with these neighbors. The waiting list for the English program of USIA usually numbers about two hundred. At one time, forty of the fifty-two men in the Chamber of Deputies were enrolled.

However, despite the success of these extracurricular classes in conversational English, PCVs have had to cajole to get enough classroom hours in which to teach such courses as part of the regular school curriculum. Conversational English is of little help, Volunteers are often reminded, in translating a paragraph in the examination for a baccalaureate degree.

The teachers must follow a formal curriculum and a rigid time schedule, especially in the later grades when pressure mounts in preparing for the difficult exams. Also, to a French country, the introduction of English as a conversational language is a radical change, and change is always resisted.

Not all the Volunteers had planned to spend their summer

working in language training. Mike Moore would conduct a summer camp at Sokodé for students from his school. Ruth Beckford would do demographic studies in the Sokodé area. Mary Jo Robinson, a petite, dark-haired New Yorker, would assist at a day camp in Lomé for eight- to fourteen-year-olds, mostly boys. In addition to classes in civics, hygiene, dancing, singing, and music (Mary Jo plays the violin), she was expecting to give evening lessons to a winner of an AID scholarship. "Time goes so fast," she said. "At first I was worried. I said to myself, 'Oh, my goodness, what am I doing here?' Then I decided, 'Well, here I am. I'll make the best of it and do as well as I can.' Suddenly, everything was O.K."

Much as they enjoyed planning and running the spare-time projects for adults, the Volunteers had found that the children in the lower three classes of school were more responsive. They had not been indoctrinated with rote learning and could be encouraged more easily to think, to reason, and to question.

PCVs were also confronted with discipline problems which they often had to handle in ways they found distasteful.

"I don't believe in corporal punishment and it's humiliating for me to have to ask for help in disciplining students," said Mary Jo. "But students here don't quake at teachers as they do in some places, and I can't give in. I have to send them to the office even if I don't approve of the punishment I know they'll receive."

The teachers in Togo had also encountered the single greatest problem of Volunteers everywhere: the lack of supplies. "I think the Peace Corps should send supplies first and after they've arrived, then send the Volunteers," one PCV suggested, pointing to the empty bookshelves in his classroom.

This shortage of texts and the lack of even paper and pencils, is probably the most frustrating condition that PC teachers around the world have had to meet. They have become shameless about borrowing and begging for books and supplies wherever they can get them.

There are more teachers than any other professionals in the Peace Corps. Most of them work at the elementary school level. Many also initiate evening classes for adults, and here again, either get along with the available books or teach from memory. They know that, as teachers—with or without supplies—they still have the greatest opportunity to influence the future of the emerging nations.

Yet, despite their feelings of satisfaction here, I think the teachers sometimes also feel that they have been overlooked in the PC publicity. In Togo, for example, they share attention with the fishermen and the medical team, both "firsts" for the Peace Corps.

The accomplishments of the teachers cannot so easily be glamorized by copywriters; their work, more often than not, cannot be measured.

"I'd love to come back in ten or fifteen years to see how my students are getting along," said Jean Mammon, who was teaching at an elementary school in Lomé. In fifteen years, the youngsters of today will have begun to assume responsible positions in their own countries.

The message received at the hospital late in the afternoon was that a man was dying. He had been bitten by a monkey. The wound was swelling, he was feverish and in pain. Two young Americans, a doctor and a nurse whom the Peace Corps had stationed at Sokodé to assist the French-trained local staff, went off in a jeep to treat the man.

After four hours of driving over unmarked, curving dirt roads, they finally located the patient. He had only a minor infection. The doctor cleaned the wound, applied medication and a dressing, gave him a shot to prevent infection, and suggested he come to the clinic in a few days.

It was dusk now, too late to drive back to the hospital. Besides, they were exhausted.

"No one invited us in to spend the night," the dark-haired,

twenty-two-year-old nurse told me later. "I guess we were just too strange. In fact, the people there didn't offer us anything —not even a mat or blanket to sleep on.

"So we found the school house—they're all open—and slept on the ground under the thatched roof. When I woke up in the morning, the yard was full of people staring at us.

"I sat up quickly and yelled for the doctor to wake up, and everyone moved back, shocked and surprised—but no more so than I was. Anyhow, we got up and drove back to the hospital. I'm sure the patient was all right."

I had heard about the medical team on which this young couple served before I had reached Togo. Theirs was not only the first medical project in the Peace Corps, it was also the largest and most specialized sent out during the first two years. The doctors and nurses in this group worked at the two-hundred-bed hospital at Sokodé, in north-central Togo, and served also the surrounding area.

There is a serious shortage of medical personnel in Togo. Near Sokodé there may be one doctor to every 35,000 persons; elsewhere the ratio may be as low as one to 200,000. That was why the Togolese government had asked, soon after the Peace Corps was established, for PCVs to help the Health Ministry enlarge and improve the nation's medical services. Sylvanus Olympio, first president of Togo, was assassinated before the achievements of the medical team could reflect creditably on his judgment.

The joint aims of the Health Ministry and the Peace Corps were ambitious: to create public health, sanitation, and preventive medical programs; to give health education to those using the Sokodé facilities; and to establish a referral center to serve the northern half of the country.

The seventeen members of the team under the leadership of a thirty-four-year-old New Yorker, Dr. Nicholas Cunningham, had been recruited from all parts of the United States, including Alaska, and represented a broad sampling of ethnic, religious, and social backgrounds. They included a surgeon, two pediatricians, a pharmacist, a sanitation expert, several nurses and laboratory technicians, and a diesel power engineer to install and maintain equipment.

The Volunteers had arrived in Sokodé on November 27, 1962, and on December 3 the project was officially started by the Ministry of Health.

"We spent the first two weeks in Sokodé unloading and cataloging drugs and equipment," reported Dr. "Nick" Cunningham. "If we could furnish the skills, AID agreed to supply the initial equipment, supplies, drugs, and vaccines. And we received private gifts of two premature baby incubators and an artificial respirator."

Within six months, the hospital was using a new X-ray unit, a hydraulic delivery table, microscopes and other laboratory equipment, a 30-kw diesel generator, a diesel water truck with pump, complete sets of surgical instruments and operating lights, suction and anesthesia apparatus, and a steam autoclave—all through AID.

The hospital, built in the style of French colonial architecture, had five units: surgery, pediatrics, men's ward, women's ward, and a polyclinic for outpatients. The pavilions were connected by covered walks. The Volunteers assigned to the different units worked side-by-side with their Togolese counterparts.

The results had come rapidly, but they were also frightening. As Dr. Cunningham explained, "The number of persons all over the area seeking care increased tremendously; the bed-occupancy rate soared, especially in pediatrics. But so did the tragically high mortality rate. Parents, hoping for miracles, now bring almost moribund children to the hospital, when it is, of course, too late for treatment."

Everyone agreed that widespread education about public health and preventive medicine was essential. Dr. Cunningham, with Dr. Aziagble, *médecin-chef* of the *Subdivision Sani-*

taire, and Margaret McEvoy, PC public health nurse, started a preventive program immediately. All the pupils around Sokodé were given complete physical examinations, including a check-up of teeth, sight, and hearing. When laboratory tests revealed an extremely high incidence of people infested with Bilharzia worms, a special clinic was set up to follow hundreds of cases individually, administer a series of curative shots, and to explain to the children how they became prey to the parasite, stressing that the only way to avoid catching it again was to avoid the contaminated waters. This program after only a few months was put under the direction of a Togolese sanitarian.

Other accomplishments during the early months at Sokodé were equally impressive: a school milk program, using powdered milk, to provide daily protein to all students in Sokodé (school directors have taken this over, too, while the PCVs hope to extend the program to outlying schools); spraying of hospital wards and local colleges against bedbugs, roaches, and other vermin; malaria control measures; construction of model public latrines; a vaccination program which provided tetanus, diphtheria, typhoid, and smallpox immunizations to over four thousand students; central sterilization of instruments instituted at the hospital, using the AID autoclave; a microcentrifuge (a device for determining the degree of anemia) set up and operated at the outpatient ward of Sokodé Hospital, contributing to improved diagnosis of this very common ailment.

Nowhere in the United States could the medical Volunteers have gotten so much broad experience so quickly, if at all. The Peace Corps doctors, for example, had been called on to perform all sorts of operations outside their specialties. A chest surgeon saved the lives of two young infants by performing stomach operations of a type never before done in Togo. Another doctor, head of the male ward at Sokodé Hospital, performed several operations for blindness. In the absence of a Togolese pediatrician, a PC doctor became chief of that service, including its ward for contagious diseases. Working with him were two Togolese nurses and two PC nurses (his wife and the wife of a teacher at the College Moderne). The nurses had virtually become experts in the treatment of snake bite, poisoning, and smallpox.

"However, we didn't come over here to run the hospital and we shouldn't have PC people heading up a department," commented Acting Rep Lucas. "It's rough to avoid this when a group of skilled Americans comes to work with a staff whose methods they consider sloppy. The Togolese are proud of their French training; they don't think they need to learn more. They give lip service to American methods and results, but sometimes it seems they don't really want to put in enough sweat to get these results themselves. They can match our skills if they'll buckle down and do the hard work, but they want to jump too fast, without the gradual growth and learning that's necessary."

Upgrading the people with whom they work was a difficult assignment for the Volunteers. Employees of the Togo Health Service received excellent remuneration, and they had many privileges; but, according to the PCVs, they had very little dedication to their work and no incentive to keep up with the improvements being made in their profession.

"One nurse at Sokodé gets 21,000 francs ($84) a month plus privileges," a PC nurse reported. "They're secure, they think they've arrived and they just don't want to make an effort to learn and improve. They don't feel it's necessary."

Imagine yourself a young American doctor in such a situation: heat, humidity, the roads washed out, and you have not been out of the place for a month or more; the hospital is inefficient by your standards, and you see more patients every day than you can possibly attend to adequately. Every time you cure a nearly hopeless patient, a dozen truly hopeless ones show up, expecting to be cured. When, after hours at night, you are called back to do an emergency surgery that only you can do, the local doctor doesn't even stand by to watch to see how it's done—so that he might try to do it himself one day after you have left his country. Or you are assisting a local staff doctor and the latter makes a careless incision—and cuts through the muscle of the hand he is supposed to be saving.

Or imagine you are a nurse accustomed to a regular shift and strict regulations. At first you come in on time every morning, even when you are still fatigued from extra duty the night before. Then you see that the regular staff appears nonchalantly a half-hour, an hour, or more afterwards. Every day, the line of patients waiting at the clinic for outpatients becomes longer than was the line the day before. You see mothers and children die when you know they could have been saved. You are lonely, and yet you observe deep emotional involvements—attractions and hatreds—flaring up all around you.

The response of PCVs to such conditions—the overwhelming needs of the people and the inadequacies of the local hospital staff—has not been good everywhere. It did not surprise me that the medical PCVs and the PC administrators admitted that a few of the PCVs had reached the point where they "just don't give a damn." Their attitude was, "What difference does it make? It's too big for me. I can't change it so I might as well go along with it." No one had a ready solution. In fact, Acting Rep Lucas had already had difficulty in regulating the activities of the medical team.

"Members of the medical team know they're key people, they know that they're needed, and they're aware that the only sanction the PC Rep can take is to send them home," one PCV said frankly. "If they come on duty late, go into Lomé for the week-end, drink too much and forget to return until Tuesday, there are few disciplinary measures the Rep can take and still maintain the project."

Working with the medical team and without a counterpart is

a twenty-one-year-old diesel engineer, John "Mike" Hofgren. Mike had done well in the eight months:

"I've installed a new 30-kw generator that gives three times the power the hospital had, but we still can't run the X-ray and air conditioner at the same time until we get another generator. We still have to use kerosene refrigerators, because the power is shut off about fifteen hours a day. There's not enough fuel for twenty-four-hour refrigeration for ice cubes and medicine. We've tripled the water truck's capacity, but we need more fuel to run that, too. I've just been showing the hospital chauffeurs how to operate and maintain the water truck. But we'll have to find me a counterpart soon if I'm going to train him to take over when I leave. The worst thing is that the Togolese have budgeted no funds to maintain the equipment they are getting."

Dr. Cunningham reported that Mike had also designed a device by which American oxygen equipment could be coupled to French oxygen tanks, and that he had contributed to the design of the filter and chlorination system for the new hospital cistern.

Mike, by choice, had not joined the dinner group that twelve of the PCVs had formed at Sokodé Hospital. "But it's so much fun," said a young nurse who was just returning to the States to be married. "I really hate to leave the gang at Sokodé. The year just flew by. We had such wonderful discussions and danced the Charleston every night."

"I object to PCVs sticking together," argued Mike. "I prefer to eat with local friends. Three days a week I have a boy cook a good meal for me, and the other nights I eat a good meal at the hotel. Every couple of weeks, I invite in some guests—maybe six—and cook for them myself. But I wouldn't take time to cook every day."

About once a month, Mike went into Lomé—a seven-hour drive by jeep although the distance is only two hundred miles —but he usually uses his free time for horseback riding or fishing. On the Lomé-Sokodé road, accidents are frequent, and on one occasion Mike and Acting Rep Lucas went off a twenty-seven-foot vertical drop. The jeep landed upside down on a flat rock; fortunately, neither man was hurt.

The Togo Volunteers—fishermen, medical team, and teachers—never merged into as cohesive a unit as other groups did.

"Some days I feel like I'm holding the group together with Scotch tape," Acting Rep Lucas said. "No one can ever say for sure when a Volunteer reaches the 'safe zone,' but I think if we can just get past the halfway mark, most of them will make it for two years. At least, that's what I'm praying for."

*Our aid programs should be designed not
primarily to counter Communism, though they will
do this too, but to create conditions of self-respect.*
ADLAI STEVENSON
United States Representative
to the United Nations

The fifteen Volunteers—eight men, seven women—whom I
visited on the island of St. Lucia late in September, 1962,
were "old timers." After a year on the island, they seemed
very much at home. As "old timers" they knew their hosts by
their first names and had come to grips with many of the
local problems and their causes. After a year of field service,
a PCV knows what is possible and what must wait—perhaps
forever. Most of the St. Lucia PCVs were deeply engrossed
in their projects. They were eager to see them established sufficiently so that their native counterparts could carry on after
they were gone.

St. Lucia, in the British West Indies, is sometimes called
the "Helen of the West Indies." A quiet, peaceful isle, its
green-forested mountains contrast sharply with the brilliant
blue sea. From November to May, the temperature ranges from
a delightful 70 to a pleasant 80 degrees (F.). The 233-square-
mile island, discovered by Columbus in 1502, has belonged
to Britain since 1814. Any discernible unrest on the island
is economic, not political. Many of the 83,000 inhabitants,
aware that the land area and the banana crop are not enough
to provide prosperity for everyone, seek to move on to countries where there are more job opportunities.

After three months of training, the group of fifteen arrived
at Castries, St. Lucia, to begin their assignments with an in-

sular people hitherto untouched by many outside influences.

The PCVs—the third group in the field—were under the joint sponsorship of the Peace Corps and Heifer Project, Inc., an interfaith self-help project that distributes livestock and poultry where agricultural assistance is needed. In addition to the six PCVs working with the St. Lucian Department of Agriculture, there were two nurses and six teachers. One, Merlin Skretvedt, worked with the department of education and of agriculture to improve the agricultural curriculum in the schools.

As Representative Fred Brancel pointed out, the small group had from the beginning been considered something of a model or pilot project. "The eight men and seven women," he said, "form a well-balanced group with a blend of the enthusiasm of youth and the maturity of experience. All sections of the United States are represented, as well as different ethnic groups. The Volunteers are all college graduates. A number hold advanced degrees."

On their arrival, they had gone out in ones and twos over the little tropical island to fill their positions as teacher trainers, public health nurses, agricultural educationists, and as aides in animal husbandry, soil conservation, irrigation, and forestry. They had agreed to keep in close touch. Even for a visitor who is unacquainted with the island it is possible to drop in on all the PC projects on St. Lucia in two days.

Tall, blond, soft-spoken George F. Askew arrived in St. Lucia from Hillsboro, Iowa, where a farm generally consists of several hundred acres of rich, rolling land that is tilled by mechanized equipment. PCV Askew was assigned to a relocation project on seventy-five acres of hill country in the Delcer area of the island. Thirty-four farm families had been moved to the seventy-five acres, each receiving a plot of from one-quarter acre to six acres. The farmers were to be introduced to contour planting.

George, however, had to wait in Castries for two weeks before being introduced to his counterpart. He was offered no means of getting to Delcer, so he set off on foot in his chino pants, Army boots, and wide-brimmed straw hat. He estimated that, although he did get rides along the way, he still walked about fourteen miles.

A year later, he was the only PCV on the island who resided with his counterpart. Albanie Noel—a senior agriculture instructor—and Noel's wife and four children gladly gave George a small room in their tiny prefabricated home that had cost the government less than three thousand dollars. The ocean, however, had to serve as his bathtub.

Noel's older children traveled thirteen miles to school. There they sat on long wooden benches in an unpartitioned barracks-like building. The St. Lucians do not partition their school rooms. Each class stands when called upon and recites in unison from memory. The Delcer Roman Catholic School, which was near Noel's home, had been closed in the fall of 1962 because it had no benches, but the priest himself was building benches, and the school was expected to open as soon as he was ready.

The farms of the relocation project were on the hills beyond Noel's place. George climbed on foot or used a jeep to make his daily visits up the steep hillsides. When he walked, he would halt along the way to admire the brightly colored hibiscus flowers, to inhale the fragrant air, and to smile to himself as he continued. At home, such obvious pleasure in nature might set him apart, but in St. Lucia it seemed normal for an American boy to revel in the beauty of the island.

The friendly way in which he said hello to the local people, his excitement at the report that a sow had finally been bred, his pleasantness as he reassured a woman that she need not dress up to receive callers, get sincere appreciation from the people.

"Why, Mr. Calderon," he might say, "that's just

wonderful that you've got nine newborn pigs. It really is. Just wonderful news."

Or, "Mr. and Mrs. Mondesir, I'd like you to meet my friend from the United States. No, no, nothing special. We just wondered if you'd care to show us your new kitchen."

As I observed the reactions of those whom we visited, I thought: just the fact that the PCVs have shaken hands with these people, have called them by name, have discussed their problems as though the problems were their very own, that they have brought their friends (other Volunteers, or visitors like me) to admire what was being done, and have given this respect and show of friendship to people who are trying to win a place in the world, may be enough, if nothing else is accomplished, to justify the investment in the Peace Corps.

George could sense the pride in these people, that they had accomplished something more this year than last year. When he brought visitors to the local farms, he showed off the farmers' achievements, not his own. However, the St. Lucians on the relocation project did not forget who had given them encouragement and praise.

Watching and listening to George Askew talk to the peasant farmers, I detected not the least trace of condescension. He genuinely felt that it was a privilege to know these people. Indeed, I have never met a PCV—even one who is no longer an enthusiast about the Corps—who does not feel that he has benefited more by his contact with the people of his host country than they can have benefited from contact with him.

Most of the farmers on the project were older men. This was worthy of note because the project required that the farmers give up their traditional methods of agriculture. One might expect the younger men to be more eager to learn the new ways, but the older folks were just as eager.

The barren, hilly land in the southern part of the island gets inadequate rainfall. The men, therefore, had started to plant their crops in curved rows that followed the contours of the hillsides and to dig curved irrigation ditches between every few rows of the crop. Feeder ditches brought the water down the mountain. And the farmers were experimenting with unfamiliar crops.

Since there is little likelihood of increasing the size of a holding or of mechanizing a farm, the St. Lucian farmer can hope only to increase the productivity of the few acres he owns. Even at optimum, however, he cannot compete with the truck gardens in Florida. Still, he wants a wider variety of produce to sell locally or to set before his own family.

In the Delcer area, two items were always big news worth discussing with George, with Noel, or with anyone else who might be interested. These were: pigs and kitchens. Pigs is the more important topic, for pigs offer a possible solution to the economic difficulties. But for the women, like their counterparts everywhere, a new kitchen is a symbol of achievement. In St. Lucia, the cement-block room which is called a kitchen bears no resemblance to the version in the pages of *Better Homes and Gardens*. In fact, the models being built in St. Lucia seem to be a refinement of the pens used for the pigs.

Nineteen pigs had been donated by Heifer Projects, Inc., which, begun in 1942 with the gift of one calf, has sent more than a million gift animals to fifty-seven countries. To be assigned a Heifer pig, a farmer was expected to comply with certain conditions. It is interesting to note that here—as in the experiments with new modes of cultivation—the older men were usually eager to try the new techniques. To obtain a Heifer pig required a financial investment, and it may be that only the older men had the necessary capital. Also, the pig pens had to be built to certain specifications: the cement floors were to be drained properly and there had to be troughs for water and feed. Local materials—thatched roofs, dried banana leaves for litter—were used whenever possible. The pig was to be washed every day, and the pen cleaned daily with antiseptic. Adequate ventilation was to be provided, and the food ration was to contain a prescribed balance of minerals, iron, roughage, etc., with grasses, breadfruit, green bananas, and other local foodstuffs making up most of the diet. The pig, in other words, lived better than the farmer.

I visited one farm where not far from what may have been the largest and healthiest of all Heifer sows, there stood a runt. Although most local animals ran wild, this undersized native pig had a pen. At first glance, the local animal might have been a young pig not yet full grown; the difference in weight between it and the Heifer sow must have been several hundred pounds. The chops, though they were bound to be small and tough, would—I was told—be eaten. The farmer was too proud of his Heifer to be apologetic for the runt.

PCV Askew and I admired Mrs. Mondesir's kitchen—really a two-room house—and George said he had never seen one better. Each room was about six by eight feet. Harry Mondesir had made the concrete blocks himself. The thrush grass for the roof had been gathered and was drying in the sun in bundles of ten or twelve strands; the strands would be woven intricately and securely before being placed on the roof. This weaving is an artistic feat, and the life of a well-made roof may be five, some say ten years. The water does not penetrate the thatch, but slides off it, and the damp thrush dries almost as soon as the sun comes out, which it always does, sometimes even before the shower ends.

Most showers in the Caribbean islands are violent but of short duration; one can get thoroughly soaked in a few seconds, but be dry again a few minutes later. For Mrs. Mondesir and the other wives whose husbands had become affluent enough to build kitchens, the weather was unimportant, for they no longer had to cook their food outdoors over an open fire.

There was little refrigeration in St. Lucia, so the cooking was done in quantity. The cooked pork or chicken dishes were eaten for several successive meals. Enough bread or cassava cakes (which had the texture of dog biscuits) were baked at one time to last for several days. Soups, both meat and vegetable, kept well. Fruits and vegetables could be picked when needed and be eaten immediately, much fresher than if they had been purchased at any market. George was often invited to eat with the farm families. Generally, he ate at home with Noel and his family.

At Volunteer Gene Hunter's house, Rosie was in charge of the kitchen. Her Kallaloo soup may well have been the tastiest on the island. Naturally inquisitive, Gene had a West Indian cookbook in which he looked up the ingredients of the new dishes that appeared on his table.

"Of course, Rosie doesn't always use what the book says," Gene said, "but whether the Kallaloo is made with tanya leaves or spinach, it's always good."

A slight, dark-haired, good-natured boy from Shreveport, Louisiana, Gene had drawn what seemed to be an ideal assignment—the Beau Sejour Research Station at the southern extreme of St. Lucia. He was to help cultivate vegetables on eighty experimental plots to determine which vegetables thrived best in the local soil and climate.

Gene lived in a house, previously occupied by an American army officer, that sat on a bluff overlooking the abandoned United States Army base at Vieux Fort and, beyond that, the bright blue ocean. From his front porch, he could watch the white breakers offshore. On his motor scooter, he could whiz down the government road—the only paved road in the area— and go for a swim after work. The house had inside plumbing and a shower. The living room walls were lined with shelves of books. When unexpected guests dropped in, Rosie could put a delicious dinner of native delicacies—plantain, breadfruit, mango, rice—on the table in half an hour.

Frequently, as when I was there, Gene had another PCV staying with him, often Merlin Skretvedt. Merlin worked with the agricultural extension service and visited every school on

the island periodically. He had received considerable publicity
for the geese he had distributed to the schools soon after his
arrival on St. Lucia.

Gene could reach the Beau Sejour Research Station in a
few minutes by his motor scooter, and came home every noon
for a meal cooked by Rosie. No one on the island, it seemed,
lived more comfortably.

Yet, if Arthur Gene Hunter had not been naturally resourceful—the sort of young man with multiple interests who is seldom bored or at a loss for something to do, as Rep Fred
Brancel described him—he might have become the No. 1 Peace
Corps problem on St. Lucia. For, one year after his arrival—
when most PCVs know that they cannot possibly finish everything they want to finish though they work at the peak of their
efficiency—Gene had little to keep him busy. A few tomato
plants on two plots were bearing, but the other seventy-eight
plots were not producing.

It seems that Gene and the boys employed at the experimental farm had applied weed killer to these plots exactly as
directed by the head of the agricultural service. Gene, appre-
hensive about the quantity he had been told to apply, had
questioned the director and had been assured that the amount
was correct and that it should be applied exactly as directed.
A few weeks later, still acting on instructions, Gene planted
seedlings in the eighty plots. The seedlings, to use Gene's
description, "just tipped over and died."

Now nothing could be grown on that land for some time.
A PCV with less enthusiasm for living than Gene might have
become bitter and disillusioned at the mistake. Morale often
nosedives when a Volunteer has time on his hands—whether
the "spare" time is due to lack of money or equipment, of
trees and seeds to plant, or of children to teach. The host
countries are sensitive about relocating PCVs since that would
be tantamount to admitting they had failed to provide the
proper environment for the PCV. When caught in such a

situation, some Volunteers become bored and hypercritical
and decide "to sit it out" until it is time to return to the
States. Gene, however, went to the station every day, took an
interest in the projects of other Volunteers, joked with Rosie,
and busied himself with his own experiments. In a fish tank
which he built from strips of wood, window glass, and putty,
he sought to determine whether salt-water fish will adapt to
fresh water if the saline content of the water is changed
gradually. Suppose newborn salt-water fish are transferred
immediately to fresh water, will they live? Gene was capable
of conducting his own projects until there was once again a
full work load at the research station.

Visiting the Peace Corps in St. Lucia—at least the agricultural projects—was like going to a country fair in the States,
except that the exhibits were spread out over miles: here a
pig, there a chicken, everywhere geese, and experimental
tomatoes fifty miles away.

As Dave Thaeler, George Askew, and I drove into the village
of Micoud, we saw Bill Hundley's motorcycle parked beside
the road and knew that he was having his daily chat with his
counterpart, Mr. Henry. They had been working together to
help the farmers on the steep slopes on both sides of the
Micoud Valley to diversify their plantings, to terrace their
lands, to lay out drainage ditches, and to graft new varieties
of fruits on existing trees.

PCVs may be impervious to the discomforts that overwhelm
most of us—heat, bugs, hunger, and thirst—but I was aware
of them. I was wet with perspiration and grimy with dust
before we left the car to hike uphill into the bush, and I had
intermittent cramps due to what PCVs call the "tropical trots."
However, I was determined to see Bill's soil conservation
program for myself.

It was banana cutting day in this part of the island. Every
now and then we met a woman who balanced a bunch of

bananas on her head or sometimes a woven tray that held two bunches. Men never carry bananas—that is women's work. The women had to make their way several miles down the rough paths to a waiting truck. Bananas might bring four cents a pound. Since a sizeable bunch weighs thirty to forty pounds that meant about $1.50 a trip. However, a banana crop ripens in ninety days, and each tree can produce three crops a year. Bananas were the lifeline of the island, a year-round crop so profitable that the two largest sugar growers were converting much of their rich valley land to bananas.

Bill and Mr. Henry had split their territory roughly in half. "It didn't take us long to find out which farmers would work and which wouldn't," Bill smiled. We climbed toward a farm he wanted to show us. The five acres had formerly belonged to a large estate, but had recently been acquired by the farmer who had worked on the estate. We passed many men, women, and naked children; some peeked out of the cottage windows and doorways, which had neither glass nor screen; others stared frankly from wherever they happened to be. We waved and spoke to everyone—Dave with his cheery "G'Day! G'Day!" and Bill calling most of them by name, asking about their families, their health, sometimes introducing his fellow PCVs and me. The responses often came in patois, most of which the boys understood.

"You realize," Bill told me, "you're probably the first white woman who has ever been up here."

When we reached the hillside farm, the owner was at work lining out new trenches. The government had agreed to pay two dollars a chain (sixty-six feet of trench) to each farmer who lined out his ditches properly. "Only a one-foot drop every 120 feet," Bill reminded the farmer, then pointed out the deep gulleys where torrential rains—160 inches a year in this area—had run straight down the mountain and had carried away much of the good topsoil.

I understood now why Bill had led us up here to view his

territory. Across the valley on the opposite hillside (which was also in Bill's area), were neatly terraced fields of coffee, avocado, and banana, each easily identifiable by the different shade of green and its distinctive leaf. Where we stood, coffee, cocoa, avocado, and citrus trees had been planted among the bananas, and not far way, pineapple and dasheen.

Bill was justifiably proud of his year's work. In what he called his nursery—a single twenty-foot row of seedlings—he and his farmer friends were experimenting with oranges and practicing plant grafts. A Julie mango tip, grafted to a less desirable type of tree, had taken. I could see sprouts underneath the cloth and paraffin that Bill had taped over the cut; he would not remove the covering for another ten days.

"I'm sort of like Johnny Appleseed," he quipped, obviously pleased with his work. Questioned further, he added:

"Actually I never grafted anything before in my life until I came here, and you bet I'm not showing you my first graft. I'm a soil conservationist from Cle Elum, Washington, so this is a whole new culture to me. I just got a book and read up on grafting fruits, tried it a couple of times, and it worked."

This ability to translate theory into practice is, I think, the secret of American know-how. It also explains how Americans can accomplish so wide a variety of tasks in the emerging nations.

On many Peace Corps projects, some one Volunteer becomes a hero in the eyes of the people.

In St. Lucia the hero was Carlos A. Naranjo, from Albuquerque, New Mexico. Carlos had introduced two activities to the island—basketball and adult education—and while the adult classes were popular beyond all expectation, it was probably the basketball that gave Carlos his fame.

"Many would say the introduction of basketball to St. Lucia is the most significant thing the Peace Corps has done for the island," said Rep Brancel.

There was little recreation of any kind in St. Lucia, and few could afford to fly to Martinique, Puerto Rico, or the United States. When Carlos, who loved basketball, saw the play space in George V Park in downtown Castries and realized that after the working day had ended, there were several hours of daylight, he went into action.

First, he persuaded a group of boys to help him build backboards, to put up the baskets, and to lay out a court. Then he taught a number of the townspeople the rules of the game, organized a team of PCVs and several local teams, and arranged to hold night games in the park. Of course, it was not championship basketball, but when the Giants drove to a narrow four-point victory over the Shamrocks, it was the most exciting sports event ever held in St. Lucia—both to those who participated and to those who watched. Carlos was a hero.

His more serious contribution, of course, came in arousing interest in an adult-education program and in pushing his plans through a local government that sometimes moves very slowly when it comes to sponsoring educational and social reforms.

Classes were set up for illiterates, beginners, and school dropouts, and the program opened in various sections of Castries and the outlying districts.

Carlos and five women PCVs had been assigned to a program designed to improve the capabilities of the local teachers. The six PCVs were especially lucky to be working with Mr. Thomas, the chief of the Department of Education, who came to his post at about the time the Volunteers arrived from the States; since their offices adjoined, communication was simple. Fortunately, the goals of the education chief and the PCVs were similar, although they did not always agree on methods or scheduling.

"We have our differences about how to succeed," Thomas said pleasantly, adding that he and the St. Lucian educators were generally enthusiastic over their six Volunteer-assistants.

"They think we move too slowly, and we're sure they're too impatient. Their suggestions are good, but we just aren't ready for them yet."

I understood, but like the PCVs, I could not observe the great educational needs of the island without feeling uneasy that there was no drive to make progress faster.

The hope, of course, of both the Department of Education and of the PCVs, was ultimately to upgrade the teaching requirements so that the approximately five hundred school teachers, then teaching more than 20,000 children, could each be certified for the grade to which he had been assigned. In 1962, three-fifths of the teachers were uncertified by local standards, standards painfully low compared to those in the United States. Most of the early grades were taught by fourteen- or fifteen-year-olds who had been drafted to teach only a short time after completing the very grades they were now to conduct.

The PCVs' teacher-training program was an ambitious one, involving much paper work and record keeping as well as classroom teaching. In the first year, the St. Lucian teachers were exposed for the first time to *methods* of teaching reading and arithmetic.

"It's sort of a correspondence course combined with class work," explained PCV Carol Watkins. She had spent the summer grading papers to determine which of the pupil-teachers should continue to teach in the fall. "We spent four days a week preparing assignments, and on Fridays we visited teachers in the schools to see how they were doing and to make suggestions.

"About five hundred teachers—they'll be given three chances to pass before they're dismissed—sat for exams in three or more subjects. To sit for exams, a certain amount of work is required. We sent out thirty assignments for the teachers; fifteen had to be returned. Of thirteen possible Saturday classes, one-half must have been attended. Of the thirty vacation classes held, attendance was required at three-quarters of them."

It was financially to the advantage of the young pupil-teachers, who were rated as PT 1, 2, 3, or 4, according to their accomplishments, to qualify for a higher grade, particularly since lack of progress could mean eventual dismissal. A pupil-teacher received from $576 to $660 a year in Beewees (BWI currency) depending upon his rating, an incentive to do lessons and attend classes.

"But they're used to a permissive system," Carol added. "The children, for example, come to school about three days a week or fewer; some children stay home because they have no clothes to wear. They don't want to sit naked next to pupils who are dressed."

If you have wondered how it is possible for American youths in the Peace Corps, many without advanced education themselves, to accomplish so much—to teach, to solve problems, to build bridges and schools, to improve crops, to raise the standard of living, to plan community projects, to get things done with ingenuity, a visit to the schools of such an underdeveloped area would provide the answer.

"I've seen a teacher draw a boat on the blackboard and ask the children to draw one like it on their slates," Carol went on. "Even if a child draws a better boat, the teacher will go over and erase it. He insists on having the boat copied exactly, otherwise it's wrong. All thinking is discouraged, and learning is nothing but rote and memory. Many students —and teachers—can recite definitions and multiplication tables, but they can't use the knowledge they have. Thinking up examples is impossible for them."

One PCV told me that a child in her class, when asked to give 3 times 4, replied, "3 times 1 is 3, 3 times 2 is 6, 3 times 3 is 9, and 3 times 4 is 12." I witnessed this type of learning in progress when I visited a large school where ten or twelve classes were all being conducted at one time. At first, I was favorably impressed. The headmaster, a man of sixty who appeared much younger, and who probably had taught every teacher on his staff, was presiding over several classes at once, extemporaneously and without any confusion. He came over, greeted me, chatted leisurely for a few minutes, explained to the pupils that they had a visitor, and then quietly went on with the lessons.

To one group, he gave a problem in arithmetic which they wrote down in their notebooks. While they were trying to solve it, he moved over to another group, whose members were sitting on long benches, glancing at their books now and then, and began to quiz them on the historical facts in the story they had been assigned to read in the previous few minutes.

The children, many of whom were barefooted but each of whom owned a brief case or book bag, stood up to recite. In unison, they gave rather stilted answers to the teacher's carefully phrased questions. Sometimes he corrected an answer which did not exactly suit him and had the student repeat it in his (the teacher's) words. I thought that he was cleverly getting in a little practice in grammar and diction along with the history, but I wondered if they were learning anything they could actually use.

The same procedure was employed in the rest of the large open room. I was fascinated by the poise of the teachers in the face of distractions, their ability to shift from one subject and grade level to another, the excellent deportment of the pupils when they were left to their own devices while the teacher "visited" another class.

Afterwards, I realized what I had seen: a headmaster who had been teaching the same classes and asking the same questions for years, who knew all the answers by heart but for whom there was only one correct answer—that in the textbook.

In countries where no one is taught to reason, to experiment, to fit facts together or to question, and where teachers for the most part have from fourth- to sixth-grade skills, PCVs —those who have the temperament for it—are bound to show up well. As one PCV put it (he was neither boasting nor criticizing, merely stating what he considered a fact), "No matter how little one of us knows, it's hard not to keep ahead."

Melinda DuBose, a nurse from Miami, Florida, saw almost immediately what she must do in St. Lucia. To her, in the year 1961, it was unthinkable that school children should never be given physical examinations as a basis for corrective measures to their health while they were still young and growing. She talked to the doctor to whom she had been assigned, and her enthusiasm inspired him. Together, they began to examine each child to determine if he (or she) could see properly, if his teeth were sound, his height and weight normal for his age, his general health good. A few months later, by mutual agreement, they dropped this preventive and diagnostic program, and went back to caring for those who were clearly ailing.

Why did they give up the broader program? Did they decide it was not suitable? Were the children and their families and the teachers uncooperative?

"No, because it was no use," Melinda explained. She was resting in bed, having suffered a bump on the head from falling off her motor scooter. "Even if two persons could have examined all the students in fifty-two schools, what would we accomplish? When we find a child who needs glasses or should have his permanent teeth repaired, what can we do? Nothing. There's no money and even if there were, there probably aren't enough optometrists and dentists on the island to take care of the need. Maybe someday—I don't know how many years from now—but right now, we can't do a thing about it."

A neat little building about eight miles north of Castries houses one of the seventeen public health clinics on St. Lucia. When I arrived, Nurse Weeks, a small, dark and attractive nurse in a spotless white uniform was standing on the porch, lecturing in patois to a group of ladies. She and her assistant— PCV Karelyn Hodges, who helped regularly at three clinics in the area—had just finished examining the dozen pregnant women who now sat on a long wooden bench and listened. The women all wore clean, colorful cottons; some were bare-foot, others wore sandals; several wore berets or bandannas on their heads.

They listened attentively and stared at a homemade flip chart which showed pictures of containers of milk and chunks of cheese that the nurse had cut out of various magazines. Her talk this morning was about proteins and calcium and how to prepare powdered milk for use. The nurse interspersed her comments about the dairy products with questions. The ladies responded in unison in patois. In this way, she assured herself that they had understood her. Once in a while someone asked a question, and the nurse responded briskly. The two children who had accompanied their mothers remained silent. The women, besides being instructed in prenatal care, were also being prepared to bring the babies in later for check-ups and preventive measures. The session lasted only fifteen minutes. Karelyn Hodges stood by quietly.

In their relationships with their counterparts, many PCVs achieve, apparently without strain, a rather interesting bal-ance. Administratively, the local counterpart is in charge and the Volunteer is there to assist, frequently being asked to follow instructions. Technically—in skills, knowledge, and modern methods—the PCV is usually superior to the counter-part yet seems to be able to take the lead inoffensively and to establish a sensible working relationship.

The flip charts and the material that Nurse Weeks used in the prenatal clinic had been assembled in a seminar which Karelyn had helped to conduct for all the public health nurses on St. Lucia. Only the day before, she had driven to each of the seventeen locations and spent from one-half to three-quarters of an hour with each nurse to check on the use being made of the visual aid material. "I wanted to make sure that the nurses were spacing out the material, not using it all up in one session and leaving nothing for the rest of the meetings," Karelyn explained. "I discovered they have a tendency to go through all the material too rapidly."

Nurses Weeks and Hodges saw a different group each day—tomorrow would be child welfare clinic day—and a different group of mothers each week. Nurse Weeks, who had six children of her own, practiced midwifery. At the clinics she not only instructed but also changed dressings and gave injections. She did not have time, she explained regretfully, to make home visits, although she felt there was a need.

Injections and many drugstore items, both of which were state subsidized, were given free. UNICEF furnished powdered milk to pregnant and lactating mothers and, when prescribed by a doctor, to malnourished children.

The reason for the carefully supervised distribution of the powdered milk, Karelyn told me, was that when it had been given out freely, everyone came, got a supply at several different clinics—and used it all to make a big batch of ice cream.

The response to the nurses' seminar which PCV Hodges was conducting—a pilot project in adult education which dealt primarily with intestinal diseases and malnutrition—had been good. "Most of the nurses were eager to learn," Karelyn said.

"An immediate, inexpensive solution to the protein supply," suggested Representative Brancel, "would be more fishing and the better use of fish. But so far, the Department of Agriculture hasn't seen fit to go along."

"Until the island has a good water supply," Karelyn added sadly, "the program can't go ahead. We can't tell people to stay out of the rivers when that is the only water they have. Yet, it's from the river water that they get liver fluke."

As though to confirm the fact that the Volunteers had settled right down into the heart of St. Lucian life, two PCVs who hoped to remain on the island even after their first tour of duty had ended got married. The bride, twenty-four-year-old Roberta Jane Napier, and the groom, twenty-seven-year-old Arthur David Thaeler III had been assigned to the Ciceron area, where they conducted evening classes for adults.

Like any young couple two weeks before their wedding, Dave and Roberta were enthusiastic about their home-to-be, which they had rented. They took me on a tour of the house, although the owner had not yet moved out.

There was still some carpentry to be done inside, and a heavy tank was to be raised to the roof to catch rain water. Then they would bring in their beds and perhaps a chair from the dormitories where they were living, and get a kerosene stove for cooking. A Coleman lantern would complete the furnishings—which would be lavish by the standards of the neighborhood.

Dave had decided that they ought to have a kerosene refrigerator—a luxury for most St. Lucians—but he had been unable to find one secondhand; even if he had, it would have cost $400. He wanted to make the marketing and cooking easier for Bertie, since she often had only an hour or two between her daytime work in the Department of Education offices in downtown Castries and the 7 P.M. adult-education classes she was teaching in Ciceron.

When I came to visit them, Dave and Bertie had just started their one-month annual leave. Besides the house to be readied —and neither was aware that Rep Brancel and some of the Volunteers were planning a bee to help them finish—there was a myriad of other details. Bertie was making her own wedding dress. Dave had to pick up the cloth for his suit and take it to a tailor; his truck, "Ole Bessie," had broken down again and was in the garage for repairs. Then there were the local guests to be invited and arrangements to be made for housing the out-of-town guests, for transportation, and for a place to go on a honeymoon. Bride and groom were both planning ahead so that their projects could continue while they were honeymooning.

Nevertheless, on the first day of their leave Bertie got up at 5:30 A.M. to prepare breakfast at the dormitory for several PCVs and the guests who were leaving for a tour of the island. She then spent part of the day working on plans for her classes. Dave spent the entire day driving me more than a hundred miles around the southern part of the island and hiking into the hills to see the agricultural projects others were carrying out. He nevertheless found time to pick up the material for his wedding suit. Bertie, I later found out, had also managed to do a little sewing on her dress. In the evening, they both taught adult classes as usual until 10 P.M.

"We can't find substitutes, and we hate to recess the classes," Dave explained. "But I hope that we can make some arrangement to have the classes continued during our honeymoon."

This was a particularly critical time for Dave to be away, too, because several of his chickens were ailing. At Babonneau in the north-central section of the island, he and Tous—a Babonneau school teacher named Toussaint—were raising 150 broilers and 150 layers under scientifically controlled conditions. The experiment, which employed modern methods, was the most progressive poultry project on St. Lucia, where chickens generally are small and run wild. Tous was to be in complete charge while Dave was on leave, but Dave was concerned because some of the chicks had developed eye trouble; the sick chicks must be segregated from the flock, with preventive medicine put daily into the water given to the others.

Dave and I went over to the Babonneau school. The principal seemed delighted to see us. He left his classes and, to my amazement, urged Tous to leave his, too, and to come along to show us the chickens.

Before they entered the screened pen on the farm, Tous and Dave both took off their shoes and stepped into slippers (kept inside the pen) so that no germs might be carried in on their feet. The floor was covered with clean sugarcane waste that was changed frequently. Adjustable feeding troughs were used since they could be raised as the chicks grew. Rain water, caught in barrels, had been piped to troughs inside the pen and the flow regulated automatically. Besides his regular school duties and work with the Babonneau Young Farmers, Tous cared for the chicks morning and night. He proudly explained the detailed records which he was keeping—under Dave's direction—in a big ledger. The figures gave the amounts of feed consumed and every cost of raising the birds, so that, when they were sold or began to lay, profits could be determined precisely. To toast this efficiency and business enterprise, we stood in the shade of a palm and drank fresh coconut milk from coconuts that had just been hacked from the tree with a huge machete.

Dave later wrote to me that the results of the experiment had been excellent. "Tous's broilers turned out extremely well, and the Young Farmers' Club has all kinds of ideas—some pretty wild—about expanding. Tous wants to set up a broiler project for his parents, who, he thinks, should retire soon. Other members are just as keen, so we'll be expanding. Figuring *all costs* except labor, we made about fifty cents per bird; actually, we made more than that since the chicks and some of the feed were free."

The Thaeler's wedding gave the fifteen PCVs who were scattered over St. Lucia an opportunity to get together to celebrate the beginning of their second year on the island. From the day of their arrival, transportation had been their biggest problem. According to the agreement between the United States and the host country, the St. Lucian government was to furnish the PCVs with the vehicles needed to get them to and from their projects.

One year after their arrival, when some were already beginning to think about the end of their tour of duty, they were still living with no permanent means of traveling around the island. Each morning seven girls crowded into a single jeep to ride down the mountain to the education and public health offices in Castries; the Rep and his wife, who drove a van provided by Heifer Project, never went up or down the hill without picking up riders. Sometimes when the Brancels went out for the van, it was not where they had left it; a PCV might have borrowed it to do an errand or to get to class. Several boys and one girl rode secondhand motor scooters they had bought for themselves. The only vehicle the local government furnished was a pickup truck, to be driven by David Thaeler only, an inflexible government ruling. To this one must add the high rate of breakdowns; not one of the vehicles was new and the winding mountain roads took a heavy toll. As a result, the Peace Corps was the best customer for rentals that Freddie's Garage had ever had.

The shortage of vehicles was acute, yet no PCV suggested that the local government might be stalling so that the Americans would have to provide their own transportation. Nor did they refer to another factor of which they were all aware, that local government officials had secured a copy of the Peace Corps agreement with Tanganyika—these agreements vary—in which the Corps was to furnish its own transportation.

To the PCVs, of course, it made no difference whether a delay was due to a lack of additional funds and aid from the United States, to the red tape in Washington, or because of red tape in the host government. They struggled against delays, and they were seeking ingenious ways to overcome them.

"Maybe there was too much emphasis during our basic training on accepting things as we found them in a country," said Roberta Napier, Mrs. Thaeler-to-be. "Sometimes, we had to do that. But then we found that if we just accept local attitudes and put up with things as they are, we will never accomplish anything. You have to deal with things as they are, but you have to be persistent to get things done."

Three weeks after I left St. Lucia, Roberta and Dave were married. The following account appeared in the *Voice of St. Lucia:*

A simple but impressive wedding took place at Ciceron Methodist chapel [capacity forty-seven] on October 3, 1962, when Miss Roberta Jane Napier, twenty-four, Peace Corps supervising teacher, became the bride of fellow Peace Corps Volunteer, Mr. Arthur David Thaeler III, twenty-seven. The bride, who was given in marriage by her father and attended by her sixteen-year-old sister, both from Oxford, Ohio, wore an elegant self-made street-length gown of white brocade. The groom's father, a medical missionary in Nicaragua, assisted the resident minister in performing the ceremony. Best man was the groom's brother, John, of North Carolina. Other relatives who came to St. Lucia for the wedding were the bride's thirteen-year-old brother, the groom's sister and brother-in-law from Pennsylvania, and his aunt from Georgia. Eighty-five guests attended the reception at the women's residence, Morne Fortune.

A short time later, I received my first letter from Dave:

"Our home is quite lovely inside but leaves something to be desired on the outside. Roberta has a flower garden and hibiscus planted along the walks. There is no vegetable garden yet (my job!) but we have some semblance of a lawn, a rock and gravel pathway, and a banana plant in the middle of our front lawn.

"The inside of the house is painted marine blue (bedroom), light green (living room and dining room), and light yellow (kitchen). The ceiling is off-white. We are having trouble storing things. Volunteers seem to accumulate so many items. I've built a small safe for the storage of food, flour, sugar, etc. This is rat, roach, fly, and children proof! We have so many, both adults and children, in and out of the place that we wish for privacy sometimes. Although we have keys to all doors, we never lock the house, and find that 50 per cent of the time someone has been in the house while we were out. We do have a lending library of sorts (250 books) and most of the people now know how to use it, so they help themselves. Contrary to popular opinion, we have lost nothing except my new wedding shoes a week after we moved in and that's pretty good in two and a half months.

"Roberta has mastered the art of cooking on a kerosene stove, and she is an excellent cook. The other day we had muckaboo pie which tasted like apple pie. Muckaboo is part of the banana family, but with a shorter finger which is very thick. Roberta also seems to be able to work eight hours, clean house, do laundry, cook, and go to four night classes a week, in addition to taking care of me, no easy task. I do the evening dishes two nights a week, but of late I don't seem to get them done. We have both been extremely busy. We have a Christmas program to do this Wednesday evening. Roberta rewrote *The Christmas Carol* as a play for the Ciceron community. It's pretty good—I'm directing it, and—well, I'll be glad when it's over. It will be a little crude in places but everyone is having a 'mick' doing it."

But Volunteers' thoughts, no matter how absorbing their personal interests, are never far from their Peace Corps projects. As Dave said:

"I could go on forever about them. Remember the hogs we were raising? Agnes' gilt had eleven little pigs—eight boars, three gilts. This is good even in the States for a first litter. Moreover, she has saved all of them; they are four weeks old today—this litter weighed 120 lbs. yesterday—not bad for conditions in the tropics where we can't get the feed that they should be getting. We are extremely lucky with this litter— I think we can make these hogs pay—perhaps make thirty dollars per head. But under present conditions—that is, the way the peasant farmers are raising most of the imported pigs—it won't work. Basically, a farmer will have to consider spending $200 or $300 to make $400 on his pigs. We are doing this with the club pigs; it's an experiment really which I'm sure will work.

"In fact, I've gotten to the point where I might stay on down here longer just to see some of the projects materialize."

Which, in fact, is what the Thaelers did; they elected to remain in St. Lucia for a third year of Peace Corps service.

Once past the halfway mark, every Volunteer realizes that it is only a matter of months before this unique experience in his life will come to an end. He could not tell when he joined how it would come out, but he feels vaguely that somehow he should know the outcome now—and he does not. Who will take over after he is gone? Are his government and the host government arranging for an orderly turnover? What can he do to assure continuity? Has he accomplished anything lasting? Will the people—can they—continue the projects he has helped them start? Who will distribute the pigs born to Heifer sows (half the females in every first litter were supposed to be given away and there was a long list of applicants)? What about feed for the animals (there is little raised on the island)? What will become of the children whose interest in music or math has been awakened? And for the Volunteer himself, what next?

It had appeared at first that the Peace Corps project in St. Lucia would serve as a prototype for all other projects. Many visitors reported that the PCVs formed an ideal unit; Washington urged reporters to visit the island to see a versatile group of Volunteers in action. These St. Lucia PCVs recognized no limit to the hours they worked and were close to their host people.

As is true of so many models designed to operate under ideal conditions, St. Lucia at the halfway mark was a successful project, but with a questionable future. Several PCVs had begun to doubt that either they or their successors could help St. Lucians develop an economy that could raise the standard of living above subsistence level.

Nature and history had not cooperated. For the resources, the raw materials, the acres of rich soil and fertile valleys do not exist in St. Lucia. Five-acre farms, on steep hillsides, terraced and irrigated to produce barely enough food for the peasant farmer and his family, cannot be mechanized. Access roads on which to bring the produce to the coast, even if constructed, would not move St. Lucia to a main shipping lane or increase the scope of her markets: St. Lucian fruits and vegetables cannot compete with those raised in Florida. Farm cooperatives, some PCVs think, might be beneficial, but not enough to bring wide prosperity.

Manufacturing is out of the question. Most of what St. Lucians themselves use is imported; it is not even practical to process cocoa oil to make their own margarine and soap. How, the PCVs wonder, can the people possibly get enough money in their pockets to become independent?

Tourism—unwelcome to some—may be the answer. St. Lucia's greatest potential is probably as a vacation place. The very features which militate against a solid, self-sufficient economy with a high standard of living—the mountains that rise to the sky and dip right down to the sea, the tropical climate, and the warm ocean—are a tourist's dream. Six thousand visitors were expected in the winter of 1963. One looks at the two-hundred-room motel being built on a georgeous sandy beach north of Castries and wonders if we should not be sending PCVs who are trained in hotel management and operation to teach St. Lucians, particularly the young people, how to please the tourists, how to take out fishing parties, how to prepare native dishes for restaurant service, how to develop and sell native crafts (which seem to be almost nonexistent).

Some Volunteers, with their eyes on practical results and their hearts on the ideal, find it difficult to accept it all without feeling that they have failed the people—now their friends— whom they came to assist. Personally, as a citizen who helped to send them, I am satisfied. I am satisfied because of the hands they have shaken, the encouragement they have given, the pride people have gained from American friends who call them by their first names, who eat with them, and who sit and talk with them, and, yes, inspire them in many ways.

The St. Lucian who has come to know one or more Volunteers from Iowa or Louisiana or New Jersey, who has been visited regularly by an easy-going American who drives up in a jeep, addresses him cordially, and asks how the sow or the peanuts are doing, will never be the same man again. He will never think of Americans as he thought of them before the PCVs came his way.

Probably not a single reader of this book has known what it feels like to spend his whole life within an area of five miles, never to have been even to a town that lies seven or eight miles away. Yet, there are thousands within a few hours flying time of your home and mine, who are thus limited, thousands who are eager to improve their lot, to whom the appearance of the PCVs has been an eye-opener on what life may hold for them— in some future.

It is not uncommon, in these underdeveloped areas, for the people to be more enthusiastic than their governments about the PCVs and about the work of the Corps. "The most appalling thing to me," said Representative Brancel, "is the indifference of the well-to-do St. Lucians to the needs of their masses. They have no concept of community development—of getting up and getting things done. The best we can do will be just a drop in the bucket."

I don't know why, but the bells ring often in St. Lucia. I still hear them.

PART III

The Seasoned Volunteer

8

*The risks are high, but so are the rewards. And
I'm sure as ever that this is the right thing to
be doing, and if we happen to die while doing it I
think it's just as worthwhile as dying for your
country in a war. By teaching poorly educated
people the dignity they are entitled to as
members of the family of man, we
are contributing to a saner, safer world.*

PCV DAVID KING
Philippines

I was fortunate to have among my correspondents twenty-six-
year-old PCV David E. King, a member of the first group to
reach the Philippines. Dave, five feet six inches tall, a light-
haired, frank, healthy young farm boy from Waterloo, Indiana,
was called "the friendly one" by his Filipino friends. He was
both friendly and frank in our correspondence, which began
with a questionnaire I had sent out to 250 Volunteers.

Dave had finished his first year of service when he wrote
in reply to me:

"Your outline doesn't begin to cover the scope of my experience. While I was attempting to comment on your questions,
I was struck with the vast inadequacy of the picture I was
able to give of what actually does happen as I go about my
Peace Corps duties. The experience is broad, but it is equally
deepening, often in very personal ways. I can predict that
you will get very little favorable reaction from us unless you
take into account the personal aspect [of our] actions and
reactions."

This straightforward criticism of any mass approach to
them I heard often from the PCVs, the majority of whom

passionately demand that they be treated as individuals, not as a group. However, my questionnaire often provoked the PCVs to send me letters of fill-in details that are invaluable for the rounded picture of their activities.

Dave, who was first a teacher's aide and then a full-fledged teacher in Nabua, Camarines Sur, south of Manila, emphasized that "each Volunteer's experiences and reactions to the Philippine Islands Peace Corps are unique," and that "no one person's attitude can reflect the whole picture."

In June, 1962, he wrote:

"During April and May (school vacation here) I worked in Jolo (Sulu), the southernmost province, in a Catholic college. I taught two classes—Speech Improvement, and Short Story and Mythology—to local students (most of them Moslems) and teachers, principals or supervisors who needed the credit.

"The place itself fulfills most people's concept of a 'tropical paradise.' I couldn't have enjoyed those two months more. When I returned to Bicol earlier this month, I stayed one night with my former housemates in Bato, then moved into the house in Nabua which I rented before leaving in March.

"I had just started getting settled in my little 'palace'—got as far as some chairs, some beds and a way to cook—when it was Friday and people started coming. It was to be this huge combination housewarming and birthday party for Nancy Jeffers (Las Vegas, Nevada), my old buddy, whom I worked with in Jolo. We've been together since Penn State. She and Charlotte Hough (Danville, Vermont), came up from Bulusan, Sorsagon—a seven-hour bus trip—for our little affair.

"At night we heard music from downtown (about a block away), so Nancy and I went out to investigate. It was an amateur singing contest and we were the unexpected guests. She's a real striking girl so we were asked to sit on the stage and sing. We belted out 'You Are My Sunshine' and 'Side by Side.' Then I had the whole town sing 'Happy Birthday' to her. By this time she'd won the hearts of everyone in Nabua, and the mayor wanted to trade me in on her (not very flattering to me!)

"We went on to a little store for a bottle of Tru-Orange, and there was a juke box. We were *forced* to demonstrate the American twist, which I'd learned in Jolo and Nancy in Manila. So we danced for them—we're pretty good, even if I do say it myself.

"You know, we'd never have had the nerve to do these things when we were in the States—but now I guess I'm not afraid to do anything I want to, so long as it's good. Most people are afraid of what others will say, but I realize now that other people usually don't even care. I've gained a great deal of self-confidence and courage.

"Who ever thought I'd be a college professor, an expert in library organization, a singer, music teacher, pianist, public speaker, writer, drama director, expert in insect extermination, and a carpenter, too? All one has to do is know a little bit and find out the rest. I'm currently involved in all these activities—and it's wonderful. I think I've lost most of my idealistic philosophy, although it still comes crashing through at times.

"Friday night Nancy was serenaded for three hours at my house. Next morning at five o'clock we went marketing. Soon eleven more Peace Corpsmen arrived, but Nancy had gone to bed with a sore throat. We had her party anyhow—got the doctor in the midst for a penicillin shot. We had a real swinging party—all stayed over sleeping with heads under mosquito nets, sheets over the rest.

"At noon next day, after cleaning up the mess, I hired a car and Charlotte and I took Nancy to Legaspi to the hospital —with acute tonsillitis. We admitted her to the dirty private room—john wouldn't flush, sink was filthy, walls were grimy, no screen or mosquito net—just bad news all the way around. Char and I went back to Nabua, and returned to Legaspi next morning to get Nancy to Manila . . . . While I was in the office paying the bill, a guy came up to me and said, 'Your companion died,' I couldn't in..gine—I'd left her shaving her legs with my razor—but he shoved this paper in my face; it wasn't Nancy, but Dave Mulholland, who had died of a liver infection and dysentery. I really broke up.

"This morning we attended funeral services for Dave, a really good friend who started with us at Penn State. It was a real horror show. PCVs came from all the provinces and many Embassy people were there as well as Filipino friends. It was interesting to see the differences. Peace Corps people wore shapeless, worn clothes, run-down shoes, hair cut short to avoid insects—the Embassy people were immaculate, and the Filipinos were all in black.

"Ambassador Stevenson and Vice-President Palaez both delivered eulogies; all was tastefully done, but it was a real time of reckoning for most of us there. We began to think, 'Is this what we volunteered for? Is it worth dying for? Is it in vain? Why be here slaving away for these strangers when we could be home?' But I think most of us came away more determined (I did) to get out there in the barrios and really work at this Peace Corps thing.

"This is part of what we volunteered for. The risks are high, but so are the rewards. And I'm sure as ever that this is the right thing to be doing, and if we happen to die while doing it I think it's just as worthwhile as dying for your country in a war.

"In spite of the title of our outfit I don't realize often that we are fighting for *peace*. The Filipinos are already quite peaceful. I guess we're here to make peace a more secure reality. By teaching poorly educated people the dignity they are entitled to as members of the family of man, we are contributing to a saner, safer world.

"I know those people down in Negros Occidental where Dave Mulholland worked will be different because he was

there. They were exposed to a lot of new things. Some the
Filipinos will like and adopt and adapt, others they won't like
and will reject. This is going on in all the towns and schools
where we work—it must add up to something in the end.
We're often called upon to do things we aren't too sure about,
but we do them—and show others how. Often our activities
seem mighty insignificant to us—and they are—telling someone
about American customs, or telling them why we think some
of their customs aren't good, or being frank when we are
expected to be tactful, or teaching someone to make a difference between *p* and *f* when speaking English, or pouring
kerosene in the open sewers to kill mosquitoes.

"And it's hard, living without electricity, water, decent toilet
facilities, and privacy. I can understand why five of us have
already gone home. It's sometimes just that bad—that you
don't want to do anything but go home where toilets flush,
where men don't hold hands, where people talk intelligently,
where you can be alone if you want to be."

A few go home, but most stay and start improvising ways
to make their quarters more like home. A PCV in Africa discussed this almost universal tendency to fix up a place: "The
Peace Corps and the local governments make a mistake putting us in second-rate quarters. Either they should billet us
in primitive huts that can't possibly be modernized or allow
us to have places similar to what we're used to at home. In
other words, don't give us any conveniences or give us ones
that function, but don't compromise."

Right or wrong, most PCVs—perhaps illustrating the democratic belief that everyone can better himself—do spend some
time improving their living quarters, and they are usually
proud of the results. Dave King was particularly pleased
when he finally added electricity to his house in Nabua.

"Today is a red letter day for me," he exulted in a letter
he wrote on July 23. "I had electricity installed! I have three
electric light bulbs and it seems better than the Waldorf to

me. By way of celebration I've fixed a little drink—a stinger with green *crème de menthe*—and it's really hitting the spot, even though I have to fish out an insect now and then, and there's no ice.

"I'm living completely independently of the 'little America' which seems to crop up wherever two or more Americans get together. I sometimes feel very alone, but I think it just takes some getting used to. I'm certainly doing emotional gymnastics, but I'm leveling off now to a point where I can begin to explore these new reactions I have.

"I like my complete independence from other Americans. My aloneness isn't physical. I'm keeping two high school boys for the year. I've had them for two months. They do the work.

"The boys are fifteen—one a junior, the other a sophomore. Lee is immature, stupid, unreliable, lazy, and ugly—but can he ever play the guitar and sing! Pete is intelligent, dependable, nice-looking and as poor as a church mouse. I really feel fatherly toward them. They address me as 'Sir' always, and this society demands that we keep that distance between master and servant. But there is a kind of feeling between us.

"I'm surprised at their profound loyalty. They protect gullible me fiercely. Even though they've been offered goodly sums in conspiracies against my meager Peace Corps funds, they've always come crashing through in my defense.

"Lee I guess I could part with easily, but Pete has really won my affection and in my magnanimous moments I've entertained the thought of bringing him back to the States with me. Being a bachelor-type, I think I could support him. There would be many problems, but what a wonderful experience for Pete! He has the ability but lacks the means. The Philippines needs him but isn't able to give him the proper breaks. Maybe I can.

"It's great fun fixing up the house. I have only the large upstairs—the downstairs is smaller. My place is 'hung over.' Up here there are two bedrooms, a large living room, one half of which I've partitioned off for a study area, a large kitchen-dining room, an entrance room, and in back there's a flush-by-pouring toilet, bath facilities consisting of two pans of cold water on the floor, and a big porch for washing.

"The house is really neat—local abstract art on the walls, sliding window panels made of clam shells, kerosene pressure-stove. I've been building furniture like crazy. I'm fantastic at making shelves. I also put together a six-foot table and two benches—crude but functional. I had a nara-wood sala set (that's a living room set, without upholstery, consisting of four chairs, sofa, and coffee table) made and my next project is to put in the rattan cane bottoms. I really enjoy being Mr. Do-It-Yourself. In fact, I helped the Seventh Day Adventist minister, who lives downstairs, to install the wiring today. Never thought I'd see the day.

"My study, too, is neat—a rattan lounge chair, a low, low table, a palm mat on the floor, colorful pillows to sit on, a kerosene lamp—now replaced with an adjustable electric light bulb waist-high or at ceiling height. I bought a wild shade for it today made of clam shells. There's a seven-foot shelving unit separating the room; I keep all my books for the public there. I've painted my three-peso bamboo chairs black and white. I'll soon be ready for a big housewarming. There'll be warm cokes and fried bananas.

"Having my own household in Nabua has meant to me the difference between living *in* a community and living *with* a community. The changes have been rather subtle but they're real.

"Right away I noticed a feeling of aloneness. There were no other Americans to go home to, to share comments and complaints with. Everyone I talked with was Filipino. Naturally many things annoyed me, but instead of being smug and analytical of these situations, I began to accept them for what they were.

"I still rebel inwardly when I feel that my personal privacy is being invaded, but I can accept the fact that this is the way Filipinos live together. It's a sign of their acceptance of me when my neighbors feel free to drop in, check my mail or count my shirts. There's no one to complain to, and I'm very much surprised at how little these things really matter when I dismiss them from my mind.

"I found, too, that as people started coming to my house and as I visited their homes, the feeling of aloneness slowly disappeared. We began to be comfortable together. It was no longer an occasion when I dropped in on them. Elaborate hospitality was reduced to coffee or *sinaput* (bananas dipped in batter and deep-fried). We began to have real conversations, too. We discuss happenings in town, we gossip, we talk about our respective countries, we even confide problems.

"I've started learning again. I had been judging Filipinos by my own American standards, making plenty of allowances because they were, after all, foreigners. It's easy to be fooled, too, because they seem so American on the surface and they claim that they are Westernized. But their basic philosophy is definitely Oriental and their values are quite different from my own. I can appreciate this whole experience so much more now that I've realized my hosts are the ones making allowance for my quaint customs and values."

A big triumph for Dave came during his second year, when he was designated as a regular teacher, a promotion from the rather nebulous "teacher's aide" status which he disliked.

"I've been integrated into the Nabua High School faculty," he reported. "I teach six classes of juniors and seniors a day— a normal English teacher's load. I have four preparations— two literature, one speech improvement and a lit-comp combination.

"By rearranging the schedule and taking advantage of me, the school will be able to save seven hundred pesos (which it doesn't have) by not hiring substitutes for teachers on ma-

ternity leave. I'll shift classes every two months as the pregnant teachers leave, with some vacant weeks to work in other
classes, to put on a play, and hopefully, to organize a chorus.
I'm helping with the newspaper after school and hoping that
by the end of the year it will be written entirely by the students. This isn't education 'aide-ing'—it's teaching—but I'm
still not convinced that I'm upgrading the teaching of English.

"Now that I have the same schedule as a Filipino teacher,
I can understand better their concerns, their frustrations, and
their problems. This, in my opinion, is a much more valid
assignment for a PC man than operating as a teacher's aide—
whatever that is. Some PCVs like being aides, but I was never
able to swing it.

"My observation is that while we're aiding, we establish
ourselves in a position of superiority. Our stated purpose is
'to upgrade teaching of English and science.' But I find that
Filipino teachers are doing a very good job.

"We don't agree with the methods they use, but perhaps
we don't fully understand the problem. We say, 'Free the
child from traditional forms. Allow him to be imaginative,
original, creative.' This just doesn't work with Filipino kids.
The social structure places children in a position of complete
dependency. Their teachers are dependent, too. When we set
ourselves up as 'upgraders' we tend to insist that teachers
follow American techniques (with which we were well indoctrinated, both at Penn State and at Los Banos by Filipino
educators), which contradict the pattern of social interchange
between teacher and student.

"As a regular classroom teacher, I follow the methods I
know; but some of them have been abandoned, others greatly
modified, and I've adopted some of the methods Filipino
teachers use. And still I wonder if I'm teaching as well as the
regular teachers are."

In the course of his teaching and at the same time studying
his Filipino associates, their lives, and their country, Dave

made numerous notes, sometimes with the intention of mailing them to his family or friends, but he did not always send them off. Excerpts from these notes, written somewhat in textbook style, give his impressions of his hosts and their customs:

"The Filipinos are not a primitive people. Almost all speak English as well as their own dialects, of which there are eighty-seven. Tagalog, the language of the Manila area, is the national language. Teachers are required to complete a four-year education course. Standards for doctors, lawyers, nurses, agriculturists, and government employees are much the same as we have in America, although training facilities are not as complete and up-to-date.

"Words such as 'primitive,' 'backward,' and 'underdeveloped' do the Philippines an injustice. More accurately the country can be described as 'developing,' 'advancing,' and 'emerging.' Democracy is firmly entrenched. The Constitution is similar to that of the United States. *Communism will never gain a foothold in a country so fiercely dedicated to the ideals of democracy.*

"The Filipinos are of the Malay race—brown skin, black hair and eyes, and flat noses. They are beautiful people, small and graceful, their color varies from deep brown to almost white. Some have intermarried with Spanish, Chinese, and Americans, producing the *mestizo*, a combination which preserves the best qualities of both races.

"Most Filipinos are fond of dancing, singing, eating, gambling, fiestas, cock fights (for men only), and parties. They never miss an opportunity to celebrate the anniversary of a birth, wedding or death. Personally, they are quite clean and dress well in American-type clothes. *For formal affairs* the men wear their traditional *barong tagalogs*, the women their sheer, embroidered over-blouses and bright wrap-around skirts.

"The land is kind. Here in Bicol it is possible to sit around and wait for the fruit to ripen, then pick it and eat it. Fresh water and ocean fish are waiting to be caught. Rice and other crops must be cultivated, but this involves only a few days work at planting and harvesting time. Since the Filipinos don't have to work in order to eat, they are not noted for being overly ambitious. They often say, 'God will take care of us,' while Americans tend to believe 'God helps those who help themselves.'

"The weather is warm—evenings remind me of June nights in Indiana—and rain is plentiful. During April and May the sun scorches everything and leaves the rice fields with six-inch cracks in the dried mud. The beneficent rains come late in May, revitalizing the earth and cooling the people. Another force of nature—the typhoon—threatens during November and December. Winds up to 120 mph and heavy rains sweep in from the south, leveling houses, stripping young fruit off the coconut trees, flooding the lowlands and destroying the field crops.

"The living standard among the masses is low. Many farmers and fishermen live at subsistence level and see very little money during their lifetimes. There is a small 'high' class that lives in great comfort, with large houses and servants. Professionals and businessmen make up a newly emerging middle class. Their financial security allows them to build houses of cement, buy electrical appliances (where electricity is available), own pianos, and sometimes drive cars. For the most part, these are the people who exhibit a social conscience, who are concerned about the underprivileged and the future of the nation.

"An avenue of life runs down the center of Bicol, the railroad and highway which connect the provinces with Manila, the cultural and business center of the Philippines. Studies have shown that along these transportation routes, the standard of living is higher than in isolated communities. People can get to Manila, and goods and ideas can reach them. Evidences of progress are not at all obvious once you leave the beaten track.

"Locally, we have bus lines which don't operate on a schedule, but I seldom wait for one more than a half-hour. For short trips, i.e. the next town, I often take a jeepney. For transportation within the town, tricycles or pedicabs are available. Philippine Air Lines operates regular flights among the major cities, and interisland boats operate on regular schedules.

"I've sometimes gone to extremely hard-to-reach places where we resort to boats, 'carabao-back' riding, or simply hiking over the mountains. One thing I miss very much is the luxury of my own transportation. The transportation companies don't sell comfort—they sell transportation only. At first, it's romantic and quaint to sit on a crowded bus with your feet in a basket of fish, a pig under the seat, and a rooster's tail in your lap. But the adventure of it wears a little thin after a while.

"In the rural areas, the introduction of transistor radios, many distributed by CARE, is a good influence. Primarily, the people listen to music, but VOA [Voice of America] transmits newscasts to all Southeast Asia from Manila and Taipei.

"The high regard in the Filipino mind for U.S. goods and ideas sometimes seems to jump all limits of self-esteem and good sense. Ever since Admiral Dewey sailed into Manila Bay in 1898, to sink the Spanish fleet and declare the Philippines a U.S. territory, the link between the two countries has been close. In the early 1900's, the U.S. government sent over thousands of teachers, known as Thomasites, who set up the present educational system. After the Japanese occupation in World War II, American troops were greeted in all parts of the island as heroes and liberators, although they may have exhibited no more courage than the Filipino guerrillas.

"In 1946 the Republic of the Philippines was formed as an independent nation, but it still bears the stamp of the U.S. in its educational system, its form of government, and in the fierce love of everything American—be it cigarettes, shoes, letters, or people. This points up sharply the responsibility Americans have to encourage and aid efficient economic development which will allow Filipinos to be independent of mind as well as government. The Philippines has been called the 'showcase of democracy' for Southeast Asia. We should see that the show is a good one.

"So far the country is not industrialized in spite of a great wealth of natural resources. There are no great leaders in spite of vast numbers of educated men and women. There is little capital investment in spite of the vast wealth held by a few families.

"As I go about my Peace Corps business in this country, with its blend of East and West, I often run into minor cultural clashes. Here are some examples:

"*Filipino time* can mean arriving one or two hours late for an engagement. This is an accepted procedure among the easy-going Filipinos. When a meeting is set for 7:00 it is understood by all (except me) to mean 8:00 or 9:00. Church services, although scheduled, start whenever people get there. School starts at 7:30 on the schedule; in actuality, it begins more often at 8:00, or when the teachers and students arrive.

"The *family system* forms a complex web of relatives by birth as well as relatives by marriage. Relationships are followed to the seventh or eighth cousin, and are quite important to Filipinos. The language reflects the importance placed on relationships. For instance our word *aunt* has the following equivalents in Bicol—sister of my father, sister of my mother, sister of my mother's mother, sister of my father's mother, etc. One good purpose this extended family system serves is that all members chip in to help financially when any member has an emergency or celebration to deal with. Produce of a family farm is often shared with all members.

"*Utang na loob* (literally, "debt already interior") is a variation of our policy of 'I'll scratch your back and you scratch mine.' In the Philippines, the idea is 'If I scratch your back, then you *must* scratch mine in return.' A favor done carries with it the obligation of a favor in return. Perhaps this helps the Filipinos to carry on their relationships smoothly.

"*Status of women* is high. Women enter freely into politics, the professions, and business. It is traditional for all women to handle the family money. It's not unusual to see a couple riding on the bus, with the woman paying the fares.

"One of the first things that I learned upon arrival was that there is a 'no touch' policy regarding females. Women are held in high regard, are courted with serenades, letters, visits to the home, and chaperoned get-togethers. Most often a lady is not kissed until after her wedding. A typical Filipina is shy, retiring, very gentle, very feminine, and very lovely. Yet they hold the purse strings!

"*Number two system* is another paradox. Divorce is illegal in the Philippines, as I am reminded several times a week. Legal separations are granted, but that's a lot of bother. It's easier to maintain a wife and her family and take a 'number two'—a mistress.

"One of the most respected teachers—he seems saintlike—has his 'number two' and two families. In another town, the mayor, who is also the doctor, maintains his wife and family, and a 'number two' nurse and family in his clinic. In another town, the municipal treasurer keeps his 'number two' in the municipal building. Even some priests are keeping mistresses and have children running around in the parish hall. I was introduced to a young man one day as the 'illegitimate son of my brother.'

"Filipinos are quick to condemn themselves for these practices, but they are seemingly unwilling to do anything about them. Perhaps the first step is the improvement of education. The Peace Corps, hopefully, will make a contribution to this goal."

In addition to getting to know others better, the majority of Volunteers discovered that getting to know themselves better was one of the bonuses of Peace Corps service. Being forced to depend upon their own resources and to endure long hours of solitude hastened the process of self-realization. Often they marveled at changes in themselves and their attitudes, as well as at the discovery of personal traits they had not recognized before.

The musings and self-analysis of Dave King—a thoughtful, introspective person—dramatize what happens to the Volunteer.

"Now that I've been Peace Corps-ing for more than a year," Dave said, "I can think of lots of reasons for joining that I didn't have when I signed on the dotted line. One reason is that I have more time than any other job ever offered—time to sit with a cup of coffee and watch the sun set, time to sit at the *sari sari* store and talk, time to think, read, and write.

"The work is slow—sometimes seemingly insignificant. I didn't know it would be like this; I imagined that I would be doing more things that show. Now that I understand how our presence will work in the communities where we're assigned, I think it's a good way. And there's time to become reacquainted with oneself.

"In addition to self-rediscovery, I've learned many things about the ambitions, values, customs, lives of people in an Oriental society. Comparisons are natural, and I've discovered many things about the States. I've even reread our Constitution. Because I'm often called upon to explain our political and social systems, I've gotten to know my own country better. Strange, isn't it, how things appear in better focus from afar. I've become better acquainted with the English language, too, because I've had to reduce it to its basic elements in order to teach it.

"I've learned to enjoy my aloneness. This is quite different from loneliness, which smacks of boredom, and I'm certainly not bored. I say aloneness because in most cases my interests are of a broader scope and, in many things, my knowledge is greater than my neighbors. My outlook is more cosmopolitan, my attitudes and values are Western.

"I've *learned* to enjoy the feeling of aloneness created by these things because I *had* to learn. It was mighty hard at first until I found outlets through reading, studying, and writing. There have to be times when I take myself apart from the community and exist for awhile in the world where I am comfortable and at ease.

"I am amazed at the way life goes. I sat for years on a tractor in the cornfields of Indiana, driving on and on in endless circles, while my mind reeled with daydreams of far, exotic places and the noble dents I would someday make on the world. Then I found myself in teachers' college with a partial scholarship and a job. With all those wonderful, interesting people around, it was like a four-year party. When I was given my degree, I was staggered by the job offers and finally chose Lake Ronkonkoma, Long Island, because it was near the Big City and paid well. I spent two great years in the East, although I didn't like the adult world until I grew up a little more. Then I got a job with the U.S. Army in Germany, teaching in schools for dependent children. I was able to explore most of the continent and find out a lot of new things about people. It was another fascinating year.

"It surprises me now to remember how quickly I accepted the Peace Corps' offer when the telegram arrived in Stuttgart. In five days I had rid myself of all my success symbols, resigned my contract with the Army, and found myself at Penn State in the Peace Corps. It was, happily, a good choice, however spontaneous. How often I've looked back and thought of those years I rode around, barefoot, in the cornfields. They were good years, but it's much more fun to be grown up!

"Life here in the Philippines is quite unlike any of my former experiences. Previously, it seems that my activities

were all self-centered. Now I operate in a realm of selfless-
ness. (I wonder if missionaries feel this way.) It's as if I've
put myself, body and soul, at the disposal of whoever wants
to take advantage of me. Anything that concerns my life,
private or public, interests the villagers. People nonchalantly
read my letters when they visit the house. Word travels quickly
back to Nabua about my activities in other parts. The Bamboo
Telegraph delivers reports of all Peace Corps members' doings
to me regularly. I don't mind because I'm a member of the
community.

"I feel comfortable here in my role. There are people I
like and people I don't like. My best friend is the janitor at
the school.

"He's a sixth-grade graduate. What fine people he and his
wife are. She sews shirts and sells them in the market place.
They often stop in just to visit or to do whatever they can to
help me. She sewed some curtains for the doors of my house,
hemmed a tablecloth, and fixed a rip in my good pants. He
cleaned the stove one day, and came to help cook for a party
I had. They still think of themselves on a lower level of
society than I—and in Nabua they are—but I'm sure they can't
know how much I value them.

"I had cocktails with a very wealthy Spanish couple in
Legaspi on Sunday. They asked me, 'Now really, Dave, how
do you like it?' My answer was 'I really *do* like it.' Great
laughter followed and 'Oh, come on now—be honest.' I was
hurt that they didn't accept my explanation.

"Next morning on the hour-and-a-half bus ride back home
I thought of that conversation. I think that for the first time
in my life I am really dedicated to my work. I wonder if it
could be because I'm *giving* my best effort where it's needed
and appreciated, with no thought of the pay check as the
reward. I'm surprised how much better a teacher I am here
than I was in New York or Germany. I like teaching much
more, too. Maybe it's like the good feeling one gets when

helping an old lady across the street. I really feel a great concern for my students.

"There's one boy—Joel Gavino—who's in my senior literature class. He's bored to death because he comprehends right away. I know it pains him to sit through the periods while I try to lead the rest of the class to some understanding of the ideas in the material we're studying. He drinks—the result, it's said, of an unhappy home life.

"He writes poetry in Tagalog, and I'm encouraging him to do a column for the school paper. I have given him books from my personal library to read. He chose Ayn Rand's *Fountainhead* and Shute's *In the Wet* and a textbook of English literature. I wish there were some way to encourage and help him because he has great ability.

"I wonder if my Spanish friends can comprehend that feeling. It just occurred to me—maybe that's what they felt when they invited me for cocktails!"

There are many David Kings in the Peace Corps.

9

*The Peace Corps in the Philippines has come
of age, the growing pains are on the way out,
and the unsteady step forward has been replaced
by a firm stride in the right direction.*
PCV LEO A. PASTORE
Philippines

As the end of his two years approaches, the PCV's attitude
begins to change. He wants to leave and he wants to stay,
he wants to get on with his own life, yet he also wants to complete what he has started. He thinks more frequently of his
own plans for the future and less about launching new projects.
He regrets all that he has not been able to do and doubts that
the work he has begun will go on in quite the way he wishes it
would.

Time now flies by. Occasionally, the emotions that have
been controlled so tightly for two years burst in heated words
with co-workers, only to be apologized for and forgiven at the
never-less-than-two-weeks of goodbye parties with their toasts,
elaborate thanks, pledges of friendship and good will, and
even tearful farewells.

One PCV said, "You can't eat and drink in one house without doing it all over town. And if you don't eat and drink,
you're being rude and ungrateful. So it's upchuck—if you
must—but on with the festivities."

As David King neared the end of his two years in Nabua,
he, too, had his moments of doubt and self-examination:

"Time passes so quickly! Soon it will all be over. I'm
beginning to wonder what will be next. Group 1 [the first
group to reach the Philippines] observed its first anniversary
in the field some time ago; it's only a matter of months now

until our contract ends. We didn't celebrate. I was in Manila at the time, and several of us uttered a rather weary Happy Anniversary to one another, followed by a sarcastic laugh loaded with so much meaning and experience that it dropped heavily into the silence that followed.

"I think all PCVs have hit ups and downs which we've never experienced before. Life for many of us has gone on with an intensity of emotion which sometimes surprises us, sometimes puzzles us, and sometimes leaves its mark (whether or not we like it) on our everyday lives. Some who came to the Peace Corps with lofty ideals, high expectations, and zealous energy (I was one of them) have had to modify their thinking, sometimes violently. Those who haven't made this adjustment find their jobs a lot harder.

"Have you found out about possibilities for ex-Peace Corpsmen? I know we're among the first to terminate, and our staff remains extremely vague on the point, so I'd like to put out some feelers. What, for instance, will be the possibility of scholarships for advanced studies? How will we be received when we return? Will we find good opportunities because of our PC experiences? Maybe I'm too eager and this is something only time will tell.

"I'll meet Shriver this week in Legaspi. Maybe he'll give us the good word. This will be the first meeting between Group 1 and him. I'm looking forward to it. I only hope he doesn't give us the same old policy speeches, although he'll surely want to clarify the memo we got saying we couldn't resign."

Reports of Sargent Shriver's visits to groups around the world varied all the way from "Great!" through "O.K." to "Awful!" and one can guess that different PCVs expected different things of their Director. When PCVs criticize, their remarks are apt to be scathing, as was this report on Shriver's visit to the Philippines:

"Shriver's visit is over. 'Anyone is free to return to the

States whenever he feels he must,' we were told. After that policy statement, several have returned—one a sad case of mental breakdown. Shriver flew to Legaspi where we were waiting to meet him in conference. It was a bad show. It would have been better if he and Representative Fuchs had never come. They managed to alienate and offend many Filipinos who attended by their curt statements, omissions of proper recognition to invited dignitaries (including the dean of the college where we met and the provincial governors), and their rush, rush, rush attitude."

These comments, it seems to me, show how much the Volunteers have learned about local protocol and time values, if not about respect and understanding for their own superiors.

"It was strictly a question-and-answer session," the report continued. "Shriver was able to repeat policy and tell us very little. Actually, the distance between us and him was never bridged, so he doesn't know, really, what's going on here. I've an idea that he did just what *Time* magazine said he did— raced from place to place eating thousand-day-old eggs and smelling compost. We were all a bit disappointed—it was like finding out that there really isn't a Santa Claus.

"After the meeting ended I went immediately to the dean of the college, a good friend and townmate of mine, and apologized for the bad show. His comment—'Well, it's all over now and that's part of our job.'

"I'm sure Shriver is good in his position and that he's running a successful organization, but perhaps he has lost sight of the operation at this low level. He didn't do a thing to improve morale here.

"Regarding jobs after termination, the word in Manila now —I don't know if they're serious or joking—is that we'll be given 're-entry orientation' when we reach the States. The explanation I got was that we'll be offered training in readjustment and aid in placement.

"I'm not awfully concerned about finding a job. I really

feel the need to study and I plan to do that as far as $1800 will reach. I'm not at all certain what I'll study—so many things come to mind. But there has to be some kind of income. I suppose I can always teach or tutor. According to Shriver, requests are already coming into the Washington office, but they have no policy yet regarding placement because there's been no need until now for such a service."

Dave King took a job as college traveler for the American Book Company instead of going to graduate school, but, of course during his last months in the Philippines he had no inkling what his final decision would be. There were some disappointments in those final months, too, about apparent successes that turned into failures—or so Dave interpreted them.

"While we were in training at Penn State, our role was described to us as being 'agents of change.' I think most of us now realize, after many bitter frustrations, that the change will not be in the form of a smashing impact or a trail of sensational improvements to which we can point when we depart and say, 'I did that.' Perhaps change will evolve because of our presence, perhaps not. Evolution and progress are extremely slow. Our time investment here is in humanity. Results won't show spectacularly unless the Filipinos bring about the change themselves.

"The events leading to the above thoughts may interest you. The library which was established in Bato, the next town, through the joint efforts of four PCVs (I was one), is now defunct. We made every effort to make the library a town project, and involved a large number of people, even though the idea was ours and we provided the push and made arrangements to have all the books donated. Now it's closed because the room where it was housed was needed more desperately for a lounge for municipal employees *and* because nobody ever used the library.

"Another related event—I'm an adopted member of the

local professional fraternity in Nabua. We Free Wheelers are a prosperous organization and we had several thousand pesos to spend. At a meeting a suggestion was made that a war memorial monument be erected naming not only those who were killed, but also every Nabuanian who served (most Free Wheelers did).

"I suggested that we invest in the future rather than the past, and present war memorial scholarships to poor but deserving students. Unanimous agreement. Wonderful idea. 'Aha!' I said, 'I'm now being an agent of change. I'm giving some of those wonderful, superior values I hold to a place where it will count.'

"This week, construction on the war memorial monument was started. I've concluded that as agents of change, our impact will be felt very slightly."

Perhaps it is easier for the Volunteers to see and feel the changes within themselves.

"I long for a chance to remove myself for some time," Dave wrote at this point, "to a place where I can think things through and discover what has happened, what changes have occurred, what kind of person has evolved in this new, altered me. I need time free from the pressure of duty and the closeness of contributing environment to sift my experiences and state to myself my new philosophy.

"At work, I'm in a rut. I teach a regular, responsible five-day schedule. Off-hours are spent primarily correcting papers and making plans for lessons. I've never really liked teaching —I like it more here—but I'm not fully happy and content doing it. The Peace Corps for me has become a routine. Maybe that's as it should be. I really don't know what I'd be happier doing.

"I've been around enough to know that most jobs are eventually reduced to routine and the repetition can become mighty tedious. Probably in joining the Peace Corps, I exchanged one rut for a different one, but I don't find ruts to be completely distasteful. There's a great deal of security and comfort in a well-established rut which allows one to discharge duties efficiently, leaving a greater amount of time and energy for things outside the rut. I want my rut, since I must have one, to be a shallow one.

"Of one thing I'm sure—I'm brave, unashamed, self-confident to a new degree. I no longer feel I must please others. Within the bounds of common courtesy and good taste, I'm free to do what I please. It's a wonderful new feeling.

"I spent some time in Manila recently, after five months here. Although it's strictly against PC rules, I stayed with Embassy friends in their air-conditioned apartment, and went with them to dinner at the Naval Officers Club, to the theater, etc.

"At first, I enjoyed the familiar environment, but after a few days, I realized that I was bored. The conversations were just plain empty. I found myself repeating meaningless comments over and over, listening to idle gossip, chatting about the Manila social scene. I remember nothing of the conversations. I found myself going places alone or seeking out other PCVs who happened to be in Manila.

"In fact, I reached a point where I just didn't have a single thing to say to the man I was staying with, formerly a good friend. I've never been like that before; I could always talk about *something*. Can it be that I've become too narrow? Is it that I no longer concern myself with pettiness? I don't know, but at this rate, I'll have a big adjustment to make to Stateside living.

"Formerly I was big on night clubs. I anticipated that life again, but I just couldn't take it. It was so damned artificial— I don't know how I ever liked it so much before. Everyone just gets drunk and talks the same old prattle. I'd rather stay home and read. And that's a mighty strange statement coming from the former me. I just don't understand my withdrawal. Is it happening to others, too?"

Projects attempted by Volunteers—even after several disappointing adventures and within a few months of departure— are often amazingly ambitious. For his second Christmas in the Philippines, David King decided on a dramatization of Dickens' *Christmas Carol* for his school's program.

"I want to make it nice," he explained, "with carols between scenes and a good stage. I'll use my speech improvement (vocational) class, hoping that something will be learned incidentally to justify the time spent practicing."

In early December, he was hard at work with rehearsals, in addition to his regular classes.

"I taught my classes about irony today, but it passed over them like a cloud—they can describe it and give back my definition, but I'm sure they wouldn't recognize it if they were surrounded by it. It's just another thing I'll have to point out again and again and again.

"Last period I resumed rehearsing for the Christmas program. It has now developed into a rather pleasing combination of Broadway musical and Greek drama. I started with a radio play and the story of Dickens' *Christmas Carol* and in adapting and Filipinizing it, I wound up with lots of Christmas carols thrown in, plus a narrator and oral chorus.

"We practiced singing this afternoon and it's really neat. We sing a capella since I think a piano sort of throws them. I learn all the parts, sing them to the sections, they memorize, then we put them together. Their natural musical instinct is wonderful. You should hear them tear through 'Whispering Hope,' a Christmas song here. I taught them *'Gloria in Excelsis Deo'* today; in less than a half-hour they were singing three parts pretty well. I'm tempted to try them with 'O Holy Night.' It's going to be a real show.

"The thing I like most is that the kids are really the ones responsible—I've delegated most of the authority to selected students who crack the whip more fiercely than I ever would. Of course, I'm still boss, but we call it adviser. After the chorus learns the songs, I'll turn it over to the son of the Seventh Day Adventist minister and he'll practice them.

"I sense that the teachers feel very uneasy about the success of the venture and maybe I should, too, but the kids seems to be proving themselves far above my expectations, and even if it isn't so good, at least it will be a bit spectacular and it will be *theirs*. My Scrooge needs a lot of work, though, but I've never seen a more conscientious kid—he practices every time he and the student director have free periods, and he told me that every night before he sleeps, he goes through the play as far as he has memorized. It's really great fun and I like most what I see the experience bringing out in the kids. For most of them, it's the first time to have such responsibilities and they're scared, but I think a little nervousness will serve as a spur to do their best.

"Saturday, December 1, marked the anniversary of our arrival in the Bicol region. Several of us had a small celebration of the event in Pili, where three girls have a house. We were able to come up with two bottles of Chianti, the girls cooked spaghetti and a fine sauce with ground meat, we made garlic toast, and hardly noticed that we lacked a green salad to complete the meal. There were seven of us, and I'm sure we all left the affair next day relaxed and refreshed.

"I was slightly surprised, but overjoyed, at the almost complete lack of bitching that entered our conversations. We all decried the fact that we've somehow established complete brother-sister relationships and that the chances for romance are nil. I ventured the opinion that this will change when we once hit the States and find ourselves in more familiar circumstances.

"Filipino-American romances exist only in rumor, since most of us find the culture gap too wide to bridge, although Heaven knows the Filipino public would be ecstatically happy should one of us make the move.

"Conversation swung—as it usually does now—to the big

question, 'What happens after?' As you surmised, quite a number are interested in some phase of government work, but
a surprisingly large number are interested in further study
immediately after. I'm now in the latter group, I suspect that
each one of us harbors a secret opinion of our own exaggerated importance due to the PC experience and thinks that
he'll be avidly sought after for all kinds of wonderful employment opportunities.

"Tales have already reached us that Coca-Cola, IBM, and
a few other firms are just waiting for us to hit the shores so
they can snatch us up. For the most part, however, I believe
that any offers will come because of individual merit or
perhaps because it will temporarily be the popular, patriotic
thing for a firm to hire a PC Veteran. I don't worry, because
so far as I'm concerned, the whole future is one big question
mark and I like it that way.

"We welcomed the chance to do group things and spent
hours playing 'Hearts' and 'I Doubt It.' One guy had learned
to tell fortunes on cards so we all learned. Then we found a
Philippine Monopoly game and stayed up until 5:30 wheel-
ing and dealing for Dewey Boulevard and Manila Airport.
I enjoyed the whole shindig tremendously, since I was in one
of my social moods."

Finally, it was time for the Christmas festivities at Dave's
school.

"The Christmas show, as far as I'm concerned, was successful," he wrote, "although some of the teachers were critical.
But the kids did well. First night was a bit shaky, but second
night they really acted and it was thrilling to see. I reacted
like a proud papa. The chorus sang beautifully, the oral
chorus felt for the first time their contribution to the total
effect, and the actors spoke with emotion, untapped until
then, and punctuated their lines with normal gestures. Spirits
were high after the final curtain and the kids invited me to
a party they had secretly prepared for me. I've been through

similar experiences in the States, but I'm sure this one will always be first in my memories."

For all his participation in so many social events, Dave still continued to write about withdrawing from others.

"The withdrawal I sensed in my last letter has been a satisfying method of finding time. Perhaps it's not really withdrawal at all; it could be a part of the process of limiting and selecting people and activities to those which really count. I feel less anxiety in my dealings with people now that I've decided to stop the show for show's sake. I've found, too, that those few whom I really value have become so much more worthwhile and wonderful since I've separated them in my mind from the masses for whom I really feel indifference.

"I think, too, that my purpose for being here is being served better, for any change I influence will come from the Filipinos themselves. Those I select for friends are the active, interested doers. Their activities can always be counted on to affect those who just stand by, whom I have neither the time nor inclination to pamper.

"It's rainy season now. It just rains, rains, rains. Everything's damp. Everything metal has long since turned rusty unless regularly polished, shoes are moldy, skin fungus is hard to control, fish are unavailable, clothes can't be dried in the sun, but most disconcerting is the fact that every filter-tip cigarette is covered with mold. It's enough to make me stop smoking.

"Today has been one of those days when all sorts of things go wrong and all kinds of people drop in. I was just thinking that since I started this letter the wiring caught fire downstairs, I've entertained three groups of teachers who came to borrow books, my three third-grade friends came to give me a Bicol language lesson, a high school teacher came to give me instructions on how to be a godfather to her baby, David, I spent the afternoon at school, the newspaper man came to collect, and I was interviewed for the school paper."

If the holidays were rough, Dave discovered that the last two weeks before departure for the States by way of Hong Kong and Tokyo, were close to a nightmare. His schedule reflects what often happens to PCVs who are saying goodbye to their hosts. The following (incomplete) list of Dave's activities reveals the strain of the parting hours:

Friday: Graduation followed by a party for the governor.

Saturday: Graduation Ball. Discovered that ten shirts, six pairs of pants, half my underwear, travel clock, pens, lighter, odds and ends had been neatly stolen.

Sunday: An all-day outing sponsored by one of the teachers.

Monday: Bus to Naga to movies, as previously promised. Five went, eating before and after. Return to Nabua by bus. Pete (houseboy) and I packed, removed wiring, rushed to get out of house at appointed time. Argument with landlord over wiring, which I had sold without his knowledge to another teacher. Paid him extra month's rent so he wouldn't complain against me for rest of his life. Bus back to Bato to spend night with friend, Wally.

Tuesday: Overnight outing with friends at their farm near Siramag. Two-hour bus ride over extremely bad road.

Wednesday: Boating and skin diving among many-colored coral formations, sea urchins and tropical fish—"ones you pay twenty dollars for in N. Y." Dinner at night with fellow teacher whose son is my godchild. Spent hours listening to stories of *aswang*, *anito* and other supernatural beings. Fascinating how these people, educated and aware of modern science, believe in the power of preposterous beings. Back in Bato, people were waiting for me with beer for another *despedida* ("celebration").

Thursday: A noon and evening affair, given by one of teachers. Mostly eating and playing bingo. Wally was immense help in carrying that affair. When we got back to Bato, discovered I was honored in *despedida* that had started at noon there. Couldn't refuse so spent night eating, twisting, making speeches.

Friday: All day outing to Buhi, lake about thirty kilometers away, planned by one of teachers. Seven of us went in her brother's jeep. Stopped at several spots, eating each time. That night, Free Wheelers gave farewell party and dance for me at school auditorium, with a band, songs, speeches. They gave me an inlaid mother-of-pearl swagger stick, but most appreciated, read a municipal council resolution listing my services to the community and adopting me as a beloved son of Nabua.

Saturday: Found all the teachers waiting for me at elementary school at 9 A.M. for another surprise party in my honor. Had to cut it short to go to wedding. Went to Wally's in Bato to go to bed, but it wasn't meant for me to sleep. His group, the Bato Athletic Association, came about 9 P.M. for another *despedida.* We sent out for rum—the only way I could have gotten through the affair, I'm afraid.

Sunday: Was entertained at dinner at teacher's home, then by more teachers in canteen at school. Too much food, but pleasant because it was family night. I went around room chatting, dancing, and feeling a bit sad to be leaving. They sang very emotional farewell songs, I gave short talk, the acting principal gave one, then we all joined hands and sang "Auld Lang Syne." They hired a jeep to take me back to Wally's because #20 bus had gone. It was much harder to leave Nabua than it was to arrive.

Monday: Pete—the one who really kept me going, carrying messages and fetching fresh clothes—and I got the morning train to Manila. I slept all day on the train.

"And that," concluded Dave, "is how I've been Peace Corps-ing for all you taxpayers. Whether or not we're worth the money you've invested in us remains to be seen. For me, it's worth it, and I'll give you my 'Thank you' for giving me two years which completely surpass anything I've ever experienced by way of understanding the U.S., our culture, myself, and the workings of the Oriental mind. I'm sure I'll be a better American for it, but it's so difficult to communicate why to any of you 'outsiders.' Maybe it is because there are so many new things in us that we feel hesitant to parade our new selves before old friends."

10

We explained that our locals had been well trained and that we hoped they would take over from us. I laughingly explained that I had come to give aid to the Lao and had succeeded in working myself out of a job. The Prince (His Highness Prince Phetserath, Viceroy of Laos, in Luang Prabang, ancient religious capital) exclaimed, "Good!" When he saw my surprise at this he said, "This is what aid should be doctor. It should not make the people dependent upon the aider, or upon the country from which he has come. Aid should work itself into a position where it abolishes any further need of itself." After thinking about this, I agree.

DR. TOM DOOLEY

from *The Edge of Tomorrow*

Few PCVs have worked themselves out of their jobs. Every country where they have served has asked for replacements and for additional Volunteers, far more than the Corps has been able to supply.

For example, since the arrival of the first group of fifty-six PCVs in Pakistan in 1961, two more contingents have gone over; yet when the Pakistan 1 Volunteers were mustered out, the government of East Pakistan asked for another five hundred. After negotiation with the Peace Corps planners, they arrived at a compromise figure of 120. In the face of such great demands and such overwhelming needs, the prospect that the Peace Corps will work itself out of a job seems far-off.

Some nations, however, have already made plans gradually to eliminate their Peace Corps programs. Nigeria, where William G. Saltonstall, former headmaster of Phillips Exeter Academy, is the Peace Corps Director (the only Representative with the title of Director), is one example. That country's plans call for 815 foreign teachers in 1965, 640 in 1966, 215 in 1968, and none in 1970. It is estimated that by 1970 enough Nigerians will have been trained to handle the classrooms. Whether or not this goal is met, the time for the final phasing out on the early projects will come eventually.

At the end of 1963, 728 Volunteers had completed their two years of service in twelve countries in Africa, Asia, and Latin America. During 1964, approximately 2,500 will terminate their service. PCVs are not required to return directly to the United States; since they may draw their funds from the Peace Corps, many have the means to put off their immediate return to the States.

For the Volunteer, the problem of turning over his task—whether to his local counterpart or to another PCV—begins to enter his thinking by about his nineteenth month of service. For those who have no local counterpart and are not being replaced by another PCV, the prospect of departure can be painful. But even when Volunteers know that others are coming to take their jobs, there is uncertainty whether the replacements will really be able to carry on.

Will the local people be capable of continuing the projects? Or will the PCV and his work fade in the minds of the townspeople into a pleasant memory? Should he stay on longer?

The Peace Corps is discouraging any extension of the two-year period of service. If a Volunteer requests an extension to complete a specific job, he may be allowed to stay on for one more year, but no longer. Warren Wiggins, Associate Director for Program Development and Operations for the Corps, has stated, "We don't want the Peace Corps to be a career." The general feeling among PC executives seems to be that the best way to promote a better understanding of other peoples on the part of Americans is to expose as many Americans as possible to such overseas experiences. Furthermore, the executives maintain, a steady turnover of personnel is needed if the Corps is to retain its enthusiasm and vigor.

However, a few PCVs do stay on. A PCV in Ghana wanted an extension, not because he liked working for the Peace Corps, but because he had become so interested in his children in the Fifth Form, which is a crucial year, that he found it too difficult to leave before they had finished their studies. One girl stayed in Pakistan; Dave and Bertie Thaeler remained for a third year in St. Lucia. But my observation is that more PCVs tend to think about re-enlisting as they have completed six months in the field than when they are actually in the home stretch. In the face of frustrations and increased tensions, enthusiasm and energy lessen, and by the last months the PCVs look toward their own futures and necessarily make decisions about what to do next for themselves.

In 1963 the Corps sent a questionnaire to all Volunteers, asking what they planned to do when they returned to the States. (Because many indicated preference for more than one career or kind of training the total below is more than 100 per cent.)

Do You . . .	_Percentage answering Yes_
Want to work—now or later—overseas?	65
Want to continue your education? (Of those answering _Yes_, 88 per cent intended to study at the graduate level, 12 per cent at the undergraduate level; 33 per cent had to have financial help if they were to study; 75 per cent wanted to study in the United States.)	60+
Want to work for the Federal Government in international service for the State Department, USIA, or AID?	34
Want to work on the Peace Corps staff?	29
Want to continue teaching as a career? (Only 13 per cent of those answering _Yes_ had been teachers before joining the Peace Corps.)	25
Plan to work for an international organization? (Of those answering _Yes_, 10 per cent indicated a preference for a non-profit private organization.)	20
Want to work for private business?	12

While the above table may reflect the multiplicity of the Volunteers' interests, it is also an indication of the uncertainty which is common among the PCVs who are about to return home. One reported that within the span of a few days, he applied for a graduate fellowship at the University of Chicago; applied for a teaching position in the Virgin Islands; decided to give up teaching; considered the possibility of becoming a writer; decided that his training and experience pointed toward library science, but admitted he would not like to be a librarian; thought about traveling through Asia, the Middle East, and Europe until his money ran out; and even dreamed about taking the Trans-Siberian Railroad from Vladivostok across Russia, then home via Europe.

"I don't know," he concluded, "maybe the best thing would be to wait until I return to the States before I make a decision."

Frequently, on large projects, new groups of Volunteers arrive while their predecessors are still at their jobs. As a pioneer PCV in the Philippines said:

"We Volunteers are in somewhat of a college situation with its strata of freshmen, sophomores, juniors, and seniors. We of Group 1 are the seniors; the older, wiser, more sophisticated Volunteers. We are listened to, questioned. I could see that those of the newer groups were experiencing the same kinds of things I did early in the experience; those of the middle groups have their devil-may-care attitude toward the Peace Corps, following our pattern of development. I look at the newer Volunteers with a bit of pity, knowing some of the things they'll have to learn and some of the hard times ahead of them."

Outgoing PCVs realize that they broke the ground in their host country and that many of the experiences they have had will not be shared by the newcomers. The old timers are glad that their successors will not have to cope with some of those original problems, but are happy and proud that they had to do the pioneering.

The early Volunteers have laid the foundations of a Peace Corps tradition and lore, complete with folktales that convey the special quality of what it means to be a Volunteer. One (true) tale concerns the PCV in Ethiopia who instituted student government. The local teachers thought it was radical and dangerous, but the PCV went ahead. The students were enthusiastic. They held an election and established a constitution, and the PCV congratulated himself on having introduced a little bit of democracy into the school activities. Then he discovered that the first action the student council proposed was the creation of a secret police force!

Another story is about the Internal Revenue Service in Little Rock, Arkansas. In April, 1963, the tax office there received their first "homemade" income tax return. It was designed and forwarded—with characteristic disregard for red tape— by John Sanders, a twenty-nine-year-old PCV in Tunisia. While unprecedented, the homemade return was accepted by the officials because it contained all the necessary information, including Sanders' social security number, and had attached to it the W-2 forms from Sanders' two employers.

In a ruled column headed I GOT, ingenious John Sanders entered his income—$135.97 from an Arkansas construction company and $229.50 from the Peace Corps, amounting to less than $600 for the year 1962. In a column headed YOU GOT, he showed taxes withheld totaling $20.80. Next to an arrow which pointed to the $20.80 figure, he wrote I SHOULD GET.

Underneath the chart, Sanders added, "No wife, kids, animals, few friends." Then he gave his Arkansas and Tunisia addresses and concluded with, "Thanks."

He received a prompt refund.

Stories like these help to shape a folklore that may inspire, if not guide, many future PCVs.

One problem that has plagued PCVs will certainly be alleviated; there will be fewer vague assignments. Their hosts know now what the Peace Corps can and should do, and the

PCVs will not have to spend as much time discovering what their jobs should be or what they should entail. And the administration in Washington has learned a great deal, too.

In addition to their fears that their successors may be inadequate, there is the usual self-evaluation: "What exactly have I accomplished in two years?" Not enough, most of the PCVs say hypercritically, but some add that it is hard to judge progress.

"We're too close to evaluate ourselves," concluded four PCVs in Somalia, although one man felt that there must be something wrong if they could not evaluate themselves.

"All I know is that more than 75 per cent passed my exam," responded a girl PCV. "My students know as much English in a year as I knew Spanish and that's the only criterion I have. After all, I never taught at home."

The fact that only a fourth of the PCVs now teaching abroad were teaching anything at home has occasioned some disappointment in various countries. "Peace Corps volunteer workers are doing a splendid service," commented H. J. Savory, University of Bristol, England, in his report on school reorganization in Somalia, "but if only they were trained teachers with the same youth and enthusiasm, how much better it would be."

Teaching, however, like road building, construction of schools, etc., can be judged more objectively than relations with foreign people, about which many PCVs are uncertain. Just how good were their relations with their host people and how much impact did they have by their presence? They wish they knew.

"It's much harder to leave than to arrive," said Dave King on the eve of his departure from the Philippines. The majority of Volunteers feel this way, I am sure, for, aside from the endless farewell parties, the PCVs are also faced with a vast array of Peace Corps procedures for departure, the most important of which is the termination conference.

This conference is actually a get-together held in the field six weeks before the two years are completed. Technically, the gathering is a "completion of service conference." At each conference, about thirty PCVs and two Washington staffers meet for two purposes: (1) so that the Peace Corps administration may listen to the suggestions and benefit from the Volunteers' experience; and (2) to help Volunteers relate their experience with the Corps to their plans for the future.

The conference is characterized as informal and, says Washington, is run primarily by the PCVs themselves.

Prior to the discussions, all PCVs are requested to fill out termination reports covering four subjects: (1) sources of satisfaction; (2) sources of frustration; (3) effect of PCVs on the host nationals; (4) changes in the Volunteers' own attitudes, values, beliefs, future plans, etc.

"Some of the reports I read were masterpieces of vagueness and generality," said a Philippines PCV. "Unfortunately, the Rep sent each of us a telegram a few days before the reports were due saying that our termination pay would be withheld if the reports weren't sent in immediately. Then word got around that our team leaders—fellow Volunteers who were chosen early in our service to make an 'in' group—were reviewing the reports. They had had little or no experience in barrio settings, so therefore respect for them among the ordinary Volunteers runs low."

This lack of respect for anyone—even their own leader— who has not had identical experiences seems unfortunate. "The conferences were interesting," said Dr. Edwin Henry, Director of Selection, "in that each PCV came believing that his experience was unique, only to find that all the others had similar ones."

"However, nothing new came out of the conferences," said a girl in Nigeria. "We just re-informed the Peace Corps about everything we've been saying all along."

Dr. Joseph G. Colmen, chief of the Research Division, who has attended conferences in several countries, feels that the discussions at these meetings may provide the basis for changes in the methods of selection, training, and programming for future groups.

"We thought the Volunteers would be guarded," said Dr. Henry. "They're not. They gripe like the Army, and that's healthy."

One of the complaints voiced most often concerned publicity. PCVs dislike being pictured as heroes. Peace Corps publications and the press (which gets most of its information, often complete articles, from PC headquarters) play up the concrete achievements, said Volunteers—the roads, buildings, pig pens—instead of the more subtle achievements within the community, such as winning the villagers' cooperation on a project.

Particularly embarrassed by the emphasis on physical hardships were the PCVs in the cities, where there are such luxuries as shops and movies, and where the results of individual efforts are hard to measure. The emphasis, said the PCVs, should be on the routine, the boredom, the fight for effectiveness, not on glamor.

In most cases, the Volunteers found that they were considerably above the intellectual or educational level of the people with whom they were working, and they therefore sorely missed intellectual stimulation. "I didn't realize the strain until I got back with people," said one girl who was working alone in a Nigerian town of 15,000 for six months.

Hoping to make up, at least in part, for this lack, the Corps adopted the practice of sending footlockers of books to each PCV household. These—when they arrived—were paperbacks meant primarily for the Volunteers' recreational reading, not for classroom use. The move was only partly successful. As Dr. Colmen explained it, "The more you read, the more you want to talk about it."

"I reached a point where I didn't even want to read anything," a PCV told him.

Perhaps this lack of intellectual stimulation contributes as much as the enervating climate to the lethargy that attacks some PCVs before their two years is over. As one remarked to me: "The thing that bothers me is that I no longer really want to work. Several other PCVs have confessed to me the same feeling. I wonder what has happened to make me so lazy."

Another gripe—and no surprise—was about the Peace Corps administration and its failure to handle the Volunteers' requests and inquiries quickly.

According to Dr. Henry, the complaints were based on three principal anxieties: regret that they had not done as much as they should have done; fear that the next PCVs will not do as well; and fear that, when they get home, no one will listen to them.

For PCVs who return early, personal interviews are given in Washington. Each returnee is encouraged to present his point of view, for the Corps hopes to benefit by learning why he returned early and where the selection process went wrong.

In some respects it is more difficult to get out of the Peace Corps than it is to get in. In Nigeria, for example, the termination procedures were set forth in a fifteen-page bulletin which instructed Volunteers in the steps to be taken regarding:

Notification of termination
Travel and transportation
Shipment of unaccompanied baggage
Readjustment allowance and other fiscal matters
Passports, visas, health cards, and Peace Corps identification cards
Disposition of Peace Corps property
Required form to complete prior to departure
Medical requirements
Work or study in or out of Nigeria after termination
Insurance

Termination conferences
Post-Peace Corps travel
Military obligations
Deferment of payment of loans
Certificate and statement of service
Mailing address changes.

As noted earlier, not all PCVs choose to come home directly. Those who intend to work or to study abroad (not merely to travel) may receive their full readjustment allowance (monies due them for two years' salary plus their return travel to the States) if they wish to remain abroad for one academic or calendar year. Those who wish to come home the long way by traveling abroad before returning to the States—and many elect to do this—may receive a cash readjustment allowance equal to the tourist transportation to return home directly. In addition, they may get their due vacation allowance and up to one-third of their net readjustment allowance (seventy-five dollars a month less taxes, insurance, allotments, etc.).

On the work table in the Acting Peace Corps Director's office in Lagos, Nigeria, was the evidence: an eight-inch-high pile of papers—requests for special money—waiting to be processed.

Jane Meleney was going home to Maryland from Nigeria by way of India, Hong Kong, and the western United States. Dave King's itinerary from the Philippines read: "I'll go to Hong Kong for five days, shop for goodies from the Orient, then do Japan in ten days, then to Alaska and home to Indiana by way of Seattle, San Francisco, Los Angeles, Las Vegas, Denver, Chicago, and Fort Wayne."

Sue Sadow, a sixty-six-year-old nutritionist, had an even longer trip planned on leaving Sierra Leone. "It will be a long, long time before I return to the U.S.A. I'm starting a long trek all over Africa. First to Conakry to pick up my boat . . . which stops at twelve ports on the western coast until it reaches Point Norie, Congo, where I get off. From then on I'll probably fly most of the time except for internal rail, car, bus, etc.

I plan to study it all from bottom to top! Africa is a mighty huge continent. It once took me nine months to cover India so who knows how long this will take. I'm greatly interested in Africa, consider it one of the most important spots in the world, as well as the most interesting for travel and learning."

Before a Volunteer leaves his host country he must undergo, in most instances, a more complete medical examination than was required when he applied to the Peace Corps. A full three days is needed (at least in Nigeria) for the medical procedures. The explanation, logically, is that the PCV has been exposed to diseases not prevalent in North America and may, therefore, require treatment before his departure.

Besides multiple chores in getting themselves ready to leave the host country, many PCVs are rushing at the same time to complete the projects only they can finish. "I'm so pressed for time," wrote Sue Sadow. "I'm writing a School Lunch Manual to be given to all schools throughout the country where CARE lunches are served. I'm also writing a Nutrition Guide for PCVs to help them feed themselves properly. And finally, I'm cataloguing all the material I've collected so that my successor will have a well-organized file and reports to refer to before she begins."

Back in the United States, what help can the returnees expect? Under existing legislation, the Peace Corps has no clear authority to undertake career-guidance counseling or job placement service. However, the Carnegie Corporation has given the American Council on Education a grant to establish a pilot placement program for returning Volunteers.

The Ford Foundation in April, 1963, announced $400,000 appropriation to provide fellowships for returning Americans with overseas experience, specifically mentioning PCVs. This grant is expected to enable about eight universities to offer up to seventy-five fellowships for advanced studies, with Penn State administering the program.

Independently, about fifty colleges and universities have announced the availability of scholarships and fellowships for returning Volunteers. Indeed, everyone—in government agencies, public schools, private business—is showing special consideration for them. The late President John F. Kennedy urged repeatedly that returning PCVs seek government careers, particularly in the foreign service, and all departments of the government are cooperating. The Department of State will consider Peace Corps service as qualifying an applicant for an initial appointment to Class 7 rather than the customary Class 8. (The lower the number, the higher the starting salary.) The State Department is doing everything to make application easy for the Volunteer, even to offering an examination overseas in any area where the number of applicants is sufficient to justify it.

The United States Information Agency has also set up special procedures to speed the hiring process. AID, the United States Public Health Service, and the Bureau of Indian Affairs all have expressed interest in interviewing returnees who have certain skills. So have many private agencies.

However, it is worth noting that a large number of the returning PCVs want to go back to school. (See table on page 192.)

"Some may change fields, too," said Director of Selection Dr. Edwin Henry. "The Peace Corps may have ruined a few engineers by making teachers of them; but they probably weren't strong for engineering, or they would have stayed home and worked at it."

Parents who had hoped that their sons and daughters were having their last fling before settling down in the family business or at a good solid job in the United States may be disappointed, for the Volunteers' characteristic desire is to study more, to wander further, and to continue to be disenchanted with business.

In sum, what does it all mean? If volunteering was—as

many in and out of the Corps have suggested—a delaying action, is the PCVs' preoccupation with more education just another way of avoiding employment in the mainstream of our business and competitive system?

Not for all, of course. As Bill and Maryl Levine wrote from Somalia: "We're more eager than ever to do graduate work. But perhaps a four-month vacation would have brought about the same results."

For some there is probably an underlying fear that they will not be accepted, that they will be unable to find jobs easily, that they are not quite fit to compete. For, overseas they have been in a superior position. For two years their only competition has been with other PCVs motivated like themselves. Many have worked alone with little close supervision and with almost no contact with any people of comparable skills. In sharply competitive business organizations, will they stand out as they did in their overseas assignments?

"Returning to the U.S. will be a bigger adjustment than going overseas," predicted Sandy McCaw, Deputy Rep in Togo. "It's fun to be a foreigner, to be different, not just one of nine million people. The attention Volunteers get and the distinctions made for them will not be made back in the States."

I watched with interest two young male Volunteers, both of whom were reputed to have no interest in business or money. After they were offered good positions with two well-known business firms, their attitudes changed. Each reported that he was on "cloud nine." It will be even more interesting to see what they have become and what their feelings will be two years from now.

In job-hunting, most returnees, with their $1,400 termination allowance in hand, can afford to take the time to find the right job. They can be cautious and can weigh the pros and cons in relation to their own needs with considerably more self-understanding and critical self-evaluation than before they

had their Peace Corps experience. Presumably personal satisfaction—not money alone—will be the strongest factor in their
final decision on what to do next.

If the returning PCVs carry out their intentions, there will
be no shortage of lecturers, discussion moderators, and slide
demonstrators after they come marching home More than
half of the Volunteers who responded to the questionnaire I
sent out in 1962 indicated that this is how they would like to
try to share their overseas experiences with the people back
home. Americans are curious about the PCVs who have been
representing them in distant lands. As one PCV told me:

"One of our members was sent home more or less by mutual
agreement between him and the staff. He was a rebel, even in
training. We liked him, but we could understand why he was
sent home. Since his return, he writes that he has been in
great demand as a speaker before civic groups, school assem-
blies, clubs, etc. His calendar for one week listed five speeches
about the Peace Corps. If this can happen to one sent home
under 'dishonorable discharge,' how much more will people
believe what successful Volunteers report?"

Certainly, the majority of Americans believe in the Corps
and wish it nothing but success. Unfortunately, the hopes of
the people back home often exceed what it is possible for a
few thousand PCVs to accomplish, which, it seems to me, may
be dangerous.

I have wondered how effectively the PCVs may be able to
communicate their experiences, especially since several expressed the view that only those who have served can really
understand. Personally, I feel that the answer that reveals
the most insight to the question, "How will you share your
experiences with others?" came from Mike Ruggiero, Togo:
"It's impossible."

Maybe not impossible—but certainly not easy.

PART IV

The Future of the Peace Corps

11

I like to go out and talk to the Volunteers in the field—I get my spiritual battery recharged so I can go back and fight the paperwork battle.

ANDRES HERNANDEZ
Field Representative
Dominican Republic

The Peace Corps involves more than the Volunteers in action; it includes also the management people: the administrators, the recruitment officers, the publicists, and the Field Representatives.

What the Field Representative does, for example, often determines the degree of success or failure in any given country. Yet, even to the most enthusiastic supporters of the Corps, few Reps—so far—have fulfilled their functions in a completely satisfactory fashion. There are abundant reasons, of course. To appreciate the nature of the Reps' problems one should turn to such a highly successful Rep as Representative Andres "Andy" Hernandez of the Dominican Republic, and see how he works.

His daily schedule may be seen at a glance at the blackboard in his office in Santo Domingo:

2:00 P.M.	Adams
3:00	Ambassador
4:00	Minister of Agriculture
5:00	Military mission

But that schedule does not begin to unfold the whole story.

Between two and three, as Andy was telling me how, during their first two months in the field, he and twenty-one agricultural extension workers had created a program where none had existed before, two PCVs who had been stationed in a

remote province dropped in unexpectedly. What they wanted
—besides a day in town—was Andy's authorization to spend
fourteen dollars for some runty chicks to get a 4-H Club
project started. Andy fired a few sharp questions, and told
them to go ahead. To me he elaborated on his plans to
increase the chicken and egg production. The eggs could be
sold to Alcoa, and the profit would go to the Dominicans who
tended the poultry.

Then the Peace Corps physician, Dr. Trumper, dropped in
for a talk, and there were also several telephone calls that
required intense discussion and decision. Andy's secretary
came in with a number of messages, and then Andy's assistant
appeared—for counsel on several urgent matters.

I listened as Andy slipped effortlessly from Spanish to
English and back to Spanish. He asked questions, reflected,
and gave instructions. Leaving me in the spacious but almost
empty office to talk with the visiting PCVs, he drove off in his
jeep to call on the American ambassador. He returned in time
for his 4 P.M. appointment. I accompanied him on the ride
past the beautiful stucco government buildings which sprawl
over several blocks. The Minister of Agriculture was not in
his office.

"I'll just keep coming back until I catch him," said Andy,
with no visible irritation. "This happens all the time."

After two months, he had become used to going ahead on
his own. "We couldn't keep the men in hotels, so I'd take a
Volunteer to a village, introduce him to the key people, teachers, and so on, and find him a house. He'd eat, unpack, and
visit a few people. Then what does he do? The community
won't even talk to him. That's where the Rep comes in. He
gets a project going, then he brings in *his assistant*—the Volunteer—and turns it over to him."

The initial project, carried out with the approval of Dr.
Trumper, had been to donate blood to the Red Cross blood
bank. For this contribution, which required no native col-

laboration, the PCVs received favorable publicity in the newspapers and in a newsreel movie, especially when it became known that, three days afterward, PCV Harvey Hartley's RH negative blood had saved the life of a Dominican infant.

Anyone who meets Rep Andy Hernandez senses quickly that this quiet, thoughtful person in his forties is a man accustomed to getting things done. He wears combat boots, smokes cigars, and gives the impression of having spent a lot of time outdoors. His honesty and integrity are apparent, it seems to me, from his lined features. Of Mexican-American parentage, Hernandez walks and talks easily with the Dominicans. If anyone is suited to weather the shifting political climate in a place like the Dominican Republic, he is.

His humility, which seems to be part of his strength, and his keen sense of what is right politically, serve him well. Both were evident in his end-of-the-year report in the *PCVolunteer* of September, 1963. He listed the accomplishments of the Peace Corps but wisely credited the citizens of the Dominican Republic, particularly the *campesinos*, or "peasant farmers," with cooperation.

His sensitive appreciation of people enabled him to inspire the Volunteers, too. When interviewing a PCV assigned to him, he might ask quietly:

"Can you make bricks?"

"Can you build a privy?"

"Can you lay out a baseball diamond?"

"Can you vaccinate a chicken?"

"Can you mix concrete?"

"When I get all *No's*—which I generally do—then I'll say 'Good! Just what we want, a nice clean sheet. The Peace Corps will write on it.' "

He felt that such questions should have been asked early in the selection period. If such data were compiled and kept on file in Washington, the records could be made available to Reps who needed PCVs with specific skills. But he had been working with government agencies too long to wait around for men who were adequately trained for their jobs. He had spent ten years with the Veterans' Adminstration and four years in the Army. Besides, he had a great advantage: he could handle people, he could make them feel that they wanted to work with him, and he knew how to train them on the job. But he confessed that he had been hired by the Corps before he knew what was happening to him.

"AID had tried to hire me, and I thought this job was part of the same deal," he said.

On the need for versatility, he went on: "A Volunteer needs to be a farmer, a lawyer, a teacher, everything. People ask a variety of questions, not just on one subject. When I was in forestry in New Mexico, people came to me for all sorts of help—how to fill out a Montgomery Ward order, how to survey land, how to fix a leaky roof, everything."

Campesinos and their simple ways of life did not shock Andy Hernandez. The ability to relate to people and that skill at "making do" came from his childhood experiences. He recalls sleeping in a bed with several other children, with coats to cover them because they had no blankets. He had gone to work early, as a small boy, and had worked at dozens of different jobs.

When his father was only twelve he had crossed the border from Mexico to El Paso. Later, he had married an American girl; Andy was one of their nine children. The father, entirely self-taught himself, had sent all his children to school and had built each of them a house. Ultimately, he became the chief machinist for the Sante Fe Railroad, but he never confined himself to any one kind of work. When the barber in town went to jail and left a large family without a breadwinner, the senior Hernandez operated the barber shop in his free time. Andy had shined shoes there. All the money they had earned had been turned over to the wife of the barber. (The jailed man eventually was pardoned.)

When he was still a child one of Andy's regular chores was to tramp over every night to a neighbor's house and read the papers aloud to them. "But it won me a 'good boy' status which I had to live up to," he mused.

He had had his first fights with the Anglo-Saxon kids in a high school that had formerly been closed to Mexicans. He had been the first Spanish-speaking boy at that school.

"We had a Spanish-speaking Boy Scout troop, but we had no money," Andy reminisced. "On the overnight hikes, the Anglo-Saxon kids brought food and equipment, but we didn't have anything to take. My Dad was put on the troop committee to furnish transportation, so one time he saw what the other kids brought.

"The next month, Dad said for me to leave one of our pigs out and to run it up the gulley. Then he picked up the hog on the railroad engine, took it to the roundhouse where he slaughtered, scalded, and steamed it—and my troop had pork chops for breakfast on the hike."

During the depression Andy's father, like so many others, was unemployed. To pass the time they went daily to watch the trains go by. One day his father said, "Well, let's go see what the Lord gives us." They went down to the railroad siding. A cattle train was letting calves off in the desert. Andy and his father voluntarily pitched in and helped. Andy remembers that his father unlocked the water tank, and they watered the cattle. One of the cattlemen pointed to a calf with an injured leg. "You can take that one," he said.

"We got a wheelbarrow to cart the calf away. Later, we butchered the calf, and we took chunks around to all the neighbors. At the time, I couldn't understand why. Another time, when we were given all the eggs we could take home, my Dad made us share those, too, with our neighbors."

In 1933, Andy joined the CCC (Civilian Conservation Corps). In camp, he learned forestry, fire fighting, how to build fences and dams, and how to control erosion. "I studied hard and got the foreman's job. Then the University of New Mexico and Carnegie Corporation hired me to do adult education work in northern New Mexico. Taos County is like Latin America. There, too, we were helping people pull themselves up by their bootstraps."

Andy's most recent job experience had been in Guatemala where for five years he did community development work for International Development Services, Inc. "I know every farmer in Guatemala," he said proudly. "I helped settle five thousand under the agrarian reform project."

Since the PCVs arrived in the Dominican Republic, they had been visited at least once a week by a member of Andy's field staff. He himself tried to see each PCV every other week, but that became increasingly difficult as the number of Volunteers grew. On alternate weeks, his deputy or Dr. Trumper called on them.

"I like to go out and talk to the Volunteers in the field," Andy declared. "I get my spiritual battery recharged so I can go back and fight the paper-work battle. When PCVs need help, they come into the office. I plan to be in on Monday and Friday, and out covering the provinces from Tuesday to Thursday."

He showed me the records of their meetings. "I have a diary on every project—its progress and its problems. Just a one-sentence entry on a file card each time I talk with a Volunteer about the status of his project. All I have to do is look at the last few sentences and I have the whole story."

His ingenuity—his skill in making do with the materials at hand—is concentrated on his present job. His chief concern was the water shortage.

Everywhere we saw people standing in line in the mud, waiting for water from a pump or a faucet.

"No wonder they don't wash much," he said. "They carry water all their lives. Of twenty-two well rigs in the country, only five work. Operators let them break down; they never do any preventive maintenance. 'It's not my property,' they say, so they don't fix it.

"We must dig a thousand wells. I'm sure we'll find water underground. In fact, we found it at eleven feet in one place. We got a motor and an old worn-out pump, just to show people. It didn't work right, but still in two minutes we'd emptied the well.

"I'm going to invent some simple equipment that'll do the job, though. We ought to be able to make some well equipment out of junk parts, local materials, and a little elbow grease."

Andy had already "invented" a number of useful gadgets, including a well digger to grind up mud and rocks. He had figured out a way, based on simple geometric principles, to lay out a square-cornered building without an engineering transit. He had designed a fruit stand which he considered an improvement over the local version (a roof on four legs, constructed at the side of a road), and he was planning a simple peanut press to enable the Dominicans to extract the oil for themselves instead of paying to have the nuts shipped and pressed. He also hoped to start the local people on profitable homecrafts, like the making of shirts, trousers, and even shoes.

"You always have to start with the home first," he said.

At "brain sessions" with the Volunteers, Andy talked about these ideas and many more—how to build a satisfactory refrigerator, how to make a baler to get the mud out of wells, how to manufacture adobe bricks, the best methods of raising chickens and rabbits. Some of the tougher problems—designing a pump that would operate on solar batteries, obtaining paint for screen wire that would not flake, finding a means to keep bread from molding—he had submitted to several professors at MIT who had offered to help solve problems in the underdeveloped countries. He was still waiting for their answers.

Some of his suggestions for overall U.S. policy on aid to

other countries might be considered "far-out," yet, recognizing his experience and his understanding of people, they sounded reasonable to me.

"Many other governments use private companies to get what they want. The U.S. should do this more. Private companies have to produce, they're always better run; they have to plan, to report monthly what they've done; their estimates have to come close.

"I think the proposal that we give the *campesinos* in Venezuela roads, schools, and so forth, in return for oil was a sensible one. But our government has to set its goals first. Our activity is too dispersed now. We need to survey our long-range and our immediate goals. What do we need to do? Who-where-why-when-how? Once we're clear about that, then we ought to take a more active part in politics. Back both candidates; then whoever wins, we can say we contributed.

"One thing we must do—somehow, we must team up the Peace Corps with money for health care, glasses, teeth, pumps, books and supplies. We can't do the job without equipment. There's already a great deal of intermingling with private aid programs, as well as with those of our government and those of the Dominican Republic. Some people worry about this, but I'm in favor of more cooperation between the various agencies.

"And another suggestion. Why doesn't each American university pick a region and set up an off-campus library? These shouldn't be government controlled, but the government could give the leadership. Students could come over for a year. This could be a vital, dynamic contribution to world peace."

While the Corps takes no active part in the politics in the host countries, Andy's interest in political matters is an asset. He has an advantage over most Reps, for he can attend meetings and mix with the crowds and bring away impressions on the thoughts and emotions of the people. In the Dominican Republic—where three changes of government occurred during the Corps' first year there—this assessment of the local mood was important.

"I go to all the riots and demonstrations," he told me. "This way I know what's happening or may be about to happen."

As to the Volunteers themselves, Andy's chief concern was for the spiritual side of their lives. "The Peace Corps has slipped up on religion," he said. "We're negligent in not providing religious outlets for PCVs. It's easier for Catholics in a Catholic country to attend mass regularly, but the other faiths have fewer opportunities for worship. The Army had chaplains; every government organization always did until the Peace Corps."

When I raised this question at headquarters in Washington, a selection officer repeated the official position: "We don't even know or ask what faith they belong to."

When I first met Andy he had been at work for two months, and admitted that the effort to get a few projects started had exhausted him. Yet ten months later, he reported enthusiastically on the activities sparked by PCVs and said he was looking forward to initiating several new projects now that the group had grown to 144.

"We can't hope to make everyone rich," he said. "All these people need is to become better political citizens in a democracy."

To help them accomplish this was his mission and his goal.

Not every group was fortunate in having an Andy Hernandez for their Rep. As Sargent Shriver pointed out, "There was no precedent for what these men would have to do in programming, logistics, and personal support for the Volunteers in their charge." A few Reps have stayed with their projects for the full term, but, in general, the Rep turnover has been high.

I was told by a Rep who had been discharged but had never been told why, that thirty-three out of 135 Field Representatives had been preemptorily dismissed by Washington; many others had left of their own accord long before their two years were up. In most of the places I visited there had been at least one change in Reps; in two instances, the Reps to whom I had talked never received my letters of thanks—by the time my letters appeared they were gone.

What makes the Rep's job so tough? That's a question PCVs ask all the time.

On the plane to Africa, I met a young couple I knew from the States. They had been teaching in Somalia and had developed an excellent relationship with the other teachers and with their headmaster. It was so good, in fact, that their fellow staffers helped them build a house. But before they moved into their new home, the PC Rep in the area asked for their resignations. They claimed they were not given sufficient reason for this peremptory action. The school staff was upset, the headmaster wanted them to stay, but the couple was brought home. However, they had been cleared for reassignment and were now on their way to Nigeria. "I'm going to stay as far away from the administration as possible this time," said the young man. "I can work fine with the local people if I'm left alone."

Unfortunately, many PCVs feel this way. Indeed, I heard almost no praise for their administrators—Field Representatives and Washington staffers alike. PCVs who were not openly critical spoke apologetically of the difficulties of setting up and running a new organization. From Sierra Leone came this indictment: "In spite of the Peace Corps office in Washington, we are out here working, making friends, and learning. In Washington, they just don't have any idea of what is happening out here, and unless someone comes out and stays at least two months they never will. I've been here six months plus, and still our PC Representative hasn't seen the place or asked what is going on up here. I am a carpenter who was sent out to teach woodworking and no one will provide any tools for the students in the school. These people have to take turns using the tools I brought with me."

The negative views Volunteers expressed about their leaders, both overseas and at headquarters, are represented by the following comments from PCVs.

"What sort of help, advice, back-up does our Rep give? None. The group is doing a good job in spite of our administrators. The happiest ones are the ones farthest from the thick of it. The leadership I've seen overseas is deplorable. Compared to a Boy Scout leader or a corporation executive, it's criminal. I'm talking about people we've seen here. It shouldn't happen. Either we overvalue ourselves and think we're awfully good and everybody else is pretty bad—but I don't think so. I'm shocked."

"I have a feeling there is a group of eager beavers in Washington, professional do-gooders or political opportunists. I almost want to disassociate myself; I don't like to be in this kind of company."

"I'm appalled by the size of the Washington staff. Every time we get a letter, it's signed by somebody new, a sub, sub, sub something or other." (More likely the new "sub" is a replacement on, not an addition to, the staff, which is limited in size by the Peace Corps Act.)

"I'm incensed at the threats that our pay may be held up, or that we may get a 'dishonorable discharge' because Washington doesn't like what we do. I heard that seven Volunteers were sent home, 'discharged for insubordination,' and the administrator sent a university official on the project a telegram listing their last names—after they were discharged."

"The kind of letters we receive here in the field—you wouldn't believe that anyone could initiate or write this kind of garbage. Most letters wouldn't get a C in Freshman English. I'd rather have no letter than a bunch of garbage like that. Say somebody spends ten minutes typing it on a $500 electric typewriter, then the PC spends 25¢ mailing it, and it's worse than useless. It's stupid to send this kind of idiot letter. And all our letters from Washington are this way—sweetness and light."

These comments are about the harshest I heard, yet they are indicative of the kind of criticism that PCVs voice about the Peace Corps administration. Even if such statements were motivated by frustration or personal grudges, the question remains: What makes the Rep's job so tough that he can apparently please no one?

The Rep is caught in a policy conflict, which inevitably affects the Volunteer. Representatives are supposed to act according to two incompatible codes. On the one hand, they are to respect the freedom and independence of the Volunteers. The PCVs should be allowed to act on their own initiative and should be permitted to make their own decisions. "Our Volunteers are truly volunteers," maintains Director Sargent Shriver. "We don't order them to do anything." Reports from the field, however, belie this, for on the other hand, there is a growing pressure on the Reps to set up standardized procedures paralleling those followed by the State Department for overseas personnel. Two of the top administrators of the Peace Corps—Warren Wiggins and William Josephson—have backgrounds in government service. So have several of the recently appointed Reps.

As David King, a Volunteer in the Philippines, wrote to me:

"About PC Representatives—I feel rather unsure of the nature of their jobs. Some, I know, sign up for only one year. Their job is surely a demanding one. All our problems are dumped on their laps and they serve as eternal listening posts. I don't know how much of that a man can stand. At first they worked for a poorly organized outfit, and even though they wanted to give adequate support to us in the field, Manila Peace Corps headquarters for the Philippines was unprepared to support them.

"Another contributing factor might be that they were col-

lege professors doing administrative work and they were learning as they went along, just as we were. Perhaps some of
them didn't fit this role, and as anywhere in any job, if you
don't like it or can't do it, you quit. I know little of the
Philippines scene, except that our new Bicol region Rep,
Charlie Dey, is well liked for his attitudes (he says that he
wouldn't want to do what we're doing, doesn't know if he
could, but is here to help us in any way he can in what we're
doing). If we want a bicycle, we get one. If our radio needs
repair, there's another one to take its place. I have the highest
respect for him and the way he does his job."

"I was replaced by a State Department career man," said
an ex-Rep college professor. "Haven't you noticed that—
except for Saltonstall—the Peace Corps is now hiring young
Reps of no prominence but who often have legal or administrative backgrounds? The trend is to standardize the post of
Peace Corps Rep. The Corps is becoming manipulative instead of adaptive. We're suggesting projects and pressing to
get into countries, instead of waiting until we're asked."

As this trend continues—and what will halt it as long as the
Peace Corps is expanding and operating as an arm of foreign
policy?—then the long-range question is: How can an organization with chains of command, rules, regulations, reports,
procedural manuals, etc., continue to attract, recruit, and send
into the field Volunteers who are able to innovate and initiate
their own projects and to act as individuals?

In practice, these two irreconcilable concepts make the
Rep's job arduous and account for the widespread dissatisfaction with the Reps and with the Washington administrators.
Headquarters has encouraged Reps to get out in the field more
often, to visit the Volunteers. Yet, at the same time, the Reps
are being pressured to spend more time in their offices writing
reports to Washington, keeping their files up to date, and
attending to fiscal matters. They are expected, on the one
hand, to encourage Volunteers to be independent and, on the

other, to ride herd on them to conform and to stay out of trouble—in other words, to avoid incidents that might result in publicity unfavorable to the Corps.

"Supposedly I was too easy-going with Volunteers, not firm enough," said an ex-Rep. "But it's pretty hard for them to grasp this dichotomy—that they're free to behave as they see fit as long as it agrees with Peace Corps and U.S. policies. I'm a college professor, not an administrator, but Shriver knew this when he hired me. I got along well with the Volunteers because I'm used to giving young people some leeway to make their own mistakes.

"Another thing—I was told that Reps would be like ambassadors who have direct contact with their chief, the President, when they feel this is necessary. For us, the lines of communication were never established, even in minor matters. For instance, I had a terrible secretary whom I wanted to fire, but I had no way to get rid of her."

The shift to more rigid organizational procedures may result in greater efficiency and better communications, which PCVs have been demanding since the beginning of the Corps, although probably few had the foresight to realize that efficiency would be gained at the price of the independence they value so highly.

After the happy confusion in the early days of the Corps, Washington headquarters gradually took on a more business-like atmosphere and appearance. When I began my research on the Corps, it was difficult to find people who had the answers to my questions, or even knew where I might get the answers. A year and a half later, responsibilities had been delegated, jobs were more clearly defined, facts and figures had been compiled and made available in printed form.

By and large, I found that the PCVs were more successful than the administrative staff in achieving the goals outlined in the Peace Corps Act. Certainly the PCVs have a better record for sticking to their jobs. But the Corps is extremely vulnerable to criticism, and when I recall the international furor generated by one little postcard written by PCV Margery Michelmore in Nigeria—which stated only facts and did not exaggerate—I am sympathetic to the Corps' administrators who want to prevent such incidents. Demands were voiced within the government of Nigeria that the Corps be withdrawn because Margery had described "primitive" living conditions.

As C. Payne Lucas, the Acting Representative in Togo, pointed out, "Individuals abroad don't have to maintain certain prescribed standards. But the Peace Corps has to build and preserve an image, and the Volunteers' actions constitute that image."

Directives from the Peace Corps headquarters in Washington account for only part of the pressure on the Rep. The PCVs, too, expect a great deal of him. I remember the routine of Rep Andy Hernandez: two days in the office, three in the field—the five days being apportioned to appointments with Dominican officials, writing reports to Washington, counseling the Volunteers, inventing gadgets, planning projects, keeping records, attending political rallies, and maintaining contacts with local people. The requests for favors Andy received from the PCVs were light compared to what I saw elsewhere.

In Togo, for example, I accompanied Acting Deputy Representative Sandy McCaw to visit three girl teachers who lived together. Within five minutes, we were asked to borrow glasses from the hostel for the Volunteers' forthcoming party; to borrow a record player from the Rep for the party; to ask the doctor for one girl's worm medicine; to tell an official at AID that one of the girls had already arranged to teach class during the summer; to notify a man in another village, if we saw him, that one of the girls was coming for the week-end; to deliver a letter to a doctor at Sokodé hospital when we went there; to send the transcript of a program about the Peace Corps that had appeared on TV.

The next day was much the same. Sandy drove one girl to the airport, drove another to school to help clarify some situation, etc. To these PCVs the Rep was obviously someone to carry messages and run errands. And while there may be a real need in countries where communications depend on word of mouth and transportation is primitive or erratic, the Peace Corps' reputation, after all, is built around the Volunteers' reputation for self-sufficiency and maturity.

At a cocktail party at the home of Acting Rep Lucas, two girl PCVs who were leaving called to a British Embassy official whose car and driver were waiting to take him home, "We're going to borrow your car and driver for fifteen minutes, O.K.?" When the official's wife appeared, obviously ready to leave herself, her husband could only say, "Not right now, dear. We have to wait for our car to come back for us."

Rep Lucas obviously enjoyed the role of father confessor to the PCVs. "I know about things almost before they happen," he said. "But it's rough. They are forty-four human beings of many disciplines—fishermen, older men, college grads, a wide age span. Teachers are used to academic freedom to do as they please. For some of the PCVs, it's their first job.

"A Rep can never predict when a PCV has passed the critical point in reaching his adjustment and will make it for the duration. The one who seems weakest, perhaps from a broken home, may be the most solid citizen in the Corps. The one who is tops in class, and who looks great, may not adjust. But the Rep's time is taken up by the marginal Volunteer. It's a twenty-four-hour job, seven days a week, and it saps your strength. A Rep can't let anyone quit if he can save him. It might ruin their careers or at least hinder them in their job-hunting later, and it will certainly hurt the project."

Often a Rep serves as a procurement officer. In Gabon, when Rep Bill Willtz and his team arrived to construct schools, they discovered that they would have to obtain the sand,

gravel, and other materials themselves (besides putting up
tents to live in, building walks, latrines, etc.). Sandy McCaw
who went to Gabon to research secondary education, had to
go off to hunt for building materials, about which she knew
little.

"We found no site and no budget. The Minister of Education agreed to the desirability of progress, but no one was
doing anything about schools," Sandy said. "I had to go out
to the gravel pits, hunting for bargains, collecting, scrounging
to get what was needed. I had to deal with two or three hundred people to get enough gravel for one school. And, of
course, I bought some that was unusable because I didn't
know how to buy it.

"But morale in that group was good; there was no chance
to live high. It took initiative just to live with leaky tents,
wet soggy grass, and equipment that didn't work. Despite the
difficulties, four school buildings have been dedicated so far."

As with the Volunteers, the Rep's endurance is often taxed
by the number of jobs he must create for Volunteers who have
arrived in a country only to discover that the positions they
came to fill do not exist.

"Just bringing about the conditions that make it possible
to do a job is a slow process and takes a hell of a lot of
patience," said one Rep. "You have to develop the host's
mentality to accept the help—he may think the local doctors
or teachers are tops—and you have to baby and cajole the
Volunteers to shift assignments. A college grad wants to teach,
not spend all his time on tact, psychology, diplomacy."

In Nigeria, the story, according to the field staff, was quite
different. "Our Volunteers need very little back-up," said
Acting Representative Bill Kruse, who had formerly been a
field officer in Ethiopia. "The Nigerian government furnishes
housing and the Peace Corps distributes kits containing sheets,
fly swatters, and so forth, and the Volunteers take over from
there."

While I was in Kruse's office, a male PCV telephoned for permission to buy a dugout canoe and a motor for river trips. Kruse approved the expenditures. "It's the only way he can get out during the rainy season," he explained to me.

But the PCV, not Kruse, had to locate and purchase the equipment.

Every director I met felt that his job would be simplified if he had some means of disciplining the PCVs, though no one could suggest any sanctions that would be feasible. One cannot impose a curfew on the Volunteers, nor reduce their pay; they cannot be demoted or refused promotion or a raise, because they are not subject to such incentives. Under present conditions, a Rep may send a PCV home for serious misconduct, but this is a drastic step, rarely taken. Some Reps feel that fewer problems of discipline would arise if the PCVs had no Reps on whom to shift responsibility for their own actions.

"If Volunteers had come over here on their own they would never have let some of the behavior problems arise," stated Acting Rep Lucas. "They simply don't take responsibility; they turn it over to the office and the administration.

"For example, there are rules about the use of PC jeeps. Volunteers know the rules, but instead of hopping on a bike or taking a mammy wagon to get where they want to go, they ask the Rep for the jeep, thus transferring the responsibility to him."

"I'd like to experiment with ten PCVs in a country without a Rep," said Sandy McCaw. "Many private individuals work overseas without close supervision. It would have to be tried in a country where the Volunteers' presence would be a minor political issue—where the government wasn't in turmoil and PCVs weren't in danger of being taken as hostages, for example. I'll bet they'd perform differently if they were completely responsible for themselves and had no one to call on for aid."

A similar view was expressed by Norman Parmer, based on his experiences as a Rep in Malaya. Writing in the *PCVolun-*

teer, May, 1963, he addressed himself directly to PCVs:

The Peace Corps in Malaya has made a *fair* start. It has been no more than that. The potential of the Peace Corps in Malaya has not even begun to be realized. Adjustment to job, climate, and the new social environment have been good, but these should not be equated with success, personally or for the Peace Corps. Such adjustments are at most only the necessary prerequisites to improving and expanding on one's usefulness, one's work.

You may ask, what work? What can I do? The answers cannot be supplied by any member of the Peace Corps administration. Each individual's work-and-living situation is different; each person's interests, initiative, energy, and personal tact differ. Moreover it would be presumptuous and ill-conceived for a staff member to tell you what you can or should do. But obviously there is a lot to be done. A number of Volunteers have found or developed useful projects ranging from book collections for school libraries, through toy collections for children's wards, leading Girl Guide troops, and helping handicapped children to working in one's spare time in a state land-development scheme. But at most, probably not more than 30 per cent of you have developed such projects . . . .

Perhaps you would say that the administrative staff should make proposals. You can be sure that the staff should make proposals. You can be sure that the staff will do its best in this respect. But the Peace Corps is Volunteers. The staff is there primarily to give guidance and assistance.

In thinking about what you can do, I suggest you start by reconsidering why you joined the Peace Corps. What were your reasons, your motivations? What did you hope to contribute, to accomplish by joining? What did you (or do you) want the Peace Corps to be? What have you done since your arrival in Malaya to contribute to the Peace Corps goals and its achievements to date? In thinking about these questions, don't shift the responsibility for any negative answers to anyone else—to the Washington or Kuala Lumpur administrators. Consider that you are in fact in Malaya; you are left pretty much alone as to your work and social relationships. How much initiative have you displayed? Ask yourself what you have done and what you can do with what you have to work with.

Giving the Volunteers greater autonomy might be an interesting experiment. But it seems unlikely that the administration would agree to that. It is more likely that the role of the Field Rep will evolve into a routinized government staff job and that the Corps will seek a less creative person to fill it. For the Corps now has two images to preserve: that of a smooth-running organization that conforms administratively to the pattern of other overseas operations of the government, and that of the band of free-wheeling Volunteers who work on a new frontier.

I can see no easy solution or compromise. I do not believe that a bureaucratic organization can attract independent, self-motivated Volunteers. However, Volunteers and Reps will undoubtedly have fewer opportunities for pace-setting in the second two years of the Corps' existence. But the Peace Corps cannot stand still.

"The way in which this project is managed and whether the enthusiasm is sustained or dies away like a juke box hit song," editorialized the *Nation* during the early days of the Corps, "will be a test of America's qualifications for international cooperation in the sixties."

12

They don't look so bad.
BROOKLYN LONGSHOREMAN
commenting on a contingent of
Volunteers departing for Colombia

Since the inception of the Peace Corps in 1961, almost every one has expressed an opinion of the Volunteers, including, of course, the Volunteers themselves.

"We're just average—don't make us sound different, because we're not," pleaded Kenneth Gibbs, a PCV in Jamaica.

"They're a cut above average," said Professor John Landgraf, PC Representative in Borneo.

"They're way below average," insisted a disappointed instructor of physical education.

"Their IQ's are well above average," said Dr. John J. Sullivan, New York University psychologist.

"Physically we're getting the average soft American," diagnosed Dr. Nicholas C. Leone, Medical Director of a U.S. Public Health Service clinic.

"If they're so average, why send them?" asked a critic.

"Why not send the average? We want the world to know us as we are, not only our best or our worst," replied a Peace Corps supporter.

James Reston, chief of the Washington bureau of the New York *Times*, wrote: "Most [of the PCVs] are young men in their twenties, just out of college, motivated by service and adventure. They symbolize a kind of protest of the postwar generation against the theory that American youth is seeking material security more than anything else. Part of the appeal of their jobs is that they are desperately needed, and are given responsibility without long years of training."

David Riesman, Professor of Social Relations at Harvard, stated: "By talking to the Japanese students about the Peace Corps . . . I was seeking to delineate the new type of young American: sensitive, not greedy or power-hungry, versatile and capable but not purse-proud about it, cooperative but not conformist, tolerant and unfanatical, not liking to throw his weight around and not liking his country to throw its weight around either."

The distinguished British historian, Dr. Arnold Toynbee, wrote in Nicosia's *Cyprus Mail* on March 8, 1962: "He [a PCV] recognizes that, if he is to establish a human relationship with the people of the country where he is going to work, he will have to do this in their language, not in his own. This is a revolution indeed, and it is to be hoped that its effects will spread from Americans who have served in the Peace Corps to other Americans serving abroad and to their fellow countrymen at home."

People who criticize the Volunteers, or judge them at all, whether favorably or unfavorably, base their judgments on their own particular frame of reference: an evaluation by a physical education coach will naturally be different from an evaluation by a psychologist or a historian. It should be no surprise, therefore, that the parents of the Volunteers express a unique point of view.

"He's always been a non-conformist, the kind of guy who has to move a golf tee over just a few inches," was Pete Wemhoff's description of his son Dan, one of the first PCVs in Colombia. "He never cared about money. Why, when Danny was a boy and I'd offer to pay him for mowing the lawn, he'd refuse. 'I don't want to be paid, Dad. I enjoyed doing it,' he'd say. Not like the other kids.

"When he was in Colombia, we sent him a hundred dollars for Christmas and he brought back about ninety dollars eight months later. He was wearing a pair of beat-up loafers that he had when he left because he didn't think the shoes in Colombia were worth the price. He doesn't want to get married and take on the responsibilities of a family, but he doesn't want to be a priest either. I just don't know.''

Dick Zecher's mother was equally bewildered by her son's decision to join the Corps. "I wouldn't have minded so much if he'd been home longer, but he had just got back from Germany two months ago," she said. "All of a sudden one day, he decided to go take the Peace Corps test."

After he took the test, the subject of the Corps was dropped for several weeks. Then a telegram came for Dick. His mother immediately forwarded it to the *Carthage Republican Tribune,* the weekly newspaper for which Dick was working. Later, she telephoned her son and asked from whom the telegram had come.

"Sargent Shriver," he replied.

"Oh, stop your nonsense and tell me," his mother retorted.

Dick read the telegram to her. It *was* from Sargent Shriver; Dick had been accepted by the Peace Corps.

I talked with the Zechers shortly before Dick was due home on final leave prior to going to the Philippines. His father was employed in the Crown-Zellerbach paper mill, the only industry of any size in their small upstate New York town. Dick has two younger sisters and an older brother—a lawyer— who thought Dick was participating in a wonderful effort.

"I just wish he wouldn't come home on leave, that's all," his mother said.

I suggested that she might feel differently when she saw and talked with him.

"Maybe, but we'll have to talk the first few days he's home because I'll be no good later," she replied wistfully.

Of course, there has been a certain degree of variation in the parental reactions, as the following statements from the PCVs indicate:

From Tanganyika: "My friends were enthusiastic, and three of them have since joined, but my parents were dubious because it cut into my graduate studies."

From Thailand: "My young friends—strong yes! Married, more settled friends—either criticism or jealousy. Many in my family and some of the family friends were against it, but they have since done an about face and feel it is good. Personally, it was my decision and I didn't much care how others reacted."

From Nigeria: "My parents said—if you really want this, then we want it for you, but we think you are taking a big chance; we admire you for taking it."

From Malaya: "My family was very pleased and proud of my being accepted, many friends thought I was crazy to take two years out of my career with no salary and no car."

From the Philippines: "They were surprised. My mother opposed the idea and my father said I should go if I thought it was the thing to do. Then I convinced my mother."

Another from Thailand: "My mother and father were dead set against the idea, but the rest of the family and friends thought it was quite an opportunity."

From Chile: "My parents felt apprehension about the effects on my health, safety, and future opportunities after service. They have since become reconciled and approve of the idea."

Another from the Philippines: "My family reacted favorably on the whole. Many friends didn't see how we could break up our home. My parents and in-laws miss us and vice versa, but are not opposed. They regard us as independent adults."

From Togo: "Everyone at home thinks I'm a nut, yet many of my friends wish they had the courage to join."

Another from the Philippines: "Some thought I was insane, others thought it a wonderful opportunity. My parents were reluctant at first because of the distance but are happy for me now because I am enjoying my life here."

Another from Chile: "My family approved 100 per cent, but many of my friends saw no value in the Peace Corps."

Another from the Philippines: "Everyone was proud that I had been accepted, some were a little envious. My father didn't want me to go, my mother would volunteer if she could, friends would also like to do so."

The parents of PCVs serving overseas are anxious chiefly over matters like: What happens if they fall ill? What happens if they fall in love? Peace Corps reassurances about such natural phenomena have done little to quiet parental fears.

"Some Volunteers do get malaria or dysentery," states a Peace Corps pamphlet, "but we provide good medical care. And loneliness may lead to some marriages of which parents may not approve. But this happens at home, too."

For parents who become panicky, the Peace Corps has provided a person whom we might call a "Parent Counselor," but who is listed in "Who's Who in the Peace Corps" as "Special Assistant to the Chief of the Division of Volunteer Field Support." This position is occupied by Ruth Olsen, an understanding woman who acts as informant and counselor to the parents.

"I have probably the most rewarding, but also one of the most frustrating jobs in the Corps," said Mrs. Olsen. "It's impossible for me to comply with many of the requests I get."

Most of these requests come from parents who are checking on the whereabouts and welfare of their children and who ask what to send and how to ship it to unfamiliar places, and, incidentally, want to discuss many of their other concerns.

Mrs. Olsen also keeps the confidential records on marriages, births, and other personal matters relating to the PCVs. She expressed amazement at the low rate of early returns to the United States—only 6 per cent yearly for all causes—and at what she considers the surprisingly few extramarital pregnancies. The figures on the latter are confidential.

The Peace Corps' attitude toward sex is very intelligent, in my opinion, although not all volunteers would agree with me. "We've been lucky so far," one Volunteer told me, "there have been no serious problems. The administration faces up to the question pretty frankly. After all, you've got men and women living together in unfamiliar surroundings. But we're treated as adult Americans who can live as we please except when our actions impinge on the Peace Corps image. But when a girl wants to leave for home, the doctor comes right out with it: 'Are you pregnant?' If she insists she isn't, then he says: 'O.K., let's take the exam right now. Go in the other room and get undressed.' "

Such instances are, fortunately, rare. Indeed, PCVs who have trained, hiked, swum, eaten together, seen each other in the most unattractive settings, been sick together, slept out together in sleeping bags, or lived in the same quarters, are bound to feel more like brothers and sisters than like romantic partners.

However, sex is a built-in problem. To set down red-blooded young Americans of the twenty-plus age group in strange surroundings, where loneliness and frustration become almost unbearable, and to expect two years of celibacy would be unrealistic. What I found surprising was not the number of attachments that had developed, or even the number of casual relationships that were formed, but the fact that PCVs don't expect adults at home to understand these associations. Whenever I brought up the subject, someone was sure to say with both surprise and relief, "You mean you know about this?"

Of course I had heard. And while many of the rumors probably exaggerate the situation, I have no reason to doubt the report that several girls in the Philippines flew off to Japan on leave because abortions are legal there.

Some of our Volunteers in isolated places have developed associations with "locals." After all, we understood when the hero and heroine of *South Pacific* found each other. Incidentally, when the party other than the PCV is a national of another country, also serving abroad, the problem can become international, with the embassies getting into the act.

There have been some marriages of necessity, but that does not imply that these unions will turn out to be unsuccessful. Look up some recent statistics on pregnancy before marriage among young brides—often of high school age—here at home; I doubt that the Peace Corps record even approaches these statistics.

What annoyed one group of male PCVs was that their Rep called them in and gave them what they termed a "Boy Scout" lecture. "It was easy for him to tell us all to cut it out and be good boys," said one. "He's got his wife with him and leads a normal home life."

One Rep told me that he had talked with his men about the precautions they should take. At least, he was being realistic. And I enjoyed the story of the Rep who, seeing a PC jeep parked outside a bawdy house, rushed in and told the PCVs, "If you're going to come in here, at least don't park the jeep right out in front."

What do people of other countries think of the Volunteers? The Corps has been sufficiently popular to be copied by the governments of several foreign countries. At the International Conference on Human Skills held in Puerto Rico in October, 1962, several nations announced that they were starting their own Peace Corps programs.

The forty-three nations represented at the conference also voted unanimously to establish an International Peace Corps Secretariat to help spread the concept of voluntary manpower as a tool of economic and social change.

By mid-1963, thirteen countries had established, or were planning, voluntary-service programs: Argentina, Belgium, Canada, Denmark, Israel, Italy, Japan, the Netherlands, New Zealand, Norway, the Philippines, Switzerland, and West Germany. Several South and Central American countries, as well as Jamaica, plan domestic corps. El Salvador's sixty volunteers, twenty of whom trained at the University of Oklahoma, combined forces with the forty American Peace Corps Volunteers to form five-member brigades to work on community development in the villages.

Most disturbed by the Peace Corps are the Communists. If anything goes wrong—if the crops fail or equipment breaks down—Communists inevitably spread the rumor that the Americans were to blame. The Communist press, in text and cartoons, continually warns against the Volunteers. Said the left-wing *Daily Telegraph* of Lagos, Nigeria: "The very idea of America offering her sons to serve . . . free of charge is deadly suspicious. What is the idea of serving without salary? Does that not suggest a drive . . . to plant their spies all over Africa?"

PCVs have their critics at home, too. Dr. Nicholas C. Leone, who put many early Volunteers through physical exams that were conducted in accordance with Army medical standards, offers the following evaluation, although he admits that it is based on a superficial clinical impression: "Malcontent, immature, grasping for something. Individualist, yes, but trying to find their niche or postponing decisions. They probably didn't have the competence to make it back here. There's no challenge of competition abroad, no pressure to work for promotion. They can avoid standards and guidelines."

As the *National Observer* pointed out in 1962, a large number of Volunteers readily admitted that they welcomed the delay of two years before making the all-important decisions about careers, marriage, and the course of their lives in general.

Dr. John J. Sullivan, a psychologist at New York University who has counseled and evaluated many of the Volunteers, does not feel that deferring a decision is the same as running away to escape, nor does he see PCVs as beatniks, as some critics have charged.

"It's true you won't get many Harvard business graduates or engineers from MIT as Volunteers, because they're hot in pursuit of a career and they don't need a moratorium to decide what they're going to do. Businessmen wouldn't understand not pursuing money, so they may call Volunteers immature. Certainly they're not working because of economic motives or drives or—except for a few who plan to join the State Department—career advancement. Travel, yes.

"But these are mostly middle-class kids with above average talent and skills. The Somalia group contained some of the most brilliant students we've ever had on campus. They're young, enthusiastic, energetic, with that blend of conviction plus service—idealism and realism—which are the best Volunteer qualifications.

"Even the forty- and fifty-year-old Volunteers who were caught in the tedium of a job and wanted to escape are charming persons because they're fighting for a meaningful life, competing with younger Volunteers. They are steady and responsive, and they know what they can expect from life."

Asked to define immaturity, Dr. Sullivan said: "Psychologically, there are two immature reactions—being too rigid or too flexible. In a culture-shock situation, which is a quick transplanting from a familiar to an unfamiliar setting, immaturity shows up either as a clinging to one's own values as superior—for example, continuing to wear a tuxedo for dinner every night in the tropics—or in going completely native. As far as I know, few Volunteers have gone to either extreme."

Sandy McCaw, who had been working with AID in Cambodia for two years, said she was not really skeptical, "but I had to be shown. After working with Volunteers for a few months, I'm much more optimistic than I expected to be. PCVs can adjust to conditions and their morale is generally good."

However, she found that the Volunteers were often hasty in their judgments. "They're intolerantly tolerant," Sandy characterized them. "They want everyone to be tolerant of the same things they are. They're not so tolerant of those who differ."

While I was in the Dominican Republic, I asked Ed Baxa, a chemical engineer with Allis-Chalmers in Milwaukee, what he thought about the Corps. Ed had just spent several months in Latin America on business.

"I was sure lukewarm to the idea of the Corps at first," he said, "but no more, since I've seen and heard the impact these young people are making. All most of these communities need is to get rolling, and that's what the Peace Corps does—it gets the locals doing something for themselves. I'm all for it."

I found it interesting that the wide response to the Peace Corps program surprised so many people around the world— friend and foe alike—to ask, "Why? Why do so *many* want to volunteer?"

Every day millions of busy Americans serve on fund-raising committees and boards of charitable organizations, do volunteer work for hospitals and social agencies, treat patients, or give legal advice without charge. It is hardly news when a person chooses a lifetime career as a missionary or a worker in one of the social service fields. No one asks, "Why?"

Why, then, have so many questioned the motives of the PCVs? I do not know, unless it is because we have lost our awareness of the basic drives that moved our forefathers to found a democracy and because we have become skeptical of any who want to help their neighbors and to serve their fellow men. Naturally, everyone hopes to gain by his individual struggles; our forefathers opened the West not only because that vast area of land offered a challenge but also because they saw an opportunity to better themselves. However, it was the spirit of mutual cooperation that brought results.

Besides, putting motives aside, what of the results? If the Volunteers have been successful in improving the image of America, should not that count heavily in their favor? Most

Americans, I think, are coming to feel that motives be damned, the PCVs are doing "a job."

Whether truly representative of the United States or not, and regardless of whether or not their parents or anyone else understand their real motivations, the Peace Corps Volunteers have won the support of the majority of American people. Headlines in small town papers and in big city dailies, and in many foreign newspapers, have proclaimed their accomplishments and have reported also on the activities of the groups at home that have organized book drives and collected gifts of tools and other supplies to help the Volunteers help themselves and their host peoples.

In Los Angeles in the fall of 1962, parents and friends of the PCVs formed the first citizens' committee and christened it the Peace Corps Service Organization. Seattle was next, and within a few months similar groups had sprung up in dozens of big cities and small towns. Besides encouraging local projects to provide funds or supplies for the PCVs, these groups conduct educational meetings with speakers and films about the various countries where the Volunteers are serving, and offer hospitality to visitors and students from Asian, African, and Latin-American countries.

Anyone interested in contacting one of the Service Organizations may obtain the names and addresses of officers from the Peace Corps Community Relations Section, Washington 25, D.C. For those interested in forming a support group, the same office has prepared a list of dos and don'ts which is helpful; it is available on request.

The strongest evidence of the regard in which Americans hold the PCVs are the tons of books that have been collected in towns and cities across the nation and shipped, in response to the pleas of Volunteers, to projects in every part of the globe.

In a summary of the Peace Corps' first year in Ethiopia— where the PCVs comprised about half the country's teaching staff—Representative Harris Wofford described the battle of the books.

"Peace Corps teachers could not rest without the essential tools. They pressed for books from local schools and central ministry officials, from the Peace Corps staff, from Americans in Ethiopia and at home, from friends, family, and home-town schools; they have searched through school storerooms; they have bought books with their own money; they have scrounged, argued, made themselves nuisances—and succeeded in getting a great number of books into the hands of their students."

At first the gifts were small and personal, as individual Volunteers wrote home to their families and friends about the millions of children and adults who had never held a book in their hands. Then the press took up the cry, publicizing the fact that even the teachers themselves were forced to teach without texts or syllabi, to write their own texts, and to copy lessons on the blackboard for their students; and Director Sargent Shriver himself, after his African tour of Peace Corps projects, expressed shock at the great need. With this new awareness, Americans went into action.

David King's mother sent thirty-eight volumes from the Waterloo, Indiana, public library to Nabua High School in the Philippines where Dave was teaching, and corresponded with some of his Filipino friends. Dave calls her a "Peace Mother." The Rotary Club of Carthage, New York, responded to Dick Zecher's appeal from Mindanao, "Send books!" with eight hundred volumes. After Sue Sadow's repeated pleas to her friends in California, she received a staggering collection of thirty thousand textbooks weighing fifteen tons and worth nearly $100,000. The books traveled twelve thousand miles to reach their destination in Sierra Leone.

Sixth-graders in Charles Allen's hometown, after he had sent a story to the local newspaper, contributed money to buy twenty English dictionaries which they shipped to him in

Ethiopia. Newell Flather's sister, Betsy, visited him in Ghana and helped him set up a school library there. "With the help of a hometown church and two high schools, I hope to have transformed the school library from thirty dirty, useless books to a functional collection of a thousand volumes by the time I leave," Newell had written to headquarters in Washington. His goal was reached and exceeded even before Betsy arrived in Winneba to help catalogue the three thousand books and to teach the students how to run their own library. It is now reported to be the second largest in Ghana.

Book collections have been especially popular with school and club groups. The Katherine Gibbs Secretarial School in New York City "adopted" Carole Sojka's class in Somalia. Carole, who is a Gibbs graduate, wrote to her mother about the complete absence of books in Merca, even in the schools. Her letter was shown to Miss Margaret Van Voorhees, the social director of the school, who manages the annual Christmas project in which the whole student body participates during three days of concentrated fund-raising. In December, 1962, they elected to make one phase of their program, "Books for Africa."

The girls sold Christmas nosegays, cashew butter crunch, chances on two tickets to Bermuda, held a Chinese auction, and served a luncheon to raise the funds. Then they voted to invest about a thousand dollars of the proceeds in books and a mimeograph machine to send to Carole.

With the aid of the African Foundation, Cambridge, Massachusetts, the books were carefully selected and approved by the Peace Corps for shipment to Somalia. The books arrived, but no one knows what became of the mimeograph machine with its supply of ink and paper. It never reached its destination; who has it or what use is being made of it is still a mystery. Such disappearances of goods in transit are not uncommon, the PCVs report.

Pat Joslyn's friends and parents in River Forest, Illinois,

became involved in an even more extensive supporting program, the Cooperative Educational Fund for students in the Bicol area of the Philippines.

"Mom and Dad, do you have any friends who would be interested in taking part in this scholarship fund?" Pat wrote early in 1962. "Would you like to ask others, organizations as well as family and friends, to contribute to a fund which will help send intelligent Grade 6 graduates on to high school? We have actually begun the fund with a hundred pesos each and are busy planning our mode of attack for raising funds here (which will probably be more difficult than in the United States, since there is much less interest here for those outside the family). We want to make it a joint thing, partly American, partly Filipino, to be taken over and continued by responsible Filipinos after the Peace Corps has left."

From then on Pat's letters were full of her activities for the scholarship fund—examinations to be given, arrangements for handling funds, information to be passed on to donors and potential donors. "It's just amazing how nicely dollars multiply into pesos—$40 is about 150 pesos, enough to completely take care of a student for a year," she wrote, adding, "of course, school really should be free; some day maybe it will be."

In 1962–63, Pat reported, the Fund aided fourteen students from five municipalities with partial or full tuition and in some cases with living expenses. Three girls were living with Pat and her fellow PCVs. "Our budget will be far tighter with six or seven instead of four," she told her parents, "but it should be interesting both for them and for us."

Requests for help from home often took a lighter tone, too. The Joslyns received one letter from Pat which read: "We'd love some Kool-Aid, for there's nothing between coke and water, and we drink far too much of the former. So send lots and lots of those precious little packages. Our guests really like it, too, and we're going broke on coke!"

The Scarsdale Woman's Club, which maintains Operation Bookshelf where they receive and sort books into balanced collections for distribution to missions, prisons, philanthropic institutions, etc., added several Peace Corps projects to their list of potential recipients.

The movement to collect books for the Peace Corps spread so rapidly that by the summer of 1963, according to Alan Emory, the Washington correspondent of the Watertown (New York) *Daily Times,* more than three million books had been shipped to Volunteers around the world. To make sure that these books are suited to the needs of Volunteers, Director Shriver set up the Office of Book Coordination to work with the private groups and with government agencies.

The greatest need is for textbooks. The Corps stresses that books must be selected carefully for appropriateness and for up-to-date information, and that the volumes should be in "near excellent" condition. *Little Black Sambo* and *Uncle Tom's Cabin* stay home.

Another channel for book donations is Books USA, a non-profit organization in Washington, D.C. For each four dollars received, Books USA will send a packet of books overseas, much as CARE packages are sent, which can be given by Volunteers to individuals. Books sent by the Peace Corps must remain in schools and libraries.

The battle of the books has been fought in the host countries as well, as is illustrated by the story that Harris Wofford, the Rep in Ethiopia told me:

"In one provincial school the Volunteers found a large supply of good *unopened* textbooks piled on the shelves. They were being carefully guarded by a school storekeeper, who was defending his perfect record with the ministry: not one book had been damaged or lost in three years. In the central ministry stores in Addis Ababa huge stocks of other books were found sitting on shelves, often unsorted, all in need of distribution to the provinces."

There is general agreement among all who know the Volunteers, and some who know them only from their written
requests for aid, that while they may ask little for themselves,
they have no scruples about asking for the tools and equipment they need to do their jobs. Peter Sigourney, teacher of
machine shop theory at the Technical Institute in Kuala Lumpur, Malaya, wrote to eight American companies, telling them
what he wanted. Five donated tools; one donor even paid the
freight. Willie Wales, a former representative of a farm
equipment factory, who became a PCV in El Salvador, explained to John Deere & Co. that no maintenance had been
done for some time on a much-needed grain combine. The
firm supplied the necessary parts in time to repair the combine
for the rice harvest.

Approval of the Volunteers and of what they are doing has
been expressed through a variety of gifts from individuals,
civic groups, and business firms. The American Hospital Supply Corporation of Evanston, Illinois, sent surgical gloves and
hemostats to Margaret Balfe, Peace Corps nurse and the only
American who has ever been in Remban, Malaya. Medical
supplies have also been contributed for Togo, East Pakistan,
Sierra Leone, and Bolivia. Seeds have been shipped to Colombia, Dominican Republic, Ghana, and Iran. King-O'Shea,
makers of sporting goods, furnished baseball equipment to
Dominican Republic Volunteers. Republic Steel donated
enough sheet steel for five thousand street signs for Addis
Ababa, capital of Ethiopia, after Sargent Shriver mentioned
that he had not been able to find his way around the city.

There is no complete list of items, but gifts that have been
sent overseas are known to have included a fire engine, a jeep,
a respirator, tools, science kits, oil paintings, folding chairs,
transistor radios, livestock, fishing nets, a water treatment
plant, baseball uniforms, pencils, pads, balloons, lollypops, and
bubble gum.

If the Volunteers need technical information, DATA International (Development and Technical Assistance) and VITA (Volunteers for International Assistance) are ready to answer questions on all sorts of subjects. VITA (1206 State Street, Schenectady 4, New York) an organization of scientists and engineers, supplies free information to persons abroad who have scientific and technical problems. DATA, 437 California Avenue, Palo Alto, California, draws on the knowledge of five hundred specialists across the country and offers a similar free service on technical questions.

As long as there are PCVs in the field—necessarily blessed with more enthusiasm than money—there will be a real opportunity for those at home to support them and to share in the work that they do overseas. Efforts to help them do a good job will undoubtedly pay much bigger dividends than time and energy spent on analyzing why they volunteered to do the job in the first place.

13

Many of us appear to be idealistic realists, with a greater emphasis on the realist part of the phrase. The emphasis on the realist part has probably increased during the time we have been abroad.
PCV JANE MELENEY
Nigeria

In the summer of 1962 I sent a four-page questionnaire to 250 Volunteers who were scattered throughout the twelve countries where the Peace Corps was then in operation: Chile, Colombia, Ghana, India, Malaya, Nigeria, Pakistan, Philippines, Sierra Leone, St. Lucia, Tanganyika, and Thailand. Washington headquarters had warned me that the Volunteers disliked questionnaires and intimated that they would not respond to mine. It is certainly true that PCVs treasure their individuality and resist being grouped or tabulated as statistics. Nevertheless, I received answers to my questionnaire from every country except Pakistan.

A number of the PCVs declined to fill out the questionnaire itself, but wrote me detailed letters about their lives, their work, and their views of the Corps. I corresponded extensively with several of the PCVs and have quoted them in these pages, sometimes anonymously. (One of my regrets is that I have not been able to write to all the PCVs who expressed interest in continued correspondence.)

The PCVs who responded had been in the field less than a year, a factor which must be considered in evaluating their replies. Many were enthusiastic newcomers, and one would expect that their high hopes for quick results would cloud their objectivity. Yet, despite the fact that they were spread over so many different cultures and faced such a variety of social

problems, their ideas and feelings—as reflected in their replies
—fell into such definite patterns that generalization is unavoid-
able. Since they are so proud of their "rugged individualism,"
the PCVs themselves may be dismayed to hear of this uni-
formity. However, they may also find that the similarities in
their criticism of the Corps and in their estimate of the roles
that they should play is comforting—for those who completed
their service found similarly at the termination conferences
that they had such opinions in common. Once aware of their
common feelings, they all felt less isolated; evidently even
common frustrations can be a bond.

PCVs are necessarily cautious with "strangers," and they try
hard not to gripe. "One area in which we've been warned to
exercise extreme caution is in our relationship with the press,"
I was told by a PCV in the Philippines. "We are frequently
reminded that we are the experimenters, the ones from whom
policy will be derived for future groups. Others will be guided
by our mistakes, our successes, our solutions to problems. I'm
afraid of being misinterpreted and suddenly finding myself on
a plane to the States."

Except for those who are too bitter to be cautious, most
PCVs apologize for, or qualify, any adverse comment or critical suggestion. Several PCVs returned their questionnaires
unanswered with the not-so-cryptic message: "See me next
year after I get out if you want the truth about the Corps."

There was clearly a good deal of pressure from the Corps
that all connected with the movement remain discreet. The
father of one PCV refused to talk with me because he feared
he might get his son into "trouble" and ruin his opportunities
in the Corps. Instructors in the PC training programs were
also noticeably uncommunicative and gave the impression that
they preferred not to discuss anything beyond the super-
ficialities of the program.

The first PCVs to return mentioned their frustrations, yes,
and how they had not accomplished as much as they had

hoped to. But they were not specific, and they evidently will not be because of a number of deterrents which they did indicate to me.

"We can't explain to people," I was told. "How could we make them understand? We didn't ask for the hero role, but we certainly aren't going to go around trying to convince people that we failed and that the PC really isn't so great, because we still think the idea is great."

"Why should we disillusion folks back home? My mother thinks the PC is the greatest thing in the world," a PCV in Africa said, "and I'm not going to try to change her mind."

There is also pressure from more recent PCVs. A friend in Group 2 told a Philippines 1 Volunteer, who was about to leave for home, "You of Group 1 could spoil it for all of us, you know, if you go home and start complaining about the Corps, flunking out of graduate schools, or quitting jobs."

The Group 1 Volunteer was surprised: "I asked what we could possibly say that would be of harm. She was concerned that we would stress the administrative blunders, the still unsettled question of the rightness of educational-aide roles for PCVs in the Philippines, the various failures, the occasionally spectacular circumstances under which PCVs are sometimes sent home, etc. I argued that even though I might probably refer to all these things, the American people would not lose their faith in the whole Peace Corps. For the nation wants to believe in it and it does. There will be enough positive comments, and the PC will continue to be highly regarded—and maybe because of the critical comments, it will become more real to everyone, with its heartbreaks and failures as well as its successes. I don't think anyone really expects 100 per cent glowing praise forever."

Judging by the returns on my questionnaire, a majority of the PCVs share this faith that the public understands the constructive intent of criticism of the Corps.

To begin with, the questionnaire revealed that the PCVs

were practically unanimous in being pleased that they had joined the Corps; of those who had doubts, not one expressed any strong regret at his decision. However, the reasons for being pleased with their Peace Corps service varied from the undefined to the practical. PCV Stephen Murray, in Colombia, said: "I have remained convinced that the Peace Corps will remain a two-way deal for all Volunteers. It's an opportunity to understand and be understood, and to help and to be helped." From Tanganyika, PCV Charles Barton wrote: "My reasons were vague for joining and are vague for liking it." One PCV was glad he joined up because "I feel a sense of being needed and wanted—in other words, secure and happy." Another young man, stationed in Sierra Leone, stated emphatically: "This is the most constructive thing I have ever taken part in." Marion Ford, in the Dominican Republic, wrote: "It's only fair to say that I hope to benefit from the knowledge I gain during these two years."

A large number of PCVs, however, cannot state exactly why they joined—their underlying motivations are too deep to be easily brought to the surface—and they do not like to be questioned about them. Furthermore, in a number of cases their reasons for being glad that they had joined had changed, for the PCVs had become aware of various benefits that they had not originally expected. Thomas Kincaid, teaching in the Philippines, wrote: "I've learned a lot about myself as well as about other people." Many PCVs comment on the warm new friendships they have developed, on their new understanding of others, and on their personal growth and development. Many of the PCVs felt that by joining the Corps they were enabled to participate in a useful service; almost all stated as well that their participation was beneficial to themselves because of the opportunity to gain experience as well as to travel. For some the Corps was a step forward in their own careers.

Concerning dropouts, the early figures released by the Corps showed that only about one in thirty or 3 per cent returned home early. Reports from the field—at least in troublesome areas like Jamaica and Somalia—were different: "If all is true concerning our dropout rate, then we are in bad shape," said a Somalia PCV, "and I suspect that there will be more before the time is up. I imagine there are problems of potential dropouts in all projects that a strong Rep can help out."

By the end of twenty-two months the Peace Corps officially reported that there had been 289 early returns for 4855 Volunteers—or approximately 6 per cent. This is considerably lower than the dropout rate for overseas workers in private industry or in other government jobs. PCVs feel a strong responsibility to stick it out, not to fail, not to disappoint the people back home.

In the beginning, the PCVs were given to understand that resignations would not be considered except in the case of a family emergency at home that demanded their presence. Pressure from PCVs themselves apparently brought about a change in this policy, for during Sargent Shriver's visit to the Philippines, he told the Volunteers that anyone was free to return to the States whenever he felt he must.

In Jamaica, one PCV was recalled almost at once, two others —a married couple in their forties—left under a cloud of security while I was visiting there and were flown back to the States, and several others returned soon after, which makes that project's dropout rate about double the figure released by the Corps. However, several large groups have had relatively few dropouts.

Most of my respondents said that if they had a chance to reconsider they would still volunteer. Less than a fifth were definitely considering a second term; this percentage probably decreases as the tour of duty comes to a close. In reply to a Peace Corps questionnaire in late 1962, fewer than 10 per cent of those replying indicated any desire to extend the length of their service. Only three of the PCVs whom I met personally were thinking of staying on: the Thaelers in St. Lucia and Tex Ford in the Dominican Republic. These three wanted to see the results of their projects and were reluctant to turn their tasks over to local assistants. I met many more PCVs who were eager to have the time pass so that they might return, although many were vague about what they would do next. One PCV agreed thoroughly with PC headquarters on the subject of re-enlistment: "I don't think Volunteers should be allowed to serve a second term. The organization's value is the freshness of approach which comes with new Volunteers." Obviously, mass re-enlistment will never be a problem for the Peace Corps; the majority of PCVs consider that a two-year contribution is enough, although what they encountered was more comfortable living, far less primitive, than they had been led to expect. Cooks, laundresses, stewards, and houseboys may be obtained easily, and PCVs who don't have household help are a wonder to the local people.

In Ghana, the fact that Americans did not have cars and the other luxuries enjoyed by the Europeans in the country caused such consternation that the PCVs were forced to live on a higher scale in order to save face. Also, the PCVs found that to do their own cooking and cleaning would take too much of their time from the work they came to do.

"Our meals are prepared by Clara, our maid, who does all of our household chores," said Geraldine Thomas, teacher in the Philippines. "She cooks on a wood-burning stove, beats our clothes clean with a wood paddle, shines the floor with a coconut husk, and irons with a charcoal-burning iron."

The Corps is obviously no place for late risers or nine-to-five workers. "We're up between 4:30 and 5:15 A.M. and go to school about 7 A.M.," said another teacher in the Philippines. "Three high school students live with us. Pigs and dogs are attached to the house, ducks all around. Road is dirt. There are floods yearly."

In Tanganyika, it's "eat in a tent, sleep in a tent, facilities nonexistent. Laundry in a bucket of boiled water. Work aver-

ages ten hours a day, six days a week, but sometimes runs to
sixteen hours, seven days. My partner and I surveyed over
eight hundred miles of road in four months."

In Colombia, Steve Murray's day begins like this: "Rise
and shine at 7:30, breakfast at 8:00 if there's time. At 8:15 we
leave for a round of visits or day of community working on
projects, such as the aqueduct. About 4 or 5 P.M. we begin
our meeting with the whole community and discuss the day's
work, finances, plans, and suggestions. Many nights we have
short classes after the meetings and arrive back home at 9:30
or 10 P.M."

"Community developers have no hours. However, it's always more than sixteen a day," explained Dennis Grubb,
another Colombian PCV.

In the table on pages 252 and 253 are some of the questions
I asked the PCVs about their lives and jobs, plus a tabulation
of their replies.

A number of Volunteers stated that not having enough to
do, or else not knowing exactly what their jobs should be,
caused problems, particularly in the beginning. Of course,
some PCVs plunged immediately into activity. Dennis Salgado
wrote from Colombia: "My first day was spent digging a ditch
around a soccer field; we had around a hundred people working real hard and fast. We kept on digging while some of the
people made bets that we would give up. We didn't give up."
Other PCVs were taken on tours of inspection in schools and
hospitals, or began work on such useful tasks as patching up
broken machinery and surveying land. But many found the
first weeks quite frustrating.

Gary Schulze wrote from Sierra Leone: "I was told to 'talk
to the boys about the Peace Corps.' It didn't really matter
what I covered in class as long as the boys were quiet. This
went on for about five weeks before I was finally given official
classes. But even then I was not given any idea of what the
syllabi for the courses were."

"Life is physically very easy," said Jane Meleney, in Nigeria. "Psychologically, it is much harder because of the isolation, the monotony of life, the slow-and-easy pace of doing everything, and the need to create from scratch any contributions we might make. One isn't asked to do much because there isn't much doing."

Peace Corps teachers in the Philippines seemed to get off to a very slow start. One wrote: "It takes about two months before you are really able to know what you can do." Another added a humorous note on her early days: "We spent a great deal of time observing classes before we did any actual work. We were fed in every classroom we came to observe, and one day I think I was offered fried bananas four or five times and drank six coca colas. Eventually, we did start to work."

Not every delay struck the PCVs as amusing. A bit of understated irritation appears in this teacher's reply: "The first day was a party—the second a conference—the third another conference. The fourth—a typhoon which disrupted the schools for about two weeks, then an athletic meet, no school —then Christmas vacation. For an impetuous person, it was exasperating."

The tempo of life was not appreciably faster in some areas of South America. One of the girls in Chile wrote: "We lived for two weeks in an unfurnished house, slept in sleeping bags and cooked on an alcohol stove. Went to the country to visit homes; in one community we invited the ladies to attend the home economics and sewing classes each Thursday. The women were shy at first and afraid to talk to me. They thought I was a spy of the Patron (employer). Because my job was ill-defined, almost everything was a problem at first—what to do and where. I had to find my own job and work at it."

This tortoise pace, and in fact, the entire way of life in many countries, was anathema to the Volunteers. When asked what they considered the most difficult adjustment to

Question	Percentage answering				Comments
	YES	NO	YES & NO	NO ANSWER	
Are you glad you joined the Peace Corps?	95.3	0.0	4.7		
If you had a chance to reconsider, would you still volunteer?	90.7	4.7	2.3*	2.3	
Are you considering a second term of duty?	18.6	37.2	44.2†		
How do you see your Peace Corps service?					*Listed in order of frequency mentioned:* chance to get experience; chance to travel; step to career; contribution prior to career; temporary interlude in career; chance to become familiar with another culture, language; chance to serve; personality development; chance to widen background, discover field to go into.
Have there been any problems you didn't expect?	69.8	18.6		11.6	*Among problems listed were:* having to plan own projects, find own job; lack of privacy; curiosity of people; lack of urgency; having to get own equipment, supplies; clothes wearing out fast.

make, several mentioned food, climate, language and poor sanitary conditions—as might be expected. But many found it hardest to tone down their Yankee heritage of constant busyness. Murray Stern in Sierra Leone recognized that his difficulty was a common one—"reducing my optimistic ideal-

Question	Percentage answering				Comments
	YES	NO	YES & NO	NO ANSWER	
Have there been any benefits you had not anticipated?	55.8	25.6		18.6	*Among benefits listed were:* being accepted; interest of people at home in sending books; sponsoring students; attachment to children; their appreciation; learning more than expected; better living conditions than expected.
Have you felt fear at any time since your arrival?	41.9	53.5	2.3	2.3	*Among fears listed were:* own inadequacy to do job; not being accepted; auto accidents; hellbent driving; unknown; typhoons; cobra; rhino; bats.
Have you written your family and friends in detail about your present life?	86.0	14.0			
Did you ask for your present assignment?	21.0	76.7		2.3	

*Don't know.
†Undecided.

istic tendencies at the start. I had a lot of energy to burn and still have some." Tom Kincaid, in the Philippines, agreed: "Our difference in background tended to cause us to expect too much in too short a time; people are slow to do things here." To Carol Valentine, it was "learning to wait hours for everything to happen according to 'Philippine time.' "

Often adjustment to the people of the host country was accomplished more easily than the accommodation to other Americans on the scene, or to "British colonial types" and to Europeans living and working abroad. Many times, PCVs reported, these people were more antagonistic to the Peace Corps than the local citizens. Also, they often seemed to rub the PCVs the wrong way.

The Volunteers attributed hostility and anti-Americanism among locals (and more than 50 per cent reported such reactions) to fear that the PCVs would take over their jobs, or simply to a general apprehension of the white man. In some instances, hostility was focused on a specific problem, such as the price of Colombian coffee, or the fact that the United States Congress had turned down the Philippines' bid for war reparations. However, Volunteers found that there was more friendliness and cooperation than real hostility. The natives in nearly every country were overwhelmingly curious about America: "How much does a chicken cost?" "How do you do the twist?" "What do you think of the President?" "Why does everyone get divorced?" "How can I get to America?"

In the table on pages 256 and 257 are tabulated the reactions PCVs observed in their host countries.

One feels, after reading these comments, that if only we stopped sending American movies overseas there would be no need for the Peace Corps to counteract the wrong impressions others get of the United States. Such widespread misinformation, even in the Philippines, which has a history of close relationship with America, astonished the PCVs. "Better to ask if we've noticed any correct information about America," wrote Evelyn Mittman. "Misinformation they have regarding wealth, religion, size of families, beauty of the United States, entertainment, and so forth." A city planner in Thailand described the local attitude: "People here think all Americans have money, big houses, big cars, big everything."

People in the host countries often have their own particular concept of certain aspects of American life. Charles Barton in Tanganyika, told me that one local man had said: "I've read a lot about cowboys and have seen them in the movies. Who do I write to join them?" Barton's subsequent importation of a batch of cowboy hats was a big success with the male population in Tanganyika.

Despite these exaggerated notions about America, many people in the countries where the Corps was working admired the United States; the PCVs in the Philippines found an almost disconcerting adoration for everything American. They were welcomed with such overwhelming hospitality that it was difficult for them to avoid being cast as "heroes" and to go about their jobs inconspicuously. Sometimes, this worship of the United States hampered, embarrassed, and even aggravated Volunteers. While few countries respect the right of privacy to which Americans are accustomed, the concept has no meaning at all in the Philippines. Barrio inhabitants feel quite at ease wandering in and out of the Volunteers' houses, reading their mail, and asking dozens of personal questions. "I sometimes think I'll scream if one more person quizzes me about why we don't have a baby," said one young wife.

The PCVs were also disturbed by the Filipinos' lack of national pride. "They never say anything good about their own country," young Americans said incredulously.

Despite an unenthusiastic citizenry, the Philippines is definitely a democracy, although a rather conservative one, according to the PCVs. In Evelyn Mittman's estimate: "We're liberal and probably the closest thing to communism these people have ever known. They're real right-wingers here."

There would appear to be no danger that the Philippines will move into the Communist camp, and according to the Volunteers, there is little to fear in most of the other countries where the Peace Corps is active. In truth, the majority of PCVs are not in situations where they are likely to meet Communists.

Question	Percentage answering				Comments
	YES	NO	YES & NO	NO ANSWER	
Do you talk much about America?	79.1	18.6	2.3		
Do you talk much about democracy?	44.2	55.8			
Do you feel qualified to answer most of the questions you are asked?	97.7		2.3		
Have you met any avowed Communists?	30.2	69.8			
Have you sensed any hostility?	53.5	46.5			
If so, were you able to . discover the reason for it?	44.2	4.6		51.2	
Have you been aware of any anti-Americanism?*	55.8	41.9			
Have you noticed any misinformation about America?	93.0	7.0			
When people have the wrong information about the U.S. what do you do?					*Listed in order of frequency mentioned:* try to explain; correct; interpret; disagree.
How would you describe most persons you meet?					*Listed in order of frequency mentioned:* friendly; cooperative; curious; reticent; hospitable; helpful; polite; shy.

Question	Percentage answering				Comments
	YES	NO	YES & NO	NO ANSWER	

On what subjects have you found misinformation about America most common?

Listed in order of frequency mentioned:

all Americans are rich;
moral standards are loose or lacking completely;
bad racial relations, segregation;
way of life, living standards;
divorce and its prevalence;
violence, lawlessness, all areas;
motives for foreign policy;
social customs;
Americans do not care about people;
cowboys;
religion;
Indians;
educational system;
excess luxuries;
foreign aid;
agriculture.

How do you think people got this wrong information?

Listed in order of frequency mentioned:

movies;†
magazines, newspapers;
lack of firsthand knowledge, education;
G.I.'s;
tourists;
United States workers;
Communists;
propaganda;
radios Peking and Moscow;
difference in money values;
suspicion of foreigners.

---

*Very little: 2.3.
†Listed by about 65 per cent.

"People who think they are Communists are more what we call socialists," said an agricultural extension worker in India, and his judgment was echoed by PCVs in many other countries. I did find it interesting, however, that several of the PCVs who said that they do have to work with Communists are stationed in our own hemisphere.

"Tom (another PCV) and I both work in a community that is said to be Communist," wrote a girl from Chile. "The Indian chief is Communist, but allows us to work there. He really knows little about communism except that it sounds a heck of a lot better than what he's got now. But we don't discuss politics with him."

"Here in Colombia, I've been asked very involved questions about *Yanquis*," said Steve Murray. "I've found the Communists' tactics very shrewd in that they either try to make you look like a fool or lose your temper."

"They're boastful of Castro's Cuba and future plans in Chile," added Elden J. Stang. "Mostly they're well informed on the United States, but they are expert at twisting statistics and at asking difficult and embarrassing questions."

Marion "Tex" Ford, in the Dominican Republic, reported on his encounters with Communists: "I met one guy, about twenty-five years old, at a party in Santiago. He told me that he believed only communism could solve his country's problems. He was, of course, unemployed. I suggested, 'Why not try democracy?' "

At another time, Tex met "two or three smart alecks who wanted to start something. They're always the type who wouldn't work if they were offered a job. Most anti-Americanism comes from people who want to blame their own problems on somebody else, so they use the Americans."

When confronted by Communists, Tex admitted, he usually acted more on his own initiative than according to his Peace Corps training. "Maybe I should have argued for democracy, but it seems to me that most of them don't really want to discuss politics; they just want to make a provocation. So I refuse to discuss it."

In Tanganyika surveyor Charles Cathey saw little strength in the Communists. "The leader of the local party of about five turns out not to know what communism is. The most radical thing he wants to do is nationalize the sisal industry."

This statement is typical of the sense of humor the PCVs feel they must develop to face the often dull day-to-day routine and the inevitable frustrations of dealing with ill-equipped, slow-moving, and often lethargic people. They manage to find amusement in all kinds of little incidents. A community development worker in Chile recollects the time she was forced to "rock and roll for an hour straight with every man in the community," and Tex Ford, who stands six feet six inches tall, contributed to the levity among PCVs and Dominicans alike by doing the merengue with a tiny five-foot local girl.

From the Philippines, a female PCV wrote me of an amusing incident that illustrates the superstitions still held by many: "During a solitary hike that I took up in the mountains near here, some children thought that I was a fairy or *aswang*; the people living below came scrambling up and grabbed me by the arm and pulled me down to their house. They had never seen anyone with red hair. After they had captured me and I had explained, they fed me a raw egg and camotes and we proceeded down the mountain."

Sylvia Jean Boecker, also in the Philippines, related the outcome of a difference in social customs: "I dated a Filipino boy this summer. In the Philippines, boys and girls do not hold hands with each other. However, boys hold hands with boys and girls with girls. But my friend knew about customs in America from the movies, so one night he held my hand. He said it was the first time he had held a girl's hand. I asked him how he felt about it and he said, 'It's just the same.' I said, 'The same as what?' He said, 'The same as holding a boy's hand!' "

Another PCV summed it up with a simple statement: "Every day is a rib tickler."

Not only a sense of humor, say the PCVs, but also determination, self-control, enthusiasm, and cheerfulness are necessary. They urge above all the cultivation of patience. Apparently they follow their own advice: when I asked what they had accomplished, most admitted that, as far as any advancement of the local people was concerned, very little had been accomplished. William Rowe in the Philippines wrote: "The results may not be visible for another ten years." In Sierra Leone, a physical education teacher admitted that he had not been able to do much "in the education field though I have been able to help a number of boys with personal and family problems." From India, a PCV stated: "Results are very slow. Probably we will never be able to see many of them."

On the other hand, the PCVs could cite the completion of innumerable small projects: a road begun, an idle machine repaired by skilled American hands, a vegetable garden to show the local people what vegetables can be grown successfully in local soil. Elden Stang in Chile reported that there was "definite improvement in the physical facilities of the school, and my hosts have become interested and active in improvement." From Colombia, Dennis Salgado commented: "If Americans had been doing this before us, things would be much better, for the results of our work are good."

It is not unusual for a PCV to think he has accomplished a task only to discover that he has not. A Peace Corps teacher in the Philippines related this story to me: "The *p* and *f* sounds are often confused. After a detailed explanation and practice session with a class I wrote the Peter Piper twister on the board and reviewed it several times, after which one of the students recited it with every single *p* pronounced like an *f*. I guess I'll have to try again."

That teacher obviously had his work cut out for him. But how were the PCVs trained for that work? Did the Corps give them sufficient information? Were they sufficiently grounded in language and in other skills they needed? The table below indicates the opinions of the PCVs on these questions.

Question	*Percentage answering*			
	YES	NO	YES & NO	NO ANSWER
Do you have all the tools and equipment you need?	46.5	53.5		
Have you received all the support you needed or asked for from PC headquarters?	67.4	23.3		9.3
Do you consider that your training was adequate?	53.5	30.2	14.0	2.3
Is your language facility adequate for your work?	86.0	9.3	4.7	

"There is no such thing as *all* the things we need," wrote a male teacher in the Philippines, one of the many science instructors who must teach without a laboratory. "My job is to help them do with what they have," explained a female teacher of English and science, while Murray Stern, a physical education teacher, in Sierra Leone, quipped: "It's like teaching swimming without water."

However, most seem to be doing the best they can, with the majority feeling that they have received sufficient support from Washington. Yet several indicated that they hadn't bothered to ask and to wait for aid: "Do-it-yourself works best," they said.

They expressed a wide diversity of opinion regarding the effectiveness of their training and offered a variety of suggestions for improving it. In general, the PCVs rated instruction in language as the most valuable element in their basic training. For the most part they found that their language ability was adequate but wished that they had greater fluency. Even the PCVs who were teaching English voiced a desire for more training in their mother tongue and in the methods of teaching it to people for whom English can only be a second language.

To many PCVs, the Peace Corps' program in Puerto Rico was the most valuable and enjoyable part of basic training. "It was the best eight and a half weeks I ever spent in my life," said Charles Gary Combs, a twenty-seven-year-old medical assistant in Malaya. "I wish all Americans could be fortunate enough to take advantage of this type of training. It gives one a very good glimpse of what we look like to other countries and individuals." Even the most rugged PCVs look awkward in their first attempts at primitive living.

The respondents to my questionnaire commented adversely on the theoretical aspects of their basic training. "We didn't have enough practical experience on what we would be doing," said a twenty-two-year-old girl. "We had too many lectures on theory. No one was quite sure what we would do, so we got a lot of false and inaccurate information on living situations and much useless information."

Others described the program as "superfluous," "overtraining," "boring," or "misleading." Naturally, in the early days of the Corps it was nearly impossible for the people in charge of the Volunteers' orientation program to provide anything but theoretical training. Charles Cathey, a PCV in Tanganyika, blamed the inadequacies of his training on the fact that he came from one of the first groups of Volunteers: "Everything was slightly confused and off schedule, but I understand the program is running smoothly now."

A few PCVs felt that no matter how good the training was, it could only go so far. A twenty-three-year-old teacher in

Nigeria remarked: "It's impossible to train. One needs flexibility and adaptability." Tom Kincaid in the Philippines agreed: "Many things confront us that no amount of training could have prepared us for." A Nigerian teacher added: "Training was as adequate as could be expected for a set of situations nobody knew much about."

Whether or not their training was as complete as it could be, the PCVs had to adapt themselves to the conditions that existed in the host countries. As we have seen earlier, they were usually able to make the adjustment. Nevertheless, every good PCV was aware of the huge problems of the host countries, even though these problems were generally beyond what the Peace Corp could solve. According to the Volunteers, the principal deficiencies of the host countries are (listed in order of frequency mentioned):

> Education;
> Development of resources—agriculture, industry, roads, irrigation, water;
> Ambition of local people to get ahead, to better themselves;
> Money, capital, aid, credit;
> National pride;
> Land reform;
> Leadership, trained personnel;
> Community development;
> Food;
> Jobs;
> Technical assistance;
> Agriculturists;
> Workers in middle-level jobs;
> Respect for labor;
> Birth control;
> A feeling of inferiority;
> Transportation;
> Consumer demand;
> Redistribution of wealth, income.

A rather formidable list of deficiencies.

When asked if the Peace Corps can help in any way to fill these needs, 48.8 per cent of the respondents to my questionnaire answered *Yes*, 41.9 per cent answered *No*; the rest expressed mixed feelings. Assistance in the educational field, of course, is the Corps' biggest contribution. There are more Volunteers in teaching than in any other capacity. To an onlooker it seems that the Peace Corps is staffing the Philippines' schools; yet PCVs say the need far exceeds what they can do. In one school in Ethiopia, more than half the teachers are PCVs.

Of the PCVs who gave negative answers, a large proportion felt that progress was being delayed because of the attitude of the local people. Jane Meleney in Nigeria wrote: "The greatest hoax foisted on the American public is the notion that all Nigerians are striving for progress and development. Many are enthusiastic about aid programs (as opposed to building their own nations for themselves), but there are many, particularly in Sokoto Province who don't seem to care one way or the other about better schools, good health, or good government."

A PCV in Sierra Leone said: "What is done in the areas of natural resources, agriculture, and industry must be done by themselves. They need to associate with people with initiative." Mike Ruggiero in Togo commented that he was astounded by the Togolese people's "complete lack of understanding or appreciation of technology. They use cars and plastic bags and have no understanding of the work, capital, and engineering behind them, and couldn't care less." A PCV in the Philippines stated that "there is enormous economic opportunity here, but the people have to be shaken out of their apathy. Leadership is needed." And, a PCV in Nigeria summed up a very common problem: "Everybody wants to be a white collar worker, but you can't build a country 'untouched by human hands.' "

Sometimes an active social consciousness rather than a lively nationalism is missing. In Chile, a community development worker says she has a "yes-and-no" feeling as to whether the Peace Corps can contribute in such cases. "The fact that we are here and, as Americans, are interested in the lot of the poorer citizens of the world will, I hope, show those nations who have the money that they should have a concern for those of their own who have less. Also, I hope it will draw attention to the citizens who are working to improve their own country, but as of now, they get little public support or money."

Even among the PCVs who believe the Peace Corps is helping, there is often a sense of futility—expressed in such phrases as "We can't make a dent"; "We can help only partially"; "Without education what can be done?" "We already make up one-third of all the qualified university teachers in Sierra Leone."

This awareness of the total need of the host country and of the miniscule contribution an individual can make is what most deeply erodes the Volunteers' enthusiasm and brings out a feeling of resignation.

Fortunately, the expectations of many of the PCVs are not necessarily as broad or ambitious as those of the people back home. The Volunteers do not think they are contributing much, if anything, to peace; many do not expect to see any results of their work—and certainly not quickly. A large number do take pleasure in simple rewards—"a child's smile when he says something correctly in English"—and feel a close sympathy for those with whom they work—"I could cry when the children stare at me." (This comment from a male PCV.)

Volunteers find satisfaction in the fact that the people of the host countries are accepting them and treating them as friends. In Colombia, a young man reported his pleasure upon "being named godfather to one of my tiny Colombian friends." PCVs are happy when they find their students becoming eager to learn, or when they themselves contribute to the pride of the community. From St. Lucia, Arthur "Gene" Hunter com-

mented on his sense of accomplishment from "helping a
peasant farmer to beat out a lot of estates in a recent vegetable
contest at an agricultural fair. He won five first places and
three seconds." A PCV in Tanganyika related his pride in
"climbing a hill and seeing the isolated towns we would connect
to the world outside by our road."

Certainly, most of the PCVs with whom I communicated
had no grandiose ideas about the contribution they were making to world peace. Some said clearly that they were contributing nothing. One, with a slightly cynical air, replied: "World
peace? I contributed to *my* peace of mind. At least I tried."
Charles Lester in Sierra Leone believed that "I'm making
friends for America, but that is about all." And from Togo
came the statement: "We've done nothing, but we'll be remembered with affection and respect."

However, some PCVs viewed the Peace Corps' contribution
to world peace in a more positive light. A PCV serving in
Africa said: "By our example we are showing the Sierra
Leonians that America is interested in helping them build
their new nation, not in exploiting them for financial gain."
One of the teachers in the Philippines wrote: "If I and one
Filipino can share a feeling of mutual respect and friendship,
the bond can expand to everyone in the world if there are
enough people dedicated to achieving it." Tex Ford in the
Dominican Republic said: "I think misunderstanding is one
of the greatest enemies of world peace. I know I have changed
and will help to change that."

It is obvious that the PCVs themselves feel that their greatest contribution lies in furthering human relations and public
relations, rather than in advancing the economic and educational welfare of the host countries. Jane Meleney summarized
the general impression I got from all who wrote to me: "Many
of us appear to be idealistic realists, with a greater emphasis
on the realist part of the phrase. The emphasis on that part
has probably increased during the time we have been abroad."

But small though their visible accomplishments may seem to them, most of the PCVs who answered my questionnaire were still strongly in favor of the Peace Corps. Some thought it should be kept the size it is, mainly to avoid red tape and bureaucracy, but more felt that it should be expanded. The great majority definitely favored its becoming permanent. Here and there was a suggestion that the Peace Corps, or a similar agency, should be placed under the auspices of the United Nations.

Most Volunteers, at least at the time I sent out my questionnaire, recommended that anybody who wished to join up, should do so; but there were also qualifying statements: "Don't plan to set the world on fire"; "Don't come out wearing rose-colored glasses and do not expect too much from anyone"; "There are many frustrations—I'd advise anybody with great hopes of reforming the world to stay at home."

Obviously, the PCVs consider the Peace Corps an experience that is highly worthwhile, but one that is not to be rushed into without careful deliberation.

14

Are we contributing? Are we learning?
Is the Peace Corps experience worth it? I think
we have difficulty seeing the forest for the trees
(or stumps). Perhaps twenty years from now
we'll realize the real value of living in a foreign
culture or being exposed to a completely different
way of life. When the revelation comes we
will know that the decision to spend these years
in this way was the right one.
PCV ROBERT J. BURKHARDT, JR.
Iran

Will the Peace Corps last? Will it, with time, "phase out" and ultimately be abandoned? The old platitude "only time will tell" is about the only answer that can be given. For the Peace Corps has been in operation little more than two years; the facts, the figures, and the opinions can be made to substantiate a case for the Corps and, *probably*, just as easily against the Corps. Yet the need for help being there, everywhere in every emerging nation around the world, and the demand for Volunteers increasing, it is unlikely that the United States would abandon the Peace Corps program. Indeed, we could scarcely give it up without losing "face."

Of course, one can, to be the devil's advocate, ask sternly, "How successful has the Peace Corps been—anyway?" The answer to that depends upon what was expected of it in the first place.

Senator Hubert Humphrey, one of the Peace Corps' sponsors, understandably finds that the Corps has done "an outstanding job." As we know, the PCVs themselves, with their field experience, have variously stated that the Corps should be continued, that it should be enlarged, and also, some have said, that it should be replaced by other services. The results, good or bad, are impossible to measure in any tangible unit—either in dollars, percentages, number of lives saved, or iotas of good will gained. And the majority of Americans probably still hope that this people-to-people movement will be a wonderful success, although some also fear at the same time that it may not be living up to their dream.

"People expect too much of the Corps," said Representative John Landgraf. "All it's intended to do is acquaint people with Americans and us with others, to broaden all horizons."

Eric Sevareid, a critic of the Peace Corps from the beginning, takes the negative position. In the *Washington Star*, Christmas Day, 1962, he wrote: "There is nothing so irresistible as pure intentions backed by pure publicity, and I am aware that in the current atmosphere of euphoric reverence an expressed doubt about the Peace Corps will receive the same treatment as a doubt expressed about virginity . . . . If fringe benefits were all that the Corps' originators had in mind, then this should be made clear . . . . If they truly believe in solid, practical, measurable results, then we ought to have a preliminary accounting . . . soon, always bearing in mind two things: the cost to the taxpayer and the proportionate good to the country involved."

Many, including Sargent Shriver, have taken issue with Sevareid on the "fringe benefits," since these objectives are clearly stated as the second and third purposes of the Corps in the Peace Corps Act.

There is another point to consider. At the end of the first two years there were still less than five thousand Volunteers spread out over the entire globe. Measured against the tremendous needs of the underdeveloped countries, how much can we realistically expect of the PCVs?

While many questions will remain unanswered, the Corps itself is not beyond independent investigation. Inquiry and criticism do not necessarily imply censure. However, with the exception of isolated editorial comments such as Sevareid's, both the American and the foreign press have been overwhelmingly favorable to the Corps and have restricted their coverage to anecdotes and episodes of the human interest variety. Excellent as such coverage is, it gives only one side of the picture. No attempt has been made, for example, to explain the sudden transfers and recalls of Volunteers, which occur frequently in every host country. On the other hand, such intramural news is not always easy to come by since the discretion and lightning speed with which these moves are made often spreads, or seems to spread, a "top security" cloak over them.

News about the Corps, in fact, is controlled by the Peace Corps itself, at least to the same extent that all news emanating from Washington is "managed." A very active public information office releases or plants most of the stories about the Peace Corps that are printed, and undoubtedly certain information is withheld. Why, indeed, should any agency give out information that is not fundamentally acceptable to it?

"Some of the articles are corny," said one of Sargent Shriver's assistants, "but Sarge believes we have to have some schmaltz—human interest—in the stories in order to appeal. We'll write a story for any type publication, just tell us what you want. Our biggest problem is to get to the public press the truth of what's happening. So much of it is privileged information."

Then he proceeded to discuss several bits of supposedly privileged information, adding, "But you can't mention this, of course."

It may be naive to expect anything but managed news from an organization that is sensitive about its "image," but most PCVs have wished it were otherwise. The "everything's coming up roses" approach embarrasses them because they know that the Corps is not free from troubles.

"Are you interested in failures or, like the PC staff, only in

successes?" a male PCV in the Philippines asked me. "For
example, have you learned of the special problems girls have
just because they are American and female?"

I had heard, but only by direct contact with the Volunteers
in the field. In this respect the Peace Corps operates like a
private business firm—if possible, it tries not to embarrass its
personnel. However the Corps also follows the business practice
of not revealing its weakness to the competition. The difference,
of course, is that the Peace Corps is a tax-supported enterprise
in which we are all stockholders.

A Volunteer with six months experience in Somalia told me:
"I don't want this to sound like one big complaint. It isn't.
My wife and I are very happy with our work and we're getting
results. We've had good remarks all the way from the little
Somali school kids to Shriver and crew. But to be honest, we
feel that it's very little like what we read in the papers and
PC blurb sheets. I think what we're doing is fine, but it sounds
better than it is. I guess this is necessary to make it easier
for the people in Washington to get the money and help
through Congress. It's put on, but I'd rather have this than
the whole story of our problems and frustrations."

Early in 1964, subways in New York City carried a Peace
Corps poster showing the happy smiling face of a Negro boy
who was apparently looking up into the eyes of an adult. The
poster read: "Why join the Peace Corps? Not to change the
world, but not to leave it the same either."

The Corps is here expressing a view of its own work with
which the Volunteers would agree and, at the same time, has
taken a step toward presenting the public with a realistic image
of its purpose. Meanwhile, I trust it will not be considered
un-American to attempt an evaluation of some of the aspects
of this movement we all hope will succeed.

If the host countries had to pay the full cost of the Peace
Corps, no Volunteer would ever have left the United States.
In each instance, the Corps makes a separate agreement with

the host country. The host may provide transportation, housing, supplies, or counterparts for the Volunteers (some observers maintain that the Corps would be more effective if all the hosts were required to supply these). Sargent Shriver once reported that "host countries have in every case made voluntary contributions to the Peace Corps programs. In Africa alone, they have supported the program to the value of $2,500,000."

Such participation may be commendable, but it does not begin to cover the United States' government's expenditures on the Corps. Technically, the Corps supplies manpower, not economic assistance. The funds are spent primarily on the Volunteers, and as Shriver pointed out, 75 per cent of the money re-enters the national economy in one form or another: after all, the trained and experienced PCVs come home to enrich our work force. Whether or not we agree with this interpretation, the fact remains that the Corps is an *aid* program; the United States should be prepared to continue to bear the brunt of the cost. Stipulating that the host countries should invest some money—such as paying for counterparts— might, however, increase not only the productivity of the Volunteers but also the commitments of the hosts to the goals of the Peace Corps.

The host countries are aware what happens when the PCVs arrive in a land where there are few tools, little transportation, no books or other necessary supplies. They know that the Volunteers will arrange to get their own equipment, often from another agency, such as AID, Heifer Project, CARE, or from individuals and business firms back in the States. Some in the Corps—Rep Andy Hernandez in the Dominican Republic, for example—believe that the ties between the Corps and other agencies should be even closer than they are now. He reasons that the Corps has the trained personnel, while AID, Alliance for Progress, etc., have the large sums of money to dispense. He favors joining these forces, for as the PCVs have discovered, high hearts and bare hands are not enough to turn an underdeveloped nation into an educated, self-supporting nation.

Some observers point out that many countries may never become self-supporting, that they must depend indefinitely on foreign (namely, on United States) financial assistance. Undoubtedly the host countries are aware of this. Perhaps some of them are tempted to ask for PCVs simply to enhance the chance of receiving huge quantities of American money. If you heard that simply for the asking you could get a free maid for a year, you would probably be tempted to ask for one. If that maid broke dishes, aggravated the neighbors, mistreated the furniture, and burnt the meals, what would you do? Would you dismiss her? Perhaps, perhaps not. However, if by keeping the maid for the year you were also assured that you would get a new house and a new car, or, better yet, a check for several million dollars, you might decide that you were not so terribly displeased—you might decide that broken dishes could be endured, that burnt food wasn't so bad, and that she was quite acceptable considering the circumstances.

One should not conclude that the Peace Corps passively permits underdeveloped nations to receive Volunteers for whom there are no plans. But, on the other hand, the representative of a foreign government who comes to Washington hoping to obtain millions of dollars in aid is not likely to ignore the Peace Corps and fail to ask for Volunteers. Foreign nations are sensitive to American pride. They know we are proud of the Peace Corps. While they are "selling" us their cause, they may see no reason why they should not, at the same time, ask for the one element of help on which we are likely to yield most graciously. And, lest someone holler "Foul!" let me add that I do not contend that the Peace Corps openly pressures countries that have no Volunteers to ask for them, but I have been told that the United States has become more aggressive in *suggesting* programs to countries where PCVs might go.

So, on the one hand, host countries may have asked for Volunteers to enhance their chances of getting financial aid, and on the other hand, the Peace Corps may have encouraged placement of Volunteers in countries that are not ready to receive them. In either case the result is the same: PCVs are sometimes stationed where they are not needed or where no plans have been made to use them effectively. The situation was summed up in a conversation with an official in one host country:

"The success of the Peace Corps," he said to me, "is much more important to the United States than it is to us. You cannot afford to have it fail. However, before any more Volunteers come, we should all get together and assess the need."

"But," I retorted, "it was *your* government that asked for the Volunteers. If there is any question regarding their work, you should talk with your own officials as well as with the PC Rep for the area."

"Our government," he said crisply, "thought it logical at this stage of our development to ask for Peace Corps help."

Governments in underdeveloped countries sometimes overestimate what changes their people are ready to make. A host may therefore, with the best of good will, create a program that will never work; and the Volunteers will suffer the consequences. In the Philippines, a PCV told me that her students were seriously confused because they learned new ways in school only to come home and be told by their parents that the old ways were best. Many PCVs stated that the people with whom they worked were fifty, even a hundred, years behind the United States in technology and general way of life. That was confirmed by a representative of the World Health Organization (WHO) whom I met in Togo. She maintained that so little progress had been made that "the last ten years of AID, UNICEF, and so forth, is money down the drain."

Trying to upgrade a society too rapidly has its dangers and, unfortunately, when the Volunteers declare that they are going to help others they only too often mean that they intend, or wish, to Americanize them. Even if Americanization were the best way to insure the friendship of the host countries, it is simply not possible to create "Little Americas" in non-industrial nations. Perhaps it is not possible to teach this in advance, but as we have seen repeatedly, PCVs everywhere have had to alter their original ideas. The gap between what they had hoped to accomplish and what they realized they could actually do proved to be so wide that they had to re-examine their situation and lower their sights. They learned to live with the knowledge that any grand success—such as a noticeable rise in the overall standard of living in the host country—would take a long time, much longer than two years, and could not be accomplished by the Peace Corps alone.

The accomplishments, as reported, seem to me more than satisfactory. But to the Volunteers themselves, they seem "miniscule," to quote PCV Boris Sojka. Or, as another young man said, "We had been warned that our impact would be small, but each one of us privately expected to be the exception, the one who would affect the entire country."

The absence of one necessary element for progressive development—namely, the lack on the part of the host people of a desire to bring about changes in their lives through their own efforts—had not been anticipated by the young Americans. This disinterest in helping themselves, this lack of individual initiative, shocked many Volunteers.

So most PCVs, after a year in the field, accepted that progress in an underdeveloped country is a long, slow process dependent upon many factors, including capital investment and agrarian and political reforms, and that, basically, the Peace Corps could provide only the element of personal encouragement. They came to understand Sargent Shriver's warning that changes would not be effected overnight, that each person's contribution would be only a sliver, with the results perhaps unmeasurable and unseen.

At this moment of truth, steeped in loneliness, disappointment and self-analysis, Volunteers tend to split into two groups —those who take the high road and those who take the low. Whichever road they take, they are probably adjusting to the realities in much the same way they would when faced by the realities in the States.

Some—perhaps the least stable and mature—become bitter, disillusioned, critical. They lash out at local government officials, at the stupidity of the natives, at the laziness, the hypocrisy, the willingness to accept without putting out any effort, at the lack of desire to improve. They criticize the Peace Corps for having put them in this untenable position and for being "so inefficient." They rationalize their own mistakes and failures, and often they blame others, perhaps justifiably.

A smaller number accept their disappointments quietly; they simply give up and sit out their time. A few—probably wisely—come home. Either they did not know enough about their own stability and tolerance level under stress to have foreseen this, or the psychologists and instructors who screened them failed to detect their potential weaknesses.

Many—probably the majority, judging from the record of achievements—surmount the problems successfully. They redefine their goals, lower their sights, accept the slowness of change, and realize that, even with help, people in backward areas cannot leap a century in two years.

My observations led me to believe that the timing of the peaks and valleys varies for each PCV; the Volunteers' adjustment went on continuously. However, Dr. Robert A. Roessel, Jr., Director of the Indian Education Center at Arizona State University, where the Colombia 2 group trained, has described the adaptation as a three-part process through which a person usually progresses in living and working with people of a different culture:

"Stage one, characterized by enthusiasm, dreams, and the

demand for prompt and quick action. People in this stage are appalled at injustice and feel the solution is both simple and obvious.

"Stage two, characterized by frustration, bitterness and unhappiness. One feels exploited and questions the wisdom of working with people who fail to respond.

"Stage three, representing a rational and logical approach to working *with* people, instead of for people. Individuals are looked upon as human, and both success and failure are expected and accepted."

It is hard for an energetic PCV to admit that his endurance —physical, mental, emotional—is being taxed seriously. Fortunately for the Corps, for the host countries, and for the Volunteers themselves, most PCVs do adjust well. They know that their impact may be slight, and yet perhaps cumulatively greater and longer-lasting than appears likely. They rally and go on to accept their satisfaction from small accomplishments.

The latter group soon discover that they get more than they give, that they learn more than they teach, that they grow more than their counterparts. They find the changes taking place in themselves exciting. They enjoy the broadening and the maturing, and their enthusiasm, tempered now by reality, revives.

Undoubtedly the administrators of the Peace Corps expected to learn a good deal from the first two years of the Corps' activities. The Volunteer's experience if analyzed carefully, should be invaluable in evaluating the program of basic training. Enabling the PCVs to adjust readily and more quickly to conditions in backward areas will certainly help improve our international friendships, and perhaps also pave the way to economic and political relationships that will help us, too, in the future.

Several years ago, Norman Cousins, in a powerful editorial in the *Saturday Review*, asked "Who speaks for man?" Perhaps with their deeds, the Peace Corps Volunteers do.

PCVs have a natural sophistication—a closeness to life's fundamentals—that makes them treat with equal dignity the poor man and the rich man, the peasant and the high official. They learn to walk in step with almost anyone. And they come home citizens of the world.

APPENDIX A

So You Want to Join

Each month, three thousand letters from persons eager to volunteer arrive at the Peace Corps' headquarters. Of those who apply, about one in six is invited to come into the training program. The chances of your being asked to train are considerably enhanced if you have a number of skills rather than a single specialty in which you excel; rate high in language aptitude; are a college graduate between the ages of twenty-four and twenty-six; and rank in intelligence in the upper 5 per cent of the population.

Of course, exceptions are made. The applicant with an unusual skill that has been requested by a host country—to cite two actual examples, a professor of bee husbandry or a chicken sexer—might get favorable consideration. At one time —perhaps because the majority of applicants were liberal arts students with human relations interests—engineers, agronomists, lathe operators and geologists, preferably with fluent Spanish or French, were looked on with special favor. Capable Volunteers who do not have an aptitude for languages have been assigned to and have performed successfully in English-speaking countries. Many older applicants have made good Volunteers; so have some very youthful ones who had not yet completed their college work.

"But the eighteen- or nineteen-year-old without college who does well overseas," pointed out Dr. John Hutchison, a PC administrative officer, "is an exceptional person who would have done well here in the States."

Despite all the applications, some openings go unfilled. There are not enough qualified applicants to meet the special requests of the host countries, such as for "riders skilled in horsemanship, public health, and Spanish, and able to build a school or repair a tractor, for a public health program in rural Panama."

The first step to take in applying for the Peace Corps is, of course, to fill out an application and to take the PC Placement Test. (See pages 12-14 for additional information on the application form and the Placement Test. Sample questions from the Placement Test are in Appendix B, pages 298-306.)

Evaluations of the application and of the Placement Test are made on the basis of the applicant's general suitability: his skills, language ability, psychological maturity, and so forth. It seems to me that the percentage of acceptances might be higher and that a good deal of heartache might be avoided if those who are eager to join made a preliminary evaluation of *themselves*. The PCVs maintain that one of the greatest benefits they gained was an increased understanding of themselves. But the learning was often painful. Some had to admit that they had made a mistake in volunteering—a conclusion that must have affected their work. So for your own protection, as well as to share with the Corps the responsibility of screening out those who may not make the best representatives for the United States abroad, I strongly suggest a rigorous self-analysis. If you really know and understand yourself, your chances of being accepted by the Corps may be better, too.

Here is a check list that may help you formulate other questions about yourself. If you can answer *Yes* to these, you will probably be able to adjust to most situations in the Peace Corps:

Do I sometimes think my mistakes and failures are funny, at least in retrospect?
Do I really like camping out?
Do I think up and start projects on my own?
Am I good at getting along without things, at making do?
Do I frequently make something myself instead of buying it?
Can I live intimately with a group, without any privacy?
Have I related easily to foreign students on campus and made friends with them?

Do I often work long hours without noticing the time?

When I'm busy, can I go for days without giving any time or consideration to my own personal need to do errands, write letters, etc.

Do I enjoy solitary activities such as walking, reading, swimming, etc.?

Do I have a strong stomach—literally and figuratively?

Am I willing to walk, ride a bicycle or motor scooter, ride horseback, or drive a jeep?

If you answer *Yes* to these, you should re-examine your motives for wanting to join:

Am I extremely fastidious about my person and my clothes?

Am I squeamish about dirt, bugs, rats, etc.?

Am I uncomfortable driving or walking through slum areas?

Am I unhappy with a good many aspects of my present life?

Do I seem to have more than my share of problems now?

Do I often think I'm doing more than my share or that someone is forcing responsibility on me?

As a child, did I often ask my parents, "What can I do now?"

Do I need a lot of appreciation and praise?

Am I concerned about how much I am paid for what I do?

No matter how much spending money I get, am I always broke and borrowing?

Do I dislike being alone for any length of time?

Are the majority of my hobbies and recreational outlets ones that might not be available in a remote area—such as music, theater, dates, discussions, church?

Am I violently affected by weather conditions—heat, rain, humidity—so that I cannot function properly?

Am I looking for a marriage partner?

Am I used to being driven places in a car, having errands done for me, etc.?

(*For girls only*)

Would I mind keeping my hair short and not having it styled for two years?

Do I dislike wearing skirts all the time, preferring to wear shorts and slacks a good deal?

After your application has been graded and you are accepted into the PC training program, you are still not a Volunteer. You merit this title only when you have successfully completed all phases of the training and have reported for work in the host country. About five out of six trainees are finally selected for overseas service.

The training program—which is an extended comprehensive test of an applicant's suitability—takes up the first four months of the two-year service. This program consists of three distinct but co-ordinated phases:

First, basic training—eight to ten weeks at a college or university in the United States. During the sixty hours per week of classes (ten hours a day for six days), the Peace Corps assures itself that the trainee has the required skill and that he can teach it to others. The trainee is given courses in technical studies, area studies, language, American studies, world affairs, health and medical practices, physical education and recreation, and Peace Corps orientation.

Second, field training—usually four weeks in Puerto Rico, or at other camps or on various Indian reservations. The purpose here, as stated in the Peace Corps Program Guide, is to make certain that the trainee can perform effectively under totally different cultural conditions and in situations of unusual stress.

Third, overseas training—contributed by the host country. It customarily lasts about four weeks and includes a general orientation to the country, with visits and introductions to the personnel with whom PCVs will work, and may include additional language training, practice teaching, and sharpening of other skills.

"The most important trait we've learned to look for," said Dr. John Hutchison, whose particular interest is in training and selection, "is a sense of humor. We've found that those who take themselves too seriously, who are overly intent or persistent, are also rigid and unable to adapt."

The Volunteer dropout rate, however, is an unusually low 6 per cent annually, or a half of 1 per cent a month, for all causes. Compare this to the ten to twelve per cent for paid employees in overseas duties. According to Dr. Edwin Henry, Director of Selection, an analysis of those who returned early has taught the Corps to look for two traits in trainees: a lack of flexibility and a lack of ego strength.

Lack of flexibility. People who perform well only in an organized program, but cannot adjust to undefined situations, will have problems adjusting their expectations to the reality that confronts them. For example, one PC teacher arrived in Africa expecting to be headmistress of a school, only to discover that the school did not exist—construction had not gone as rapidly as the Minister of Education had expected. This particular PCV was unable to adjust to the change in her status and returned home almost immediately.

Host countries often ask for teachers in one subject and then assign them to teach completely different subjects, even subjects for which they may not be prepared. The school systems, for the most part, stress rote learning and memorization, whereas American-trained teachers favor reasoning, thinking, questioning, and conversational techniques. But the PCVs are judged abroad on how well they teach under the existing systems. Consequently, Peace Corps administrators are looking for persons who can adjust their expectations quickly to fit reality.

Lack of ego strength. According to Dr. Henry, a person with insufficient ego strength is one who depends too heavily upon others for emotional and intellectual support. In an unfamiliar society such a person will soon come to feel sorry for himself and become depressed.

Certainly it is possible for applicants with one or even both of these weaknesses to convince PC recruiters and the selection board to take a chance on them. Those who do the evaluations do not claim that their judgment is infallible. But the recruits

who get by the board only fool themselves, for they are the
ones who are miserable overseas or who return home early.

What would an ideal PCV be like? "Don't look for a prototype," I was warned. "You'll never find him." Perhaps not,
but I can indicate some of the characteristics he should have.
He should have youthful enthusiasm and idealism—tempered
with a maturity of spirit that cannot easily be discouraged.
He should want to travel and to live outside the United States,
but he should not be merely an adventurer—he should be willing to settle down and to adopt a new language and lower
living standards. He should be skilled, but more than that, he
should be resourceful and willing to try anything. He should
have a strong "stomach"—one PC doctor in Central America
refused to take me to visit his hospital because conditions
there were so bad; apparently he did not want to gamble that
I, as a reporter, would be able to view the situation stoically.

The ideal PCV certainly should believe in the American
way of life, but not with any sense of superiority, because in
the culture where he will serve, the American way may not
always be the best way. And no matter how strongly he favors
democracy, he should remember that in the host country he
is there to help, not to indoctrinate or to propagandize.

He should be able to get along with all kinds of people. "If
you love people and do not worry about how you are doing,
you'll love the Peace Corps," said a PCV in the Philippines.
"It'll be as exciting or as monotonous as you choose to make
it. But life in any country can become routine if you do not
really have a desire to work with, to live with, to grow to love
and to know the people of your host country."

Frustration is a familiar word in the vocabulary of every
Volunteer. The term covers a wide range of annoyances and
has a special connotation for each PCV, depending upon the
aspect of life that he finds it hardest to tolerate in the host
country. Frustration, of course, implies a situation that cannot
easily be changed. So if you plan to volunteer be prepared to

live with some of the following:

No privacy. People may wander in and out of your house freely, read your mail, count your shirts, check on every detail of your existence. Your houseboy will live with you and know your every move. Neighbors may ask very personal questions: "When are you going to have a baby?" "Why don't you have a woman?"

No American-type dating or socializing, probably no theater, music, or spectator sports, little recreation except for the games you teach to the local people and such solitary pursuits as reading, walking, or just "thinking." Get-togethers with other PCVs are infrequent. Invitations to local celebrations where you may be required by etiquette to eat and drink quantities of undigestible foods or at least ones you don't care for, are common.

Not enough to do. Nothing takes the edge off enthusiasm and lowers morale faster than idleness. Oddly enough, despite their need and desire to have Volunteers, many host countries have not been ready to make use of them effectively. In Malaya, traditional courtesy prevented the PCVs from getting down to work. An exasperated PC engineer asked, "What was the use of all that hard preliminary training, when all they do is shake their heads and say, 'We wouldn't dream of letting you put yourself out'?" In Pakistan, the local administrators were not prepared. Either they did not want or need, or didn't know how to use, the services the PCVs were trained to provide. Over half of the Volunteers—after eight months of doing nothing constructive—had to be reassigned.

Delays, delays, delays. Everything takes so long, no one ever hurries, or arrives on time, or expedites anything. "It's an accomplishment to get a basketball court built in two months," said PCV Mike Wilson. "Or four hundred yards of road in two weeks, or a well dug and finished in six months. Everything's a slow, slow process. I sincerely feel that we won't see results of our work for ten, twenty, even thirty years, because it's going to take Colombia that long to catch up to our standards." And in the end, the project may not be successful because the people are not ready yet for a library, a democratic town meeting, or a cooperative market for local handcrafts.

Unrelieved physical discomfort. For Mike Wilson, it was fleas. "There are more dogs than humans in Tenjo, and I've picked up about four million fleas. The only way to get rid of them is to scratch them to death. Nothing, not even a cold shower, gets rid of them. You just itch and itch, and scratch and scratch; and when you get in bed at night, it gets worse, and when you get up in the morning, it's just as bad. That's one of the many nerve-wracking problems we have down here."

In addition to the above, you will usually have to work without sufficient equipment, your hosts will generally be slow to follow your lead and to help themselves, and in some host countries you may even be shocked at the low value placed on human life.

Although you should be prepared for hardship of every kind, you will probably find that your actual living conditions are reasonably comfortable. Maryagnes Thompson, a PCV in Nigeria, wrote: "I believe the Peace Corps image of Volunteers living in great hardships has been exaggerated. For most of us life couldn't be more comfortable physically: large, spacious houses, stewards who clean and cook and an adequate allowance. The greatest difficulties are the differences in cultures and values."

PCV Jim Fisher's description of his schoolroom in Nepal shows another side of PC life:

"My first class begins at 6:30 A.M. in an unheated room with four unfinished brick walls and several rows of rough wooden benches. The temperature is likely to be about forty degrees at that hour, and the shivering students sit there and suffer, though I have the prerogative as teacher of pacing up and down, thus keeping my blood circulating. Despite the chill, a brave handful of students continues to show up (total enrollment of the college is forty-five). In the fourth-year class, there is only one girl, but in the first-year class there are a few more. Only in recent years have girls been enrolled in school at all, but the winds of change are blowing. The air is comfortably warm by the time the high school opens at 10:30."

When living conditions or a task assignment are so unacceptable that a Volunteer cannot function effectively, adjustments can sometimes be made. Shifts in roommates are arranged when PCVs who have been housed together turn out to be incompatible. Sometimes, too, teachers entering their second year of service are shifted to new locales to give both them and their hosts broader experience. And a few unhappy Volunteers have been reassigned successfully to other countries, although this has been done only in unusual circumstances. But within a country, the Field Representative can usually work out whatever arrangements best suit the PCVs.

Don't be scared off, however, by the misconception that the Peace Corps wants only rugged athletic types and recreation directors. This is not the case, except for physical education projects, such as the one in Colombia which called for fifty instructors in baseball, basketball, swimming, track, and gymnastics. When the Peace Corps asks for people who can endure the rigors of overseas life, they want much more than strong bodies.

This is exemplified by the way trainees are judged on the obstacle course at the Puerto Rico training camp. The *attempt* to do—the willingness to try to climb over rocks, to swing from a rope over a ravine, or to jump from a tower into a pool—counts for more than how well one does it. Two handicapped girls qualified for PC service, and a blind PCV taught in a Dominican school for the blind.

"Of course we want them to get in shape," said a PCV instructor in Puerto Rico, "but we also want them to gain self-confidence, so that they don't worry about strength or lack of it. To understand themselves better and know what they can do is like preventive medicine; it prevents panic."

Training camp dormitories are barrack style—one for men, another for women—with husbands and wives separated during the twenty-six days. "If they can't take it, maybe they better examine their marriage," a staffer said unsympathetically.

Before the trainees leave camp, most of those who were afraid of heights, afraid to jump, or fearful of sleeping out overnight, have conquered their fears.

The purpose of the careful screening, right up to the time of departure, is to protect both the individual and the group from heartaches and failures. But group loyalties become so strong during training—as the strain and tension and fear of "washing out" builds up—that other PCVs in the group will protest vigorously if the Corps decides that one of its members should not go overseas.

Now a few paragraphs "for girls only." Although PC administrators maintain that they see no difference between the way the male and female Volunteers adjust overseas, the gentlemen make no secret of their feelings that the girls have a rougher time. Bill and Maryl Levine, PC teachers in Burao, Somalia, considered themselves fortunate to be together. They saw the problems of the unmarried girls very perceptively.

"Loneliness among the single girls here is great," said Bill, "and they thrive on any company that comes to Burao. We think that life for a girl in her middle or late twenties can be especially painful, for after the glory of leaving home and getting settled, she begins to realize that she is twenty-seven and single, and the prospects for two years are exceedingly dim. And she realizes that being cut off from home for two years will probably mean no company to come home to."

As several male PCVs told me, "Most of the girls want to get married and most of the men don't. We're bachelor types for the most part and we're busy."

"The female PCVs have special problems," said PCV David King, speaking of the girls in the Philippines. "They've been accustomed to a rather active social life including dating, having men visit their homes, and living in situations where they could dress up, put on some perfume and feel like real girls. Dating is out of the question here in the provinces—no transportation, no respectable place to go, and they are alien to provincial Filipino custom.

"The image our girls present, since Americans are naturally more outgoing, independent, and self-sufficient than the shy, retiring, flirting-behind-the-fan Filipina, seems in the eyes of Filipino men to verify the image the movies have given them. Consequently, at public dances where our girls go unchaperoned, the men feel free to dance with them intimately, often in a rather amusing version of check-to-cheek, and sometimes to make smutty conversation. The point is, Filipino men don't treat their own women that way. The standard is a double one."

In their work, the girls more often than the men act the part of pioneers. Their roles may be exciting but not without occasionally being hazardous. Among the early groups at least, it was common for a PCV to discover that she was the first woman teacher in her school, sometimes with an all-boy class. Or she might be the first white woman her hosts had ever seen, certainly the first one who had ever driven around in a jeep or ridden a bicycle through town, talked to the men of the community, or attended civic and social functions. And because she is a woman and the spotlight is on her, she has to exercise more discretion than the men.

Volunteers going to an established project generally have an easier time than those starting a new task in a new host country. However, several PCVs pointed out that this might depend on whether the person is "a pace setter or a follower." Others maintained that the second or succeeding waves of Volunteers would not be regarded as curiosities and would be accepted faster into the local society and have fewer problems getting started.

The Corps' psychologists view it somewhat differently. "To go now, Volunteers need a much stronger motivation," said Dr. John Hutchison. "The first group has proven it can be done. The later ones will need a very strong basic philosophy, a real spiritual consecration to serve in order for them to volunteer."

Dr. Edwin Henry expressed a similar opinion. "The early Volunteers had it easier. They were in a glamor situation— no one had done this before and they were building the way. The second ones have something to live up to. Because they need stronger motivation now, we may get better Volunteers as time goes by—if they get enough attention."

Lack of recognition, of course, is the reason strong self-motivation is necessary. In the early days of the Corps, a great deal of publicity was lavished on the PCVs. While the Corps is still very much in the news, the stories of individual PCVs no longer receive heavy coverage. Ann Olsen, a PCV in the Philippines, described the most successful Volunteer as the one who disappears into the day-to-day existence of his community. "His success is not in doing something spectacular, but in going unnoticed."

The experience of PCVs in the field has shown that your reasons for wanting to join the Peace Corps need not all be unselfish in order for you to do a good job. I see nothing wrong with the philosophy of the sixth grader who was quoted in *The New York Times Magazine* of November 25, 1962: "I wish I could travel around the world but traveling from one country to another is costly. So for my travelings I want to join the Peace Corps. *Then I will also be helping people.*" (Italics added.)

The first Volunteers seemed to be ashamed of their personal motives for joining. Only after months of practical success in the field were they able to admit frankly that they had wanted to see some faraway places about which they had read; that they wanted to defer settling down in a job or deciding upon a career; that they were postponing marriage; or that they were not doing well in their jobs in the States since they did not yet know in which field they would like to work. There were many other personal motives, though, of course, never a desire for financial gain. Only when Volunteers joined in the expectation that they would find the ideal job, or that the grass overseas was greener, or that they could escape from themselves and their inner problems (which they inevitably took with them), did they become a problem to the Peace Corps. Their own problems multiplied, too.

Despite all the talk of dedication, joining the Peace Corps is not like being called to the ministry, and I doubt that anyone volunteers for one single, overwhelming reason.

The motives, recognizable or not, are many and mixed. Perhaps the original Volunteers gave the reasons they thought they should have for joining, without mentioning some of their real reasons, because the concept of the Peace Corps was so idealistic. After responding to President Kennedy's "Ask not what your country can do for you but what you can do for your country," and having the hero role thrust upon them by admiring families, their communities, and the press, could they admit that they looked forward to the experience of living in a totally different culture or that they wanted to test for themselves whether it is really possible for the peoples of the world to live and work together?

In stressing that the recruits they are seeking are pragmatic idealists, the Peace Corps recognizes the need for more than the service motivation—although that must be strong indeed. PCVs must be idealistic enough to want to contribute to the long-range and often intangible goals of peace and a better life for all, but they must also be capable of translating their idealism into practical contributions to their host peoples. If you want to serve and serve well, don't feel guilty if at the same time you intend to get all you can from the experience and to bring back some ideas which may influence other Americans who have not had your opportunity. I cannot understand why some critics of the Corps find it disturbing if PCVs should get as much as they give, or should learn as much as they teach, as long as they do the job the Peace Corps and their host countries expect them to do.

"The other night at a cocktail party in Mogadiscio," wrote PCV Boris Sojka, a photographer who went over to teach but, naturally, took his camera along with him, "Carole and I were both asked separately by two different people why we joined the Peace Corps. When we tried to answer, we found it wasn't there any more. The answers I gave in New York and California all sounded trite over here with the people who know the score. I really had to go back to one of my secondary answers but probably the truest: For as long as I can remember I've always wanted to go to Africa."

If one of your motives is to mix with the ordinary citizens of a country, there is no better way than service as a PCV. Many Volunteers have seen that the diplomatic personnel abroad do not have their opportunity to get acquainted with the people.

If you are interested in politics, however, be warned that you will be observer only. PCVs are taught to steer clear of intelligence activities and to stay out of local politics; their only political activity is limited to finding ways to obtain the cooperation of the local officials.

"The Peace Corps," said Secretary of State Dean Rusk, "is not an instrument *of* foreign policy, because to make it so would rob it of its contribution *to* foreign policy."

Many companies and organizations are cooperating with the Peace Corps by granting leaves of absence to workers who want to volunteer. Schools and colleges are frequently willing to release teachers for two years, with the privilege of returning to their jobs upon successful completion of their service.

Teachers in New York City schools, for example, will not lose service credits for raises and other benefits; and the latest contract between the United Steelworkers of America and the National Can Corporation includes a Peace Corps "leave-of-absence" clause.

"This is the best clause to date with full protection rights of the Peace Corps Volunteer in terms of re-employment rights," said Sargent Shriver. "I hope such a clause will be incorporated into all collective bargaining arrangements."

Neither the Domestic Peace Corps nor the proposed National Service Corps, incidentally, have any connection with the overseas Peace Corps. If you are interested in serving in a particular country, write to Washington for information on the program there. The Peace Corps issues brochures describing most of its projects. You can get these for the asking.

PCV Tex Ford, in the Dominican Republic, said, "I wouldn't take a million dollars for my experience in the Peace Corps." If you know yourself and understand your reasons for volunteering, this may also be your evaluation. Good luck!

Sample Questions
from the Peace Corps Placement Test

After you have filed an application with the Peace Corps, the Corps will instruct you to take the Placement Test. Your local post office, Civil Service Commission, or Peace Corps headquarters can tell you the time, date, and place of tests. The questions below are selected from the "Sample Questions" booklet which the Corps makes available to applicants *before* they take the actual Placement Test. (The answers appear at the end.) These questions may appear difficult to you, so it is important to remember: *there is no passing score.* The results of the test merely help the PC Division of Selection evaluate your abilities in certain specific skill areas. The Placement Test is an hour and a half long.

I. VERBAL APTITUDE
Directions: In each of the following questions, a related pair of words or phrases is followed by five lettered pairs of words or phrases. Select the lettered pair which best expresses a relationship similar to that expressed in the original pair.

TORCH : LIBERTY :
- (A) tray : waiter
- (B) scales : justice
- (C) candle : poverty
- (D) bars : punishment
- (E) levers : power

II. AGRICULTURE
Directions: Each of the questions or incomplete statements below is followed by five suggested answers or completions. Select the one which is best in each case.

1. Which of the following is most commonly used in the United States for feeding swine?
- (A) Clover
- (B) Wheat
- (C) Alfalfa
- (D) Corn
- (E) Lespedeza

2. After a seven year period of drought, an area had so much rain that floods were common. However, farms in these areas were still

considered to be drought-stricken because

    (A) Farmers had not had time to plant and harvest any crops
    (B) The water table had not been raised significantly
    (C) The economic losses had not been made up
    (D) The floods had washed away the topsoil
    (E) The larger reservoirs had not yet been filled to capacity

III. ENGLISH

Directions: The following sentences illustrate problems of grammar, usage, and word choice. Some sentences are correct. Others contain errors; no sentence has more than one error.

In each sentence four portions are underlined and lettered A, B, C, and D. If there is an error in a sentence, the error will be in one of the underlined portions.

You are to examine each sentence and decide which underlined portion, if any, is wrong. After each sentence are the words: No error. Accordingly, if the sentence is correct, E is the answer.

1. The wind would of blown down the house had it not been for the
           A   B   C
special reinforcements. No error.
  D   E.

2. He spoke bluntly and angrily to we spectators. No error.
      A   B   C D   E

IV HEALTH SCIENCES

Directions: Each of the questions or incomplete statements below is followed by five suggested answers or completions. Select the one which is best in each case.

1. Which of the following would be the most satisfactory nutritional substitute for fresh orange juice?

    (A) Fresh apple juice
    (B) Fresh carrot juice
    (C) Bottled prune juice
    (D) Canned pineapple juice
    (E) Canned grapefruit juice

2. The chief danger from being cut or scratched by rusted metal is that one may contract

(A) tetanus
(B) trachoma
(C) hydrophobia
(D) meningitis
(E) encephalitis

V. MECHANICAL SKILLS

In this part solve each problem, using any available space on the page for scratchwork. Then indicate the one correct answer in the appropriate space on the answer sheet.

What does 28 feet of wire weigh, if 154 feet weighs 11 pounds?

(A) 2 lb.
(B) 2-8/11 lb.
(C) 1-1/2 lb.
(D) 7 lb.
(E) 14 lb.

VI. BIOLOGY

Rudolph Schoenheimer and his associates were among the first to use isotopic tracers in biology. Molecules or portions of molecules were "tagged" by incorporating into them isotopic nitrogen (N^{15}) or deuterium (H^2). In one series of experiments mice were fed on a diet of 20% fat and 80% carbohydrate. This fat was prepared by treating linseed oil with deuterium so that the resultant fat was 5.74 atom per cent deuterium after having been fed "tagged" fat for 2 to 8 days, the mice were analyzed for the deuterium content of their stored (depot) fat. The average figures per mouse for each experiment are presented in the table. (Ordinarily fat has 0.02 atom per cent deuterium.)

EXP. NO.	FEEDING PERIOD, DAYS	AMOUNT OF FAT CONSUMED, GRAMS	CHANGE IN BODY WEIGHT, GRAMS	TOTAL AMT. OF FAT IN DEPOTS, GRAMS	ATOM % DEUTERIUM IN DEPOT FAT
1	2	0.54	—1.8	2.06	0.27
2	2	0.58	—0.1	0.42	2.17
3	4	1.12	—1.3	2.00	0.71
4	4	1.28	—0.4	0.39	2.61
5	8	2.61	—1.1	0.97	2.71
6	8	2.72	0.0	0.94	2.36

Each of the following possible conclusions is to be judged in relation to the above data. Categorize each conclusion according to the following KEY.

KEY
(A) The data given support this conclusion.
(B) The data given refute this conclusion.
(C) The data given neither support nor refute this conclusion, but the conclusion is correct.
(D) The data given neither support nor refute this conclusion, but it is incorrect.

1. Although the mice were fed insufficient food to maintain body weight, some of the ingested fat was stored instead of being respired.
2. Some of the ingested carbohydrate may have been stored as fat.

VII. CHEMISTRY

The solution containing which of the following pairs of substances would be the LEAST satisfactory buffer for acids and bases?
  (A) $C_6H_5OH + C_6H_5ONa$
  (B) $H_2CO_5 + KHCO_5$
  (C) $CCl_3COOH + CCl_3COOONa$
  (D) $NaH_2PO_4 + Na_2HPO_4$
  (E) $HCOOH + HCOOK$

VIII. PHYSICS

A helium-filled toy balloon is tied by a 3-foot string to the bottom of a closed box so that the balloon occupies the exact center of the box. The box is then given a sudden shove. While the box is accelerating, the position of the balloon is

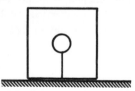

  (A) in back of its starting position
  (B) in front of the center of the box
  (C) between the center of the box and its starting position
  (D) at the center of the box
  (E) at its starting position

IX. PHYSICS

A double Atwood's machine is shown in the figure. The numbers refer to the masses of the various parts in grams. Consider the string to be weightless. The system is released from rest in the position shown. Which of the following describes the subsequent motions?

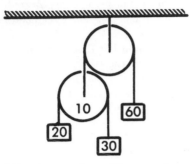

  (A) 60 moves down, 30 moves down, 20 moves up
  (B) 30 moves down, 20 moves up, 60 moves up
  (C) 30 moves down, 20 moves up, 60 remains stationary
  (D) 30 moves down, 60 moves up, 20 remains stationary
  (E) No motion occurs since the system is in equilibrium

X. MATHEMATICS

$(1 + i)^9 = (?)$, where $i = \sqrt{-1}$
(A) $-16 - 16i$ (B) $-16 + 16i$ (C) $16 - 16i$ (D) $16 + 16i$
(E) $-512 - 512i$ (F) $-512 + 512i$ (G) $512 - 512i$
(H) $512 + 512i$

XI. WORLD HISTORY

1. "The Calvinists were inclined to a democratic outlook by the circumstance that, for the most part, they remained a minority and were thus not able to prescribe the mode of life and religion of a whole region."

Which of the following was probably among the regions which the author had in mind when he made this statement?
  (A) Scotland
  (B) French
  (C) The Dutch Netherlands
  (D) Geneva
  (E) New England

2. The policy of the "open door" in China was designed to
   (A) divide Chinese territory among the great powers
   (B) compel the Chinese to open their ports to foreign trade
   (C) preserve equal trading rights for all foreigners in that
       country.
   (D) give the United Sates control of Far Eastern markets
   (E) restore full sovereign rights to China

XII. LITERATURE TEST

'Tis late to hearken, late to smile,
But better late than never:
I shall have lived a little while
Before I die for ever.

Among other things, in these lines the poet is expressing his belief
that
   (A) a man should counterfeit cheer in preparing himself for
       death
   (B) life is bitter, but must be endured
   (C) old age makes a man impatient for death
   (D) it is never too late to repent one's misdeeds
   (E) there is no life after death

XIII. UNITED STATES HISTORY AND INSTITUTIONS

Directions: Each of the questions or incomplete statements below is
followed by five suggested answers of completions. Select the one
which is best in each case.

1. Which of the following was the primary objective of the nations
   which signed the North Atlantic Pact?
   (A) To form an alliance for military conquest
   (B) To insure economic stability in democratic states
   (C) To replace the Marshall Plan with a new alliance
   (D) To destroy the effectiveness of the Soviet veto in the United
       Nations
   (E) To unite for collective defense

2. Upon which of the following did Jefferson base his argument for
   American independence in the Declaration of Independence?
   (A) The right of the colonists as Englishmen and British sub-
       jects
   (B) The natural rights of man everywhere

    (C) British neglect of the American colonies
    (D) The absence of a written British constitution
    (E) Britain's indiscriminate disregard for procedural rights

XIV. MODERN LANGUAGE APTITUDE

1. Each item below has a group of words. The word at the top of the group is not spelled in the usual way. Instead, it is spelled approximately as it is pronounced. Your task is to recognize the disguised word from the spelling. In order that you recognize the disguised word, look for one of the five words beneath it that corresponds *most nearly in meaning* with the disguised word.

  L U V
    (A) carry
    (B) exist
    (C) affection
    (D) wash
    (E) spy

2. The following items test your ability to understand the function of words and phrases in sentences.

   Below you will find a key sentence in which there appears an underlined word in capital letters. Immediately following the key sentence is a second sentence containing certain underlined words or phrases. Look over the underlined choices in the second sentence and find the one which *functions* most nearly like the capitalized word or phrase in the key sentence.

   Mary is cutting the <u>APPLE.</u>

   <u>My brother</u> <u>John</u> is beating <u>his</u> <u>dog</u> with a stick.
       A   B   C D

Answers

I	B
II	1-D, 2-B
III	1-A, 2-C
IV	1-E, 2-A
V	A
VI	1-A, 2-C
VII	C
VIII	B

IX   A
X   D
XI   1-B, 2-C
XII   E
XIII   1-E, 2-B
XIV   1-C, 2-D

INDEX

ABOUT THE AUTHOR

Velma Adams confesses that if she were not so completely absorbed in her professional career as a writer and editor she would seriously consider joining the Peace Corps herself. She feels that she has done the next best thing: she immersed herself in a study of the entire project, started correspondence with Volunteers who were already at their posts in countries around the world, and then spent two years in traveling to see for herself how the Peace Corps fared in the field. Only after that preparation in depth did she feel ready to sit down to write this story of *The Peace Corps in Action*.

Fascinated as she was by the spirit of adventure and service inherent in the Peace Corps idea, she says it took all her training as a reporter to maintain an objective point of view. With her admiration for this unique venture in international public relations, it has not been easy, especially since many of the Volunteers have become her friends.

Mrs. Adams (her full name is Velma Arthur Adams), is today the Editor of *The American Salesman* and thus has brought to her book a full appreciation of those qualities that help to create good will in practical business situations. She was the first young woman to co-edit the college paper when she attended St. Lawrence University in Canton, New York. For fifteen years she resided in and around Boston; for five of these she was assistant to the director of *Harvard College Observatory*. Subsequently, she lived in Boulder, Colorado, for two years, but with all her moving around the country Velma Adams never in her life did as much traveling as during the two years when she was following Peace Corps projects overseas.

Although many of her articles have appeared in leading national periodicals, this is her first published book. She now makes her home in Brooklyn Heights across the East River from the towers of Manhattan. Here, or in a Cape Cod retreat overlooking the dunes and the ocean, she does most of her writing.